Just Another Laowai

Living, Working & Playing Football in China

Ross Hamilton

Laowai – Chinese for foreigner. It is made up of two Chinese words, *Lao* meaning "old", and *Wai* meaning "outside". There is some debate as to whether this is a derogatory term or not.

Published by Fast Buck Music Ltd
1 Harrow Way
Charlton Village
Shepperton
Middx
TW17 0RX

Copywrite © 2007 Ross Hamilton

Pictures
Front Cover - Authors Collection (Ed Hamilton)
Back Cover - Authors Collection (Sarah Hall)

To Sarah, for sharing this adventure with me

With thanks to my Father for all of his help

Part 1 – Introduction

I never considered myself to be one of life's great travellers. After University, I wasn't struck down by the travel bug that seemed to affect so many of contemporaries. Even though I had acquired some stamps in my passport over the years, nothing could quite prepare my family and friends for the revelation that I was about to spend six months living and working in the People's Republic of China. It might be apt at this juncture to explain the reasons behind this seemingly out of character sojourn.

I have always been interested in history and for a time I had worked in the museum industry, but after a couple of jobs which I took solely for the money (mainly to fund my trip to New Zealand to watch the disappointing Lions tour of 2005); I felt that I should be doing something that would give me a sense of purpose as well as utilising my knowledge and skills. After careful consideration, I set my sights on a career as a history teacher.

I first applied for a PGCE at the beginning of 2005 but my application failed. I put this down to the fact that I didn't have any experience of teaching or spending anytime whatsoever in schools since I was 18. Unlike the past where subject knowledge and the confidence to stand up in front of a group of children were enough to secure a job in the teaching profession, today is a different story. A teaching qualification is important if anyone wants to become a teacher, especially if you wish to work in a state run school. The private sector is still an option for people like myself who don't have a qualification, but luck plays a big part as the headmaster needs to be willing/foolish enough to take a chance on you.

After arranging to spend time in some local schools, an old work colleague of mine informed me that she now worked for a company which would send me to a foreign country to teach English as a secondary language in a school or university. I was instantly interested, no doubt because I was drunk at the time!

After making contact with the company (called IST Plus), we were given the option of going to either China or Thailand. I didn't fancy the latter due to reports of foreigners being put in prison for alleged drug smuggling. Not fancying even the remotest possibility of seeing the inside of any sort of prison, I picked China. The fact that I was exceedingly interested in visiting some of the historical sites I had only ever read about in books also swayed my decision.

The other thing that made my mind up about where I would like to go was when I was told that I didn't need a teaching qualification to teach, just a degree and the ability to speak clear English. I had the necessary degree and even though some of my friends would state that my spoken English is a bit on the poor side, I was sure that my south of London accent would get me through the interview. Sarah (my partner) was fed up with what she was doing and she fancied trying something a bit different so she was quite happy to join me, especially if she was going to go somewhere she had never been before.

The interview turned out to be a brief telephone call (designed no doubt to test our speaking voices), we were both accepted on the course so I knew that by September 2006, I would have almost six months of teaching experience under my belt. With this, I applied for another PGCE hoping that I would be able to spend the summer chilling out before starting on my course.

There were a lot of things we had to do before we went. It was not as straight forward as getting off of a plane in whatever establishment we were to teach in and turning up to class on Monday morning:

1) Medical – the form was sent over to us in an interesting mix of Chinese and English. The most curious thing was that my GP had not heard of some of the expressions used and just guessed at what the answer might be. This was either a worry or just a poor translation but I hoped it wouldn't come back to haunt us.

2) An STD test – having never done one of these before, this was a bit of a worry especially when

sitting in the waiting room seeing people who had obviously had bad news when they came out of the consultancy rooms. It was nice when the results were clear.

3) Visa – The company that we were going through sorted this out for us, for a small fee of course.

4) Find someone to look after our flat. Luckily, one of Sarah's friends had sold her house and was looking for somewhere to buy. Whilst she was looking, she would stay at our place which she only moved out of a couple of days before we came back.

We decided that we would only go for five months (the other option was 10, but we thought we would see if we enjoyed it first before committing ourselves that far in advance and I had a PGCE application that I hoped would be accepted).

We had asked for a University in Beijing, but we really didn't care where we ended up so long as we were together. IST informed me there wasn't anything available in Beijing, but we would be going to a place called Chongqing[1] instead. However, after reading up on Chongqing and everything there was to see in the local area (including the only museum in China to portray the Americans in a positive light[2]), we were informed by IST that we were being placed in the Flying College of Beihang University, Beijing. All we would have hoped for is that we were in the same city, but to actually be teaching at the same University was great news.

The University sent us our contracts via a courier with instructions that they needed to be returned to Beijing within the next couple of days. This did not give us much time to read and digest their contents. We did see that there was mention of an appendix to this document, but it was either not sent or did not exist. They were desperate to have them back and the IST

[1] Chongqing City was the Captial of the Republic of China between 1938 and 1945 during the Sino-Japanese War, which co-incided with the Pacific Theatre of Opertions during World War 2.
[2] This is the Stillwell Museum, named after Joseph 'Vinegar Joe' Stilwell who commanded the Allied forces in the China-Burma-Indian theatre in WW2.

representative in China was emailing Sarah stressing this. We sent them back in time but the courier company we used could not find the Flying College. Fortunately for us, the IST representative took over their delivery and they arrived in one piece. We did wonder how big the University was upon hearing this.

Once news of our trip became common knowledge, it was amazing how many people we knew had friends that taught English abroad and gave us all sorts of tips. One advised us that the trick with a prolonged stay like this was to take the minimal amount of clothing with you and to buy most of what you need when you are out there. This sounded good as we were keen to take a load of chocolate with us to give to the Chinese staff at our college as gifts. We had been told that this was seen as good etiquette in China and we were keen to get off to a good start on the working relationship front.

IST organised a meeting at their offices for Sarah, I and the other participants to talk to some experienced teachers who had already made the trip. We were the only ones local to the IST Offices as all the others had come from all over the country to attend. They had come down to London to make a weekend of their visit especially as there was a Chinese exhibition at the Royal Academy of Arts called 'The Three Kingdoms' we were all keen to see. Present at the meeting were two people who had been on the course a couple of years before. One of them had been there during SARS and with Bird Flu all the rage in the news, everyone was very keen to know how this situation had been dealt with.

There was also a slide show on a continuous loop showing teachers that had gone on the last orientation along with a couple of amusing pictures I had seen before as humorous email attachments. Bikes covered in bags, donkeys pulling trucks, that sort of thing. The experienced teachers told us that discipline could be a problem. With the one child policy, there were quite a few spoilt children in China these days[3]. Their mobiles would

---

[3] Since the adoption of the one child per family policy back in the late 1970's, there has been a tendency for parents (and grandparents) to lavish their

go off in class and they would spend their time talking on them to their friends/girlfriends etc. They would also criticise their teachers in Chinese believing that they could get away with it. The experienced teacher who was telling us this was of Chinese descent so he was able to understand and answer the student back, which earned him the respect of the class. It also meant the student lost face, but this aspect of Chinese life is something that will be touched upon in greater detail later.

They also told us that we were getting a reasonable wage for China and that it should go a long way, as long as we didn't go mad with it. It was stressed that the students would be very interested in where we lived and our families. In preparation for this, we spent time wandering around London taking photos of the most mundane things (taxis, buses, phone boxes etc) in addition to well known local landmarks (Houses of Parliament, British Museum etc). Before the meeting finished, we were all given a Lonely Planet guide to China. As Sarah and I were going as a couple we went to the local travel bookshop later that weekend and swapped one of these for the Beijing guide as well as a couple of other China related books.

In the weeks before we left, Sarah decided that it would be a good idea to teach herself Mandarin. I remembered trying to learn French and Latin at school and as I had been terrible at both I didn't make any effort to learn any myself. By the process of osmosis, I did find that I had learned one word; Pijiu which turned out to mean beer (always best to have the most essential words to hand). Due to Sarah's keenness, for weeks prior to us leaving the flat was covered in labels with pinyin[4] written on them. I couldn't even go to the loo or take some food out of the fridge without being confronted by a label telling me what the Chinese word for it was.

With languages not being my strong point, I bought loads of history books in an effort to learn a bit

child with everything they could possibly want. This is affectionately known as 'Little Emperor Syndrome'.

[4] Pinyin is a way of leaning Chinese useing Roman letters to represent sounds in Mandarin.

about the place. These books included 'The Complete Illustrated History of China' by J. A. G. Roberts (a very long tome, a bit dry and in depth as it did try cover the whole of Chinese history, which is at least 5000 years) and 'A Brief History of the Dynasties of China' by Bamber Gascoigne (a lot thinner, a good deal easier to read and not very dry at all!).

I also bought a laptop. I assumed that the University would provide us with a means of accessing the internet and this would also allow us to contact home in the privacy of our own apartment. Key to this was the internet telephone service, Skype. I had used Skype at one of my previous jobs and knew that this would be a great way for our family and friends to keep in contact with us (as long as we had the aforementioned internet connection). Just being able to email whenever we wanted to would be enough though. I had also debated buying a computer game for it, but I hoped that I would be so busy that I would not have the time to play it. However, in the last few days before we left, I succumbed and bought a football management simulator. I found upon loading it that it included the Chinese leagues so I thought that this would be a great way of learning something about the game in China. I had been led to believe that the Chinese were football mad (a game I also enjoy), so at least I would have something to talk to my students about.

We spent our last two weeks in Britain saying goodbye to family and friends, including a massive piss up in a local pub. It felt a bit weird saying goodbye to so many people at once, but our time away would no doubt fly by and we would be back before we knew it.

A (Very) Brief History of China

China's history is very long and complex, so it is very difficult to give a brief over view, of the country's history. However, I feel that having a section dedicated to it would make some of the areas covered in this book easier to understand. China can trace its history back to as long ago as the 16th Century BC. It also has historical records that refer to events in and around 3000 BC and

9

evidence of the character based writing style is still in use today, starting at around 1500 BC.

The year 221 BC is that which historians consider to be the beginning of the Imperial Age, when the first emperor of China, Qin Shi Huang, defeated the warring states and unified them for the first time as an empire. The Imperial Age lasted until 1911. During the 2000 years of imperial rule, there were numerous wars, dynasties fell and new ones were founded, either by conquest or revolt. China also cut itself from the rest of the world in the 15th century which led to stagnation of ideas and military prowess. This was to become more apparent with the rise of the European Empires during the 18th Century. Attempts had been made to open trading links with China, but the Emperors felt that their 'Mandate from Heaven', which they believed gave them the right to rule all under heaven, so they were only interested in tribute rather than trade.

The clamour for Chinese goods was high in the West and Chinese merchants would only accept payment in silver. With silver stocks diminishing, they felt that they needed to find a way to supply a product that the Chinese would want instead of precious metal. They chose opium. When the Chinese government tried to stop the opium trade, the British declared war. This became known as the first Opium War. The British navy was, at the time, the most technologically advanced in the world and the Chinese were still reliant on wooden ships and they were easily defeated. With China's defeat came treaties which favoured Britain.

Hong Kong was ceded to Britain and other trade concessions were forced upon China. Britain was not the only power to take advantage of the government's weakness. France, Germany, Japan, Russian, Italy as well as others were granted foreign sections in China's ports, usually after the Chinese government had been forced to sign an unequal treaty. This was the age of semi-colonial rule.

The Chinese government still ruled the most of China, but they did not rule the foreign sections in their ports. This loss of territory, rebellions and defeat in wars, were the reasons, mostly, that the last imperial dynasty faltered until it was finally deposed. Imperial rule ended after 2000 years to be replaced by a Republic.

The birth of the republic was not without its upheavals. It took until 1928 for the Kuomintang (The Nationalist Party) under the leadership of Chiang Kai-shek consolidated its power. The Kuomintang had once been allied with the Chinese Communists, but in 1927, Chiang Kai-shek turned on them and therefore started the Civil War that would rumble on until the Communists won in 1949. The Kuomintang retreated to Taiwan and the Republic is still to this day in power there. Back on the mainland, Mao Zedong, (the communist's leader) proclaimed the foundation of the People's Republic of China and they have been in power ever since.

Part 2 - Orientation Week

<u>London to Shanghai</u>

With our bags packed and our wallets bulging with Renminbi[5] (or RMB for short), we made our way to Heathrow for our flight to Shanghai. Our outward journey didn't have the smoothest of starts. The security at Heathrow had been 'seriously enhanced' because it had failed a random efficiency test a few days before. This meant that the check in queue started outside of the terminal building inside a hastily erected marquee and back into the terminal for even more queuing. Apart from the fact that they asked for our belts to be removed and the queues were long, it was difficult to see what this serious enhancement was. The check in gave Sarah an opportunity to play one of her favourite airport games. This involves tutting loudly and pointing at people who seem to think that luggage the size and weight of a small elephant is appropriate for the overhead compartments on a plane. All this queuing did mean that we didn't have to wait very long for our flight to take off

The journey itself was as boring as any long haul flight I had ever been on. I had stayed up late the night before hoping that I would be able to sleep on the flight and hopefully not suffer from jet leg too much when we reached the other end. Even though I managed to drop off not long after we had taken off, we hit a pocket of turbulence and that was it. There was not a chance in hell of me falling asleep after that. It was therefore necessary to check out the in flight entertainment, which was very poor. I read a magazine I had brought with me, watched the same episode of Top Gear three times and wished that the battery in the laptop I had brought with me lasted longer than fifteen minutes. Playing a bit of my football game would have killed the entire flight instead of the boredom nearly killing me!

---

[5] The RMB is the currency of the People's Republic of China and translated, the name means 'People's Currency'. For the time we spent there, the exchange rate was roughly 14RMB to £1, which was great for our friends who came to visit but it did mean that the money we would earn would be virtually worthless if we had any left over when we returned home.

Though we were going to be based in Beijing, our initiation would take place in Shanghai. When we arrived at Shanghai airport, we were asked by customs to sign three forms asking all sorts of questions including did we have bird flu, a cold or the sniffles. I had not heard the expression 'sniffles' since I had been in infant school, so I could only assume that the person that had translated this form into English had been using an archaic dictionary. After negotiating customs, we were greeted by Janie, a very enthusiastic Chinese girl who worked for CIEE[6] and she was overly excited to see us. In all my years, I have never met anyone who smiled as much as Janie. Even though her English was a bit disjointed, we could understand what she was saying. She gave us some lanyards with our names on them as well as a message in English and Chinese stating our final destination in the city centre. We were told to show this to a taxi driver. We were then put on a public transport bus (which was a bit unexpected as I thought we would be getting in a taxi) and told where to alight. Thankfully, Janie spoke to the bus conductor so she could also tell us when we needed to alight. Once the bus pulled away, Sarah took out our pristine Lonely Planet guide to see if she could find any landmarks as we went, but as reading on moving vehicles makes her ill, it wasn't very successful!

The bus journey seemed to take an age, but it was most probably only an hour or so. Eventually, the conductor came over and started pointing at the door. We took this as our cue to get off and we saw a sign in English that Janie had mentioned earlier so we knew we were at the right place. As the bus pulled away, we were accosted by one of numerous taxi drivers that had parked in the bus stop, which prevented any buses from actually stopping in it themselves. We decided to get in the one making the least noise, showed the driver our lanyard and we sped off towards the city centre. The first thing we noticed was everyone seemed to drive at great speed

---

[6] CIEE are an American company that specialises in sending people, like Sarah and me into either teaching or study programmes in foreign countries. IST Plus is the British subsidiary of this company.

and use their horn at every possible occasion. Passengers of a nervous disposition should think twice about travelling on China's roads.

When the taxi finally came to a halt, we were outside a massive gate with a man in some sort of official looking uniform standing guard (it turned out that they liked their uniforms in China). This was not what we had been expecting. In our minds, we thought we would be staying at a hotel. Fortunately, Sarah had thought to ask for the phone number of the CIEE contact we were supposed to be meeting when we were still in Britain. This turned out to be a brilliant piece of forethought. Sarah gave the contact a call and a minute or so later, she appeared out of the gate and introduced herself as Hattie. She then turned to the taxi driver and told him where the entrance he could drive through was. We jumped back in the taxi, drove around the corner and into the complex.

The complex itself was rather large and we were staying in rather a nice hotel located in one of the corners, right next to the gate we had only been outside moments before. After a couple of quick introductions to some of the other teachers, we checked in and were shown to our room. We then made the mistake of going to sleep for a few hours. This would really screw up the rest of the week for me because I would always wake up at some ungodly hour in the morning and would be ready for bed by about seven in the evening.

When we awoke we still had some time to kill before dinner, so we decided to check out the local area before meeting all of the other participants and CIEE staff. Shanghai[7] to me looked like something from out of a Manga movie. All 'bright lights, fast moving traffic and too many people walking around'. We didn't spend long looking around, but we did have our first experience of a

---

[7] Shanghai was once nothing more than a sleepy fishing town, but by the 1930's, it had become one of, if not the most important city in China. It was also the largest commercial city in the Far East as well being the third largest financial centre in the World after London and New York. After the Communists took over the country in 1949, Shanghai became a shadow of its former self but since the Central Government allowed a more free market economy to develop, it has once more become an economic powerhouse.

bootleg DVD/CD shop, which was on the main road and not, as expected, down some seedy back alley.

Once we were back at the hotel, we got ready for the evening meal. Here we were introduced to James and Lisa from IST Plus as well as Dr. Wu who was in charge of the Shanghai end of CIEE. There were also three teachers who had been in China for at least six months. All of them were from Britain, which was odd as most of the people that were on the induction week were from the USA. Janie also joined us from dinner, having returned from the airport brining with her a chap called David. Janie and David were both students who were working at CIEE during their holidays.

Over dinner, we spent most of the time asking questions about what to expect from our forthcoming experiences and Dr. Wu talked us through all of the dishes we were eating, which were all very nice. There wasn't anything too out of the ordinary either. Sarah did embarrass herself by using the soup bowl instead of the rice bowl to put her food into. At this stage, a bowl was just the same as any other bowl as far as we were concerned. We evidently had a lot to learn.

It turned out that our arrival coincided with the 15th day of the 1st lunar month. This signified the end of the New Year celebrations and is called the Lantern Festival. Part of the dinner was some special sweet dumplings which we were informed are only ever made on this day each year, but subsequently seemed to appear at the breakfast buffet every morning. By 10pm, jet lag was beginning to get the better of all the prospective teachers (including those who had already been there for a couple of days), so we called it a night.

When we returned to our room, we could hear fireworks exploding outside our window but we were too tired to go out and watch them. As these were being launched in celebration of the Lantern Festival, we hoped that they wouldn't keep us awake or continue on the subsequent evenings. Our decision to have a nap came back to haunt us as we both awoke at 2:30am. That was annoying as neither of us could get back to sleep. The hotel had a free broadband connection so we were able to listen to the radio on line to pass the time.

Breakfast consisted of almost the same food as dinner the night before (i.e. noodles, dumplings etc). The first day would be the template for all the ones that were to follow whilst we were in Shanghai. First thing, we would have a quick Chinese lesson, learn something about either teaching techniques or how to survive in China, go on an excursion to some local tourist trap and then go out for dinner. One of our survival classes was about the difference between education systems in the UK, US and China. The main difference seems to be that the Chinese style involves the teacher telling the students something, they memorise it, take an exam in it and if they pass, they promptly forget it feeling that they wouldn't need to use it again.

Our daily excursions took us to a few interesting places. Whilst we were walking around, both Janie and David carried small flags to lead us around hoping that we wouldn't get lost. Janie did seem to be holding on to her pink flag as though her life depended on it and was very upset on the one occasion she was given a different coloured one to carry. We thought this flag carrying was just for our benefit but when we were out and about every other tour group we saw was doing the same thing.

The places we visited included:

1) *Shanghai Museum* - According to the Lonely Planet, this was a state of the art museum, but when we were there, most of the exhibitions were shut for no apparent reason, so we spent most of the time in the refreshment area.
2) *Jin Mao tower* - The tallest building in China and at this time, the forth biggest in the world. We only saw the top floor accessible to tourists, but the view was rather impressive.
3) *The Oriental Pearl Tower.* This odd looking structure was the TV tower and allegedly had fantastic views but by the time we got there it was pitch black so we decided to go down to the basement and look at the Shanghai Municipal History Museum. This had a detailed history of Shanghai and was very interesting, but the English captions were unintentionally hilarious

(see Chinglish). What wasn't so funny was the sight of one of the bins billowing with smoke. Some bright spark had decided to dispose of their cigarette in the aforementioned bin, but had not thought to put it out first. What was more disconcerting were the members of the museum staff that walked past the bin as though this was an everyday occurrence. It wasn't until I literally grabbed one of them that anyone did anything about it. This was also the first place we saw some negative notices about the foreign powers that had a prominent role to play in China during the late Imperial years and the days of the Chinese Republic.

4) *The Bund*. Well known for its historical buildings that line the Huangpu River, this was China's Wall Street in the semi-colonial days.

5) *Water Town (or Zhouzhuang as the Chinese call it)*. Shanghai's answer to Venice but without the smell. This really was a water town as it rained on us the whole afternoon but the tour guide was a right character. He wore a portable speaker with a microphone headpiece and would continually start ever sentence with "My friends". This was also the home of the most ornate post box I have ever seen (it was made of bronze and had a dragon wrapped around it) and the now infamous 'Bum Café', which according to the sign next to the door 'Welcomes You'. I wasn't tempted to find out what was on the menu though.

6) *Yu Yuan Gardens*. These ornate gardens (which were quite spectacular) had even more signs critical of the Western Powers and their treatment of the Chinese during either the Opium Wars or after some other infringement during the semi-colonial days.

7) *Acrobatics show*. This was very impressive, even though some of the performer's bodies moved into very unnatural positions. It was finished off by five guys driving motorbikes in what was called the Ball of Death. As impressive as it was,

we were right in front of the stage and so we took the full force of the exhaust fumes, which were almost overpowering.

8) *Xiangyang Market*. This was the first time we went to a Chinese market and saw the amount of bootleg clothing; DVD's, watches etc. that were readily available. We were told that it was going to be closed down as the government felt it sold too many fakes, even for China!

<u>The First Shopping Experience</u>

Whereas I didn't buy anything from the market, Sarah was quite keen to buy a watch. After catching the underground to the station nearest the market, she realised that she didn't actually know where she should go once she was there. This would turn out to be an interesting and in some ways educational experience and showed how safe she felt in Shanghai as she acted in a manner that should would never dream of doing back home.

Looking completely lost, a Chinese man approached her (no doubt having seen foreigners looking lost on many an occasion) and asked if he could help her find what she was looking for. When Sarah said she was looking to buy a watch, the man said he'd take her to a place where she could buy what she wanted. Having lived in Greater London for most of her life, she freely admits that she is not the most streetwise person in the world but she is not usually naïve enough to follow a complete stranger into a strange place.

For some reason all the natural instincts built up back home disappeared in Shanghai and she willingly followed him. He took her into a shop (and not a market stall as would be expected, seeing as it was located in a market) which was full of clothes, but no watches. There was a door at the back of the shop that Sarah assumed was for staff only, but she was lead through it to another room which was full of sunglasses. Not stopping long, she was led into another room and this one was full of handbags. This network of rooms continued up stairs, down corridors all the time passing other westerners on the way similarly being escorted by Chinese guides.

Sarah felt like she had stepped into an exceedingly cheap production of Alice in Wonderland as she was led through all the different rooms. Another part of her was in disbelief that she was happily following this stranger into room after room without a thought for her own personal safety. The fact that she wasn't the only Westerner in the building did allay her fears slightly. Finally they reached a room full of watches.

After her guide had pulled out endless trays of watches for her perusal, Sarah felt a bit guilty that she didn't like any of them. Feeling a little concerned and unable to just walk way, she explained to the guy the kind of watch she was after. He then took Sarah all the way back to the outside world, across the road and into another shop where the whole thing started again. After going through more rooms full of stuff than Aladdin's Cave, she finally reached the room with watches in it and once again, she didn't like the look of any of them. She did admire the guy for his persistence and determination to make a sale but Sarah would be the first to admit that she is a fussy shopper. There is a theory that if she went shoe shopping with Imelda Marcos, it would be the former dictators' wife that gave up first.

Eventually, both parties gave up and parted company. Sarah headed into the main open air market itself which was awash with tourists. She went to several stalls and finally found a watch that she liked. Sarah found that all of the stalls had the same watch for sale so she tried some haggling techniques we'd been taught at the induction sessions. After a few minutes of haggling, she walked off with what she thought was a bargain. Feeling chuffed with herself; she made her way back to the hotel where she swapped market stories with our fellow inductees. It was here that she realised that her watch was not as much of a bargain as she had first thought. What made it worse was that she saw the same watch in a supermarket in Beijing for a fraction of the price she had paid for it in Shanghai.

Needless to say that after this experience, we were a good deal more careful about not only what we bought, but the amount we were prepared to pay for it. We also learned the unwritten rule of market haggling is that you never disclose the price you paid for something because someone is bound to have negotiated a better/been ripped off (delete as appropriate) buying the same thing.

The End of Orientation Week

At the end of the week we were sent out on a scavenger hunt. My team leader skills came into action as I managed to get nearly half of the participants to act as one big group making it easier to pool resources. This was not the sort of thing the organisers had hoped would happen. They had envisaged lots of small groups or individuals making their way through Shanghai ticking off items on the list. As it turned out, the big group contained everyone that was actually taking part in the scavenger hunt so Hattie asked the group members to vote for the people that had done the most work because they had some prizes to award.

Everyone voted for me to receive first prize, which was an ornamental vase. The box it came in was quite big, especially compared to the item it held, which wasn't. It was also a little on the ugly side. It was a bit of a struggle trying to pack the damn things in our already overstuffed bags and I did bring it back home with me, but at no point has it ever been taken out of the box. It is always nice to win something though.

The induction was notable for the range of food we were taken out to try. None of it was anything we had eaten from our local Chinese take away and included:

1) *Eel* – Okay, not so strange for some people, especially those in the East End of London, but they were not jellied.
2) *Sea Cucumber* - We didn't like it very much.
3) *Pigs Brain* – Unlike sweetbreads, this was exactly what it said it was and was served intact so you were left in doubt as to what you were eating. The sight of the brain on the dish made me feel a little queasy. The fact that it was served raw didn't help my stomach much. Like a fondue, it was supposed to be cut into small pieces that were then put onto the end of fork and dipped in

20

boiling fat for a minute or so. There was absolutely no way I was going to try this, but Sarah decided to give it a go. After spitting out the mouthful she had taken, she said it had the consistency of blancmange, but the thought of what she was eating was just too much to bear thinking about.

4) *Root of the Lotus plant* - Tasted really nice and a bit crunchy like sweet potato.

5) *Smelly Tofu* – We cannot remember the proper name for this dish, but whenever smelly tofu was mentioned after this night, people would shudder just from the memory of it. It smelt terrible and tasted about the same. No one liked this at all. I actually turned grey from the smell of it, but I think this was down to the effects of jet lag than anything else.

The strangest food of all was in a Buddhist vegetarian restaurant where everything was made of tofu, but was designed to look and taste like meat. This wasn't particularly nice and everyone was in agreement that they would much rather have had the real thing. I did wonder how they knew what the meat tasted like in the first place so they could make these vegetarian equivalents and on reflection, I don't really see the point in a restaurant like this.

The Saddest Thing I Saw In China #1

In the front window of a restaurant we passed in downtown Shanghai, we saw a shark swimming around a tank that was just big enough for it to move its tail once before it had to turn around again. It sounded similar to the stories of Polar Bears in zoos where they have gone mad from pacing along the same bits of their cage everyday. Considering the conditions it was living in you just had to hope someone would order it soon and put it out of its misery.

The Last Night in Shanghai

Everyone was invited to a meal in the hotel as a way of reflecting on the week and saying goodbye to everyone. This was really nice and everyone made an effort to look their best, except for Dr. Wu who wore the same blue 1970's style tracksuit he had been wearing all week. After the meal, we all agreed that we should go out for a drink as this was more than likely to be the last time we would all be together in the same place. After a short discussion, nobody could agree on where we should go, so I did the only thing I knew that would get us out of the complex. I spoke as loudly as I could without shouting so I could to get everyone's attention and proclaimed that we were going to the nearest bar. Luckily, it was only over the other side of the road so off we went. The bar had a free pool table (which most of the men stood next to all evening) and we all had a few drinks. This was a great way to end our stay in Shanghai but also a sad occasion because we were saying goodbye. Email addresses were exchanged and everyone agreed that we should try and visit each other before we all went to our respective homes.

The last thing to mention about Shanghai was the weather which was a bit crazy. When we first arrived, it was very sunny and warm enough to walk around in a T-shirt but by the morning we were leaving, there was a layer of snow on the ground and freezing. We were told that Beijing would be colder, so we thought we might need to buy cross country skis to make our way across campus.

Part 3 - Culture Shock

Shanghai to Beijing
      Our departures from the hotel were staggered depending on the time each method of transport was leaving the city. Some were going by plane, others by train and one was staying to teach in Shanghai. When we were picked up from the hotel by taxi, I assumed that it would be taking us to the airport. We soon realised that the taxi was only taking us to a bus stop not far from the hotel. After a short panic and a little confusion, we were shoved onto a bus whose route terminated at the airport, so we didn't have to worry about getting off at the wrong place unlike our journey in earlier in the week.
      Our second flight within a week was just as much of a pain in the neck as the first. The flight was meant to take off at 2pm, but it was delayed for almost two hours. There wasn't a single announcement to inform us of the delay and it was only when we asked one of the ground crew that anyone would admit that there was a delay. We hoped that the delay had been relayed to Beijing so that the person who was picking us up would not wonder where we where, get bored and leave.
      The flight itself was uneventful, and the onboard meal was nothing to write home about. In fact, there wasn't one; just a pack of peanuts to eat and a choice between orange juice and water to drink. We were greeted by a member of the Flying College staff. He said his English name was Louk and that he would be looking after us for the rest of the day, or at least that is what we think he said. We found his Chinese accent to be a little on the strong side for us to fully understand what he was saying. We didn't have a clue what he said his Chinese name was. He told us that the Flying College was a separate department at Beihung University (or BUAA as it is abbreviated) and we would meet the Dean, our Waiban[8] and other members of staff in a couple of days. What he didn't tell us was when this meeting would take place and

---

[8] A Waiban is designated to look after any foreign national in their educational facilities. We were told that the Waiban would be our go to guy/girl if we had any problems or needed anything.

we actually forgot to ask. This lack of supplying us with all of the details we would need to know would become a real feature of our time in China and it didn't become any less annoying the longer we were there.

On arriving at Beihang, we were shown to our apartments as we had been given one each, which was unexpected as we just assumed that we would be sharing. The apartments we were assigned were on the 14th and top floor of the building, which was near the North Gate of the University. We had taken the lift to get there, even though there were stairs just in case we fancied keeping fit at any stage. In the lift was a young woman (in a uniform of course) to press the buttons, just in case we were incapable of pressing them ourselves.

We had been told that there was a surplus of labour in China, but employing someone to work the lift in an accommodation block was to my mind, a little over the top. Over the coming days, we would see all the 'lift girls', as we affectionately called them. We discovered that they were paid only 600RMB (or £43 in real money) a month. From this pitiful amount, they were expected to pay their amenities bills, eat and live. A real subsistence wage and I never worked out how they were able to survive on it.

On exiting the lift, we were confronted by a massive and pretty solid looking metal door, no doubt erected to keep out the riff-raff. We were foreign teachers (or experts as we were known in the official paperwork) and couldn't expect to be disturbed unless we wanted to be. The door reminded me of pictures I had seen taken from inside prisons, especially as the front door to our accommodation was behind yet another metal door. The prison motif was continued because the room number had been sprayed on the door using a prison style font I had seen in films, rather than personal experience!

After checking out both apartments, we decided that we would use the one I had been designated as our permanent residence because it didn't have a damp smell lingering in the air. There were no obvious reasons for the smell, and we had a look around for anything that had crawled into a corner to die (rats, previous teachers, that sort of thing) but to no avail. In an attempt to get rid of the smell, we left all the windows open but it took about a month or so to dissipate completely. It also had more useful stuff (pots, pans, shower curtain, coat hangers etc.) left by the previous occupant. We weren't complaining about having the extra apartment though, as it would mean our friends from home that were planning to come out could use it instead of sleeping on our floor.

Having left us alone to put our bags down and check out our new surroundings, Louk came back to take us out for a meal with another member of the Flying College staff and their respective girlfriends. Louk's colleague introduced himself by his Chinese name as he said he hadn't picked an English one for himself. We would know him as Mr. G., the name the students called him. The restaurant specialised in spicy food and fish. I wasn't particularly happy about this as I don't like either very much. Fortunately, there was some beer and freshly squeezed watermelon juice available to put out the fires that would soon be raging in my mouth.

Out of the corner of our eyes, we could see all of the Chinese having a good laugh at our faces as some of the food turned up. Fried cuttle fish and pigs trotters are not my idea of a meal but as the menu had been printed in Chinese, we had to trust our hosts to order for us. There were also some smiles at our attempts to use chop sticks. We hoped we would have an opportunity to get our own back by taking them somewhere they would have to use a knife and fork. At least the Flying College paid for the meal as it sounded expensive by our limited knowledge of Chinese prices, though I was still hungry when we left.

After dinner, our hosts were good enough to take us to the local Wal-Mart so we could pick up some much needed supplies as it was within walking distance of BUAA. It had everything that we needed at prices we could actually see without having to haggle. It was a bit disconcerting that we couldn't go anywhere within the supermarket without having all of our hosts follow us around, scrutinising our every purchase by pointing and whispering to each other. Sarah suggested we split up and meet them in twenty minutes at the till as it was a bit weird being followed all the time, but they just laughed at us; to them it was a ridiculous idea believing that two Westerners couldn't possibly be left alone to do their own shopping as we might need help. Wal-Mart was one of the few places we saw that accepted credit cards, so we knew we would be able to buy some essentials if we were ever short of cash.

On the way back, they all helped carry our shopping and told us that the two supermarkets on campus were very expensive and not very good. When we returned to BUAA and finally left in peace, we realised how cold the apartment was. There were radiators in each room but they were all lukewarm at best. There wasn't a way of adjusting the temperature either, which seemed to defeat their purpose of having them in the first place.

Good Morning Beijing

Our first full day in Beijing did not start off well at all. We couldn't figure out how to turn the boiler on which was doubly annoying as we were both keen to have a shower. I kept an ear open all morning in case I heard anyone else moving around so I could apprehend them. The first person I heard was an American called Andrew who was nice enough to come along and help us out. After showing us that all we had to do was plug the boiler in to get it going (how stupid did we feel!), he started to tell us about his time in China. He came across as rather jaded by the whole experience.

The longer he spoke for, the more I could see Sarah's face drop further and further in horror at what she had volunteered herself for. He asked us which department we would be teaching in and after we told him, he told us a frightening story about Chinese domestic pilots. Andrew, it turned out, liked to spend a lot of time looking for blogs about China as he said that it was the only way to really find out what was really going on. His story related to a plane crash that had occurred in the most western extremities of the country. When the black box recorder was recovered, the last thing the pilot was heard to say was "What does pull up mean?" The idea of doing all of our travelling around by train suddenly sounded very appealing.

26

He did impart some useful information and warned us that we would have to pay for electricity, gas and water even though CIEE had told us that we would not have to pay for anything like this. We also found out later that we would be expected to pay an 800RMB deposit on the property, which we just couldn't afford at that time. As we had been warned at the induction week, once your honeymoon period is over, it is definitely over! The culture shock was beginning to hit us hard. We were a long way from home and we only had each other (for the time being at least) to rely on to keep our spirits up. There were some plus points to the day.

All of the rooms had just had Broadband lines installed so we downloaded Skype and rang home so our parents knew we had arrived in one piece. We soon learned that we would have to pay for the Broadband as well. Was nothing free? We did get the impression that we had not been told everything during our induction week that we should have been. Andrew decided to take us to a couple of shops that stocked Western food, which were all expensive. They were mostly full of American goods, but it was nice to know they existed.

In the cold light of day, it became clear what type of building we were in. It was also clear that it was not in the best of conditions. Andrew told us that it had only been built five years ago, but it looked a good deal older. There were massive cracks in the walls which made me think that the metal security doors might have been added for our safety, but the structure looked so unsafe that I was surprised that they didn't fall off. Our balcony was prone to flooding when it rained, especially in the summer months when there were some quite violent storms. This seemed to be the way they did things in Beijing, and I assume the rest of the country. Build things as quickly as possible, without a thought to the long term. The older buildings around campus which were about 50 years old were in a much better condition and actually looked newer. I hope that they have done a better job with the Olympic stadium!

We also met a few of the other foreign teachers. They were mostly American but there were a couple of other nationalities thrown in for good measure. They were all very friendly and all said that everyone acted as a kind of support group for all the others, which was reassuring. One of the other teachers stood out for his friendly nature. Doug had only just come back to Beijing after six months away, but he showed us all around the city giving us tips about the best places to shop. The fact that he could speak the lingo also helped.

Doug was also a great source of information regarding the Flying College, even though he had not taught there himself. Most of it sounded very positive indeed. The Dean of the college had a good reputation for looking after his foreign teachers, and organised trips for them to places such as the Great Wall. Doug also warned us that on occasions, the Dean would ask his foreign teachers to help his wife with her English and in return, she would take the teacher out in her car and buy dinner. This sounded like a nice perk. We found out later that one of the other teachers was already doing this so we were never asked.

Doug also gave us some tips on surviving in China. These included:

1)   Don't get into a taxi stinking of booze if you can help it, as you are more likely to get conned if you do.
2)   Rules don't really exist. They might be written down but in general they don't apply. If you do get caught out on rules, just play the innocent foreigner and say that you didn't understand or didn't realise there were any.
3)   Don't be afraid to say no. If you don't want to do something, then don't. The Chinese don't have a word for no and don't like confrontation, so if you start saying no, they are more than likely to stop pressing the point.

Needless to say, we did not meet the Flying College staff on the day we were told we were going to, and never received any communication as to tell us why not and when we could expect this to be re-arranged.

* * * * *

The First Week in Beijing

The Flying College had not been totally aloof and we were told that we wouldn't be doing any teaching for the first week so we decided that we should do a bit of sightseeing. It would also give us an opportunity to get some bearings on our surroundings and put our feet under the table. Being out of the apartment would also mean we could avoid Mrs. Yang. She was employed by the University to look after the wash room as well collecting money for our amenities[9] (gas, water and electricity) as well as sorting our any maintenance issues. She would clean the communal areas from time to time as well supply us with a free supply of the English language government run newspaper. She was also tasked with collecting the deposit. As we only had 800RMB between us and we weren't sure if the Flying College would pay our salaries in advance or in lieu, we thought keeping out of sight would be preferable for the time being.

Our first stop off was Tiananmen Square[10]a decision we instantly regretted it as it was freezing and extremely windy. As the square is little more than a wide open space, we decided not to stay very long. The square is enormous and the only buildings on it are Chairman Mao's Mausoleum and the Monument to the People's Heroes. There are also numerous security cameras (which were all powered using solar energy) and police, no doubt there to stop anyone from demonstrating like those in 1989 that had been brutally crushed by the government. I always thought it would be a good idea to come along looking my best because you would never know who will be watching. As a last aside, it must be said that the Square looks quite impressive at night when it is all lit up.

---

[9] Unlike amenities back home, there were no paper bills. All the apartments we ever saw, whether they were on the campus or privately owned would have credit keys that could have money put on them. I suppose that the sending out paper bills would in a country of this size would have been a logistical nightmare.

[10] Tiananmen Square lies directly south of the Tiananmen Gate which is the entrance to the Imperial City. Tiananmen literally means 'heaven' 'peace' 'gate' (Tian = Heaven, An = Peace, Men = Gate) but is more commonly translated as 'The Gate of Heavenly Peace', a rather ironic name concidering some of the events that have happened on it down the years.

As we made our way back to one of the three underground stations that serve Tiananmen Square, we were picked out from the crowds by street vendors trying to sell us watches, cheap DVD's and the like because they thought that as we were westerners, we would have lots of money[11].

This was one of the more annoying sayings we would hear from the Chinese markets sellers. It wouldn't matter how many times I pulled out my teachers ID card and said I was being paid a local wage, they would reply by saying that they knew I had money and would also try to keep their prices high. We were also accosted by sellers of Mao's Little Red Book[12] which looked cheap and was definitely over priced. Tiananmen Square really was a hub for some of the worst souvenirs I have ever seen. When we arrived back at Beihung, I noticed how much my neck was hurting. Due to old sports injuries, I have had some back and neck problems in the past and was hoping that I would not have to find a 'physio' to sort this out because we wouldn't know where to start trying to find one.

We were finally called to the Flying College after sitting around the apartment trying to keep warm. We made the effort to look smart, feeling that making a good first impression would be to our benefit. We were so busy talking on our way over to the College that we actually walked past it and had to be called back by Louk who luckily had seen us. Louk told us that that he was going to take us to an International Hospital where we were to have our medicals.

I was very happy about this as I didn't want to have another blood test as I really hate needles. We had heard some particularly nasty rumours about Chinese hospitals and we were both beginning to get worried. Our nerves were not helped by the fact that our driver did not

---

[11] We would encounter this view of Westerners a lot, especially when we were trying to haggle in the markets.
[12] The books official title is 'Quotations from Chairman Mao Zedong and is a collection of quotations from Mao that had been presented in speeches or publications. There was a time when producing a copy of this book when challeneged would have resulted in a beating or hard labour and is believed to have sold close to a billion copies.

know where the hospital was. Fortunately our medical forms from Britain were sufficient so all we had to do was to sign a couple more and then we could go back. Louk told us to come back at 4pm so we decided to stay in the flat as it was absolutely freezing.

Trudging back to the college as few hours later, we were introduced to Sara, who was from the US and had been teaching at the Flying College for the previous six months. She was really helpful and told us a good deal about the College. We also met Tana, the fourth teacher at the Flying College. It turned out that Tana was being royally 'screwed' by the Flying College. She was timetabled to teach every evening (except Saturday and Sunday) and even had classes on Saturday morning. Due to the fact that she had not had not yet gained her degree, they were also paying her 1000RMB a month less than us, which was an absolute disgrace. Eventually, she would kick up a fuss about this and managed to get a pay rise so she was paid the same as us.

We were introduced to Amanda, a Chinese teacher who gave us our lesson timetables and told us that she was our first point of contact if we had any questions. Sarah had also been stitched up with lessons starting at 7:30pm and finishing at 9:30pm on Monday, Tuesday, Thursday and Friday. The classes were two hours and we were told we could take a ten minute break after 50 minutes and we could also finish ten minutes early. This seemed a bit daunting but we got use to it and in the end I would finish 20 minutes early and not have a break in the middle.

Sarah was less than pleased with her timetable but thought she would see how it would go for a couple of weeks and then see if they could be changed to give her more time off in the evenings. We were also told that even though we were contracted to teach for sixteen hours a week, we were in fact timetabled to do eighteen. To make up for this, we were told that we would not be teaching in July. We had been warned that because we were new and didn't know the ropes, we would be taken advantage of. I knew Sarah was seething at her timetable but I was quite pleased with mine as I was only teaching in the mornings and afternoons but it did mean that we wouldn't have many evenings to do things together.

We were shown one of the class rooms and they were very basic. It was like something out of the Bash Street Kids with a chalk board, a lectern and desks. At least I would be able to throw the chalk around if the students were not behaving, something that had happened to me when I was at school. We were also given text books, but they were the same editions as the students had. I was a bit perturbed that we had not been given any teachers' versions and Amanda said we could use them if we wanted to. We all tried to use them, but gave up as they were pretty poor and had been printed in America which didn't help. It was also a surprise that we were not given a syllabus or any guidance on what to teach. It really did feel like a case of 'here is a class room of kids, teach them but don't expect any help from us'.

We were then taken to see Mrs. Lu (who it turned out was responsible for paying us) and William, who asked us to pay our deposits but we told him that we didn't have it. He said they would talk to Mrs. Yang to wait until we got paid, which would be in advance. This was the best news we had all day.

The rest of the week was spent either meeting the other teachers who lived in our building (that had started to turn up for the start of classes the following week), checking out the local area, looking for a Beijing based Chiropractor/Physio etc. on the internet and chilling out. As my neck was started to become more painful I did not go out much. Sarah went on a couple of excursions including one to the main shopping district of Wangfujing and concluded that only a tourist or a very wealthy local would be able to shop there as all of the prices were the same as those back home.

We did spend a lot of our time watching DVD's on a player Andrew had been kind enough to lend us. We had been warned that we may well become real film buffs during our stay. Judging from the amount of bootleg DVD's available in some of the shops and the collections already in the possession of some of the other teachers; we wouldn't be short on choice.

The first week finished with a trip to the local hospital. The pain in my neck had become too much to bear, so after a quick call to CIEE in Shanghai explaining exactly what I needed, the Flying College duly got in contact. The hospital doctor couldn't speak any English and Louk did his best to translate what was wrong with me, but either there was a break down in communication or they both simply ignored me because all I was given were some patches to put on the affected area and told to try and keep warm. Louk was convinced that it was due to the cold that my shoulder was painful but he did say that if the pain didn't subside, they would organise a trip to a physio or acupuncturist. Having had these sorts of problems before, I knew these patches were about as useful as a eunuch at an orgy but I did at least give them a go.

It was no surprise to me that after a day of wearing them, they had not made a blind bit of difference. We had not had any joy ourselves finding a Physio and in the end, Sarah rang the British Embassy but they could only point us in the direction of a Western Hospital, which mean paying Western prices which I couldn't afford. It got to the point where I thought I would have to return to Britain just so I could get some treatment.

The Other Teachers

There were twenty apartments on the top floor of our building, but not all of them had people in them. Sarah's was empty as she shacked up in my room, and bizarrely enough, the two rooms next to mine were also empty. One of them had the washing machines in it and the other, according to Doug who had actually been in it, was a mess in need of a lick of paint and some maintenance. The only time I saw this room open was at the end of our trip and the floor was covered in a layer of dust so thick that I could see the footprints of the people that had walked in there.

Even though everyone was civil enough to each other, Sarah and I quickly found a couple of like minds who became our social group.

1401 – Tom (American) – Tom has the most shocking red hair in the whole of China. We had been told that he was a bit of a legal eagle back in the States and therefore, he commanded a much higher salary than anyone else. He also always seemed to be going to or coming back from some private tuition and his rather nice sofa bought from Ikea showed his rather large income. Tom quit Beihang and went back to the US at the end of the semester.

1402 – Stephen (British) – It wasn't only Sarah and I that shared a room. Stephens' girlfriend (who was Japanese) didn't teach at Beihang and so she was always sneaking in and out trying not to be seen by Mrs Yang, who no doubt knew about Stephen's other half but said nothing. They did keep themselves very much to themselves and I couldn't help but call them John Lennon and Yoko Ono. Stephen (and his girlfriend) both went to Britain at the end of the semester.

1403 – Ray (Canadian/American) - His parents were from Malaysia and Singapore. He had been born in the French areas of Canada but had most of his teenage years onwards living in Los Angeles. We didn't really speak to Ray much for the first month or so but once we got to know him, he became part of our social circle and a great friend to the both of us. Ray's only complaint about the room he was in was that he had to put up with the noises of almost constant shagging from the two rooms next to him. That might explain why he was so sociable.

1404 - David #1 (American) - David looked very much the stereotypical Santa Claus. He had a big round stomach, red cheeks and a long white beard. We didn't really have much time with David as he was a lot older than everyone else but this didn't stop him from having quite a few Chinese girlfriends.

1405 – Andrew (American) - China's grumpiest man and a member of the Ohio mafia, even though he didn't think of himself as American anymore having spent the last ten years teaching in the PRC. His teaching methods were infamous throughout the college because he was always challenging the students to think that their government was corrupt and full of shit. He had been at

34

Beihang for five years and his apartment looked well lived in and homely. He was a keen audiophile and had vinyl records displayed on his wall and like Tom in 1401, he would have a succession of Chinese students come to him for private tuition. No one was sure why Andrew had stayed in China as long as he had because all he would do was slag the place off (as well as North Korea and any other so called communist states you would care to mention), but after a short discussion, it was decided that he quite liked the lazy lifestyle that the PRC offered. Andrew left (or was asked to leave) at the end of the semester and we were all amazed he had lasted as long as he had done at Beihang.

1406 – The Washroom - Mrs. Yang would occupy this room Monday to Friday from 8am until 5am with a couple of hours for lunch, or that was the theory anyway. We thought that she kept her own timetable some of the time but we didn't realise that she looked after more than one building. We found her a bit difficult to deal with on occasion but we didn't have any major issues, which turned out not to be same for everyone.

1407 – My room – This room turned out to be a perfect location. We never heard the neighbours below us, there were no rooms above us and after the washroom had closed no-one on either side of us. Nice and quiet, just how we like it.

1408 – The empty room

1409 – David #2 (American) – David had come to China on the CIEE programme the semester before this one. We didn't see that much of David and he decided to go home at the end of the semester.

1410 – Hermes (German) – The Beihang bohemian. Hermes was an interesting fellow who always had a story to tell. It seemed that he had spent his entire adult life moving from country to country. He was always on his way somewhere, checking out new and exciting places to hang out. I was quite surprised to meet his wife one day, who still lived in Germany. I was even more surprised because I had seen Hermes with a young Chinese girl on his arm on more than one occasion.

1411 – Doug (American) – What can I say other than that he was the single most important person during our stay in China. Doug hailed from Michigan in the US and always had a measured put down for anyone who came from Ohio (which at Beihang was quite a few). A great bloke. He had come back to China to set up some business interests, and was working as a teacher to bring some money in whilst he built up his contacts. China would have been a lot harder for us without his wisdom, guidance and wonderful company.

1412 – Gareth (New Zealand) – He hung out with his neighbour Alistair most of the time, but he was friendly towards us whenever we saw him. He did have an issue with Mrs Yang near the end of our time here and because of it, he went to teach at a New Zealand school in another part of China.

1413 – Alistair (Brazilian/American/British Passport Holder/God knows what he was) – A man of many opinions that seemed to be solely based on how much it would wind the person he was talking to-up! Once you got past the bullshit, a nice guy who had a side line selling 1980's boom boxes that he found in the markets on eBay, to people in the US. He became a bit disillusioned with China. He was especially fed up with not being able to speak his mind without the fear of arrest or deportation. He found this too much of a strain on his life and decided to go back home at the end of the semester.

1414 – Mark (American) - Mark was trying very hard to loose his American-ness and seemed to be doing his best to go native. He would refuse to eat in most places that weren't selling Chinese food and the only time he would speak any English was with us. He stayed at the end of the semester and we envisaged Mark never going home. We have since learned that he has married a Chinese girl.

1415 – Sam (British) - A Scottish lady that had been in Beihang for the previous five years, but she was a bit of a mystery. I only ever saw her on a couple of occasions and even though she was friendly enough, she didn't hang around with anyone that we knew of.

1416 – Sarah's Room - As we turned up as a couple, but not a married one, we were given separate rooms. However, we decided to make my room our permanent home and this one was used for our guests.

They all stayed here, and even a friend of Ray's made use of this room.

1417 – Karen (American) – Another of the Ohio mafia, but we didn't really hang around with her much. Karen and Gareth had had a bit of a falling out over something that neither seemed particularly keen to talk about so there was always a chilly atmosphere when they were around each other, but she was friendly enough to us. We didn't see much of her though, especially when she got herself a Chinese boy-toy to entertain herself with.

1418 – Tana (American) – Another member of the Ohio mafia (out of the twenty two teachers we met at Beihang, four of them came from Ohio), and a real life saver for Sarah especially with the amount of testosterone on the floor. Normally at the butt of most of our jokes, she needed to work on her time keeping but she was good company.

1419 – Mysterious teacher (might have been Japanese) - I think I only ever saw her once or twice, and then only for a couple of seconds each time. Ray, who had spoken to her before we arrived, said that she spent most of her time with her boyfriend. God knows what she taught, and I cannot even confirm that she was even Japanese. That's just what Ray told me.

1420 – The Other Tom (American) - This was another teacher we didn't see that much of. He was another teacher that went home at the same time we did, but unlike everyone else, it was not through choice. Tom was rumoured to have spent some of his free time taking cycling trips in top secret military areas and for turning up to class wearing a full Chinese military uniform bought from the local market. He did seem surprised when his visa was not renewed and he had to leave the country.

Rob 'The Token Aussie' (Australian) - Rob lived in a property in Wudaokou[13] and I couldn't really tell how we got to know him. He always seemed to be around and

[13] Wudaokou was the nearest Beijing district to our home at Beihang. At the time, it housed a sizable foreign student population (mostly Korean) and was the home to some Western style bars (such as Lush) that we would frequent on the odd occasion.

became a member of our social group. He was a great bloke and always up for something. He also went home at the end of the semester.

Sara (American) - Another member of the Ohio mafia. She was the fourth teacher at the Flying College and she lived in another building in Beihang. She did keep herself to herself even though she would hang out with Karen occasionally. God knows what happened to her at the end of the semester.

The First Week of Teaching

Doug, who we were starting to spend a considerable amount of time with, was turning out to be an utter star and gave me a few tips to help me get through the first week or so of teaching. These were:

1) To shave my head as this is seen as a sign of great wisdom (since my hair has been receding for many years, a shaved head is my normal look so this one was easy).
2) The Chinese are afraid of facial hair (so I grew a goatee!)
3) Be extremely strict with the students to begin with and over time, become more relaxed about things. "The students will love you for it" is a direct Doug quote.

For my first lesson, I thought I would spend the time introducing myself and then, have all the students to do the same to me. I thought this would take up the entire two hour class without any problem and be a nice relaxing start before the proper teaching began later in the week. I went to the college early as I wanted to see Louk about my shoulder, which was still hurting. He wasn't there and having arrived early, I had to wait for almost thirty minutes for my class to turn up. Ten o'clock came and went and there was still no sign of the students so I was beginning to wonder if I was in the right place. After another ten minutes, they all started to troop into the classroom. The first thing I did (and I did this in all of the classes) was to find out who the class monitor was.

We had been told that the monitor was the most important student in the class as he was responsible for their behaviour, liaising between the students and staff (especially if they were ill) and generally being helpful.

I thought I would start the class by telling them my rules. These included:

1) Anybody caught talking when they shouldn't, will stand up.
2) Anybody caught talking twice will stand up with their hands on their heads.
3) Any student standing up through punishment would only be allowed to sit down if someone else was caught talking out of turn, meaning that there was the potential for a student to stand up for the entire class. I would normally let them sit down after five minutes or so but anyone who did stand up was laughed at by the peers, who were no doubt relieved that it wasn't them.
4) I said I would make late comers pay me money, but I never actually went through with this.
5) Anybody caught with their mobile on would have it confiscated.
6) They must raise their hand if they wished to ask a question.
7) They must have a doctors' note or let the monitor know if they weren't able to attend class. Monitors were very influential people.
8) No eating or drinking (except water)[14].

It was only after this that I introduced myself and gave the slide show presentation of my life in Britain, which actually took all of ten minutes. On reflection, I think I have should spent more time planning my lesson because for the rest of the hour the students introduced themselves to me. The ten minute break gave me a

[14] I stuck fast to my rules for about a month or so, but the first one I did let slide was no drink other than water. Nearly all of my students had a Chinese style water bottle. The only difference between these and the ones I would see at home is at the top of the bottle was a filter, which allowed them to drink tea out of it without swallowing the leaves (no tea bags here).

chance to think of something to do for the following fifty. I thought I would have a Q&A session and this turned out to be very funny.

One of the questions they asked was 'How many girlfriends do you have?' to which I said one, and that she was also teaching at the Flying College. They all thought it was Sara but I put them straight on this one. They also asked me to sing to them, but I countered this by saying that they would never have enough money for that to happen. One of them also put me on the spot by asking me what I thought of Chairman Mao. Not wishing to say anything that might cause offence or get me into trouble (especially at this early stage) I said I didn't really know enough about him to have an opinion. I was glad that I was never asked this question again for the remainder of my time in China.

I felt very good after class and managed to meet up with Louk who said that the college had organised a place for me to have my shoulder treated after I had finished teaching for the day. The second class proved to be a bit tougher then the first, mostly due to their English not being of the same standard. One of them was asleep and another one turned up twenty five minutes late because he had been snoozing in his dorm. After giving him a bit of a dressing down (that did get a few smirks from the rest of the class), I went through the same routine of introducing myself and getting them to do the same to me. The second half really dragged on because they seemed more reluctant to ask me any questions.

After class, Louk took me to the area outside the Universities West Gate to what I can only describe as a Chinese Witch Doctor. Louk explained to the guy where I had the most pain because he didn't speak any English. He spent half an hour massaging my shoulder and then he used his thumb nail on the acupuncture points in my arm which sent a shooting pain all the way up to my shoulder.

After that had finished, I spent another half an hour lying on a massage table. I couldn't really see what he was doing but out of the corner of my eye, it looked as though he was putting a lighter into a series of jam jars that were then put on my back. As soon as they were put there, I could feel the skin being pulled up sharply and it was quite painful to begin with, though I felt quite relaxed during the process and would have fallen asleep if the place wasn't absolutely freezing. I was really glad when I could put some warm clothing on and even happier when I felt all the pain had gone away. Even though I didn't realise it at the time, my back looked as though it had five enormous love bites on it.

As a way of celebrating a good day, Doug took me to Ivy's, the best DVD shop near Beihang, which was located just outside of the North Gate. Ivy's was a very small shop but she was more than happy to order in any DVD for the foreign teachers, as long as it was available. There I bought the first four seasons of CSI which turned out lasted us for a couple of months and saw a few other bits and pieces that I would go back for at a later date.

Sarah's day was the complete opposite of my own. She had spent the whole day being nervous and it didn't help that I came back from my lessons buzzing from having had generally a positive experience. Once she arrived at the Flying College, Sarah was told that some of her classes had to be moved because they had to make room for some other 'important' lessons. Understandably, she was very annoyed about this because it would mean teaching every evening of the week. Her first class was not the best either. The students were restless and kept talking all of the time[15]. Needless to say, Sarah was having serious doubts about being here.

Sarah decided that she would need to nip this evening teaching situation in the bud so the next morning she steamed over to the college to see Mrs. Lu. Using the little Chinese Sarah knew with the even smaller amount of English that Mrs. Lu knew, they managed to negotiate a change in the timetable, mainly by a series of over exaggerated facial expressions along with some vibrant and firm hand gestures. As an added bonus, Sarah was given her first months wages but she was worried that

---

[15] Sarah decided to adopt the rules that I had come up with, but due to the indiscipline of her first class, almost half of them were standing up by the time the class finished.

my timetable would be changed to accommodate her as Mrs. Lu wanted to see me straight away. However, all she wanted to do was to give me my wages. Sarah has a very suspicious mind which actually proved to be a real handicap in China where a lot of the deals are based on trust, gentlemen's agreements and 'Guanxi[16]'.

The longer the week went on, the more confident we both became at teaching. They were all enthusiastic young men and when Sarah asked one of her classes to each introduce the person next to them, about 90% of them commented on how handsome their friend was. Sarah followed this up by asking the students to tell her something interesting about themselves. One student said he slept in the same bed as the boy next to him and another one said he liked to sleep on top. Sarah wasn't sure if they realised what they were actually saying and when she tried to clarify it by repeating back to them that they actually slept in the same bed and shared the same blankets, the rest of the class fell about laughing. It turns out that they were talking about bunk beds.

All of our students were obsessed was with girls. They all bemoaned the fact that the Flying College didn't have any in it, and because of that, you could really smell the testosterone in the air, or it could have just been their body odour! When we asked them what topics they'd like to talk about in the English lesson all classes wanted to learn how to talk to girls and how to get a girlfriend. Unfortunately neither of us are experts in this field (especially Sarah who has never felt the need to get a girlfriend) and our students were all disappointed!

One of Sarah's students said he was very good at chatting up girls and at the beginning of the next lesson she got him to demonstrate two of his favourite

[16] "Guanxi is a central concept in Chinese society and describes, in part, a personal connection between two people in which one is able to prevail upon another to perform a favour or service, or be prevailed upon. The two people need not be of equal social status. It could also be a network of contacts, which an individual can call upon when something needs to be done, and through which he or she can exert influence on behalf of another. It can also describe a state of general understanding between two people: "he/she is aware of my wants/needs and will take them into account when deciding her/his course of future actions which concern or could concern me"" (http://en.wikipedia.org/wiki/Guanxi).

techniques. One of his class mates pretended to be a girl who on both occasions played very hard to get, much to everyone's amusement.

We also got first hand experience of the English names they had chosen for themselves. The most bizarre ones we had were:

Power, Rambo, Rocky, Azone, Season, Future, Merry, Vicky (this is meant to be an all male college!), Tiger, Xinzer, Unicorn, Ice, Ivy, Only, Grom and NT.

They were all quite surprised that we found some of their names out of the ordinary to say the least. Some even asked me if they should change them but I told them not to bother because as long at they liked it, it was fine.

For the first couple of weeks at least, there were loads of emails flying around from everyone who had been on the induction week. They shared some of our experiences. How they were all settling in and telling us about the funny English names their students had chosen for themselves. These included:

Hedgehog, Ice Cream, Adolf, Hamburger (a girl), Harry Potter, Donut along with Black and Blue (who really should have been introduced to one another).

One of the most amusing notes from one of the other teachers (who is about 5ft 10") said that she was asked by one of her students if she would grow as tall as her if she ate potatoes and she wasn't a child, but an University student. It did beg the question, what were they teaching these kids?

These emails calmed down very quickly and the only time we would hear from anyone was when they were coming to visit, or we were trying to visit them. I suppose that it is quite hard to stay in touch within a country as big as China.

We had been advised by nearly every non Chinese person we had spoken to that it would a good idea to buy a mobile phone. Doug came along with us and we went to the massive market that was outside the

West Gate. As soon as we walked in, we attracted quite an audience especially the group of six Chinese people who just stopped what they were doing and were stared at us to see what we were going to buy, eagerly awaiting the outcome. We didn't like to disappoint our audience so we made a show of pulling faces and trying to haggle. When we did finally buy one, it was the cheapest phone in the market because it was also the oldest. Everyone here is keen to have the latest phone so the old ones, if you can find them and most importantly if they work, can be picked up for a bargain price. We thought we would only need one between us. We would soon find out our mistake!

Chinglish

Chinglish is a curious mix of English and Chinese. The Chinese had used their own words to come up with a phonetic equivalent of the English word. A good example of this is Coca-Cola which is known in China as 'kokoukole', which translates as 'Happiness in the mouth'. It wasn't always thus as the slogan originally read 'Kekoukela' which translates as either 'Female horse stuffed with wax' or 'Bite the wax tadpole' depending on the pronunciation. Chinglish became a by-word for poor translation and there were so many examples of this when we travelling around with signs the most obvious source of mirth.

Some of the funnier signs are as follows:

1) 'Police Tips - Less Numbness More Loss' - Seen on the Shanghai Underground, nobody at the time knew what the hell this meant and even now, it still doesn't make any sense.

2) 'Watch the Escalator over you Head' - Seen in one of the Shanghai Museum's, we assumed that in English, this would have said 'Mind Your Head'. The danger with a sign like this was that you would be concentrating on the escalator above you that you wouldn't see the end of the escalator you were on causing all sorts of problems.

3) 'No Tossing' – Seen on the mountain of Hua Shan near Xi'an. If it didn't have a little diagram

of a figure throwing litter away, the connotations of this sign could have been slightly rude.

4) 'Please Don't Huddle Together' – Also seen on Hua Shan, this sign was on a fence designed to stop people from falling over the cliff, so we were not entirely sure what this was trying to warn us about.

5) 'Police Tips – Being Cheated because of Credulous Believing' - Seen in Shanghai. I have one tip for the Chinese police (well the ones in Shanghai anyway); have a few English lessons before looking words up in the dictionary and putting them on a sign.

6) 'Punch Place' - Seen on the Tiananmen Gate. This wasn't a place where you would be randomly hit, but as we got to the sign and there was no one by it we didn't know what it was for. We could only I assumed that this would be the place where tickets would be punched

7) 'For High Tower, Steep and Smooth Stairs Pay Attention to Safety Please. If Need be, Please Ask Attendant for Help' – Seen on the Bell and Drum Towers in Beijing, we think this was a warning that the steps were a hazard, but when we asked an attendant for help, she looked as puzzled as us.

8) 'No Burning' – Seen in the Temple of Heaven Park, I thought this was a warning that people could spontaneously self combust. On closer examination, it had a no smoking symbol on it as well so we could only assume it was for that.

9) 'Be Careful when Tanking Elevator' - Seen at the Polar Aquarium and Tiger Beach Park in Dalian, the spelling mistake was humorous but it was actually trying to warn people about an escalator.

10) 'Be Careful of Slip' – Seen in one of the many KFC's I visited, I can only assume that should have said 'wet floor'.

11) 'Aggressive Service' – Seen in the local Western Brand Supermarket (name withheld because they have a bit of a litigious reputation). I am

sure it should have said that the staff would be happy to help instead of wanting to attack you.

<u>Life at Beihang</u>
Apart from orientation week and the odd trip to another part of the country, Beihang University was our home for our stay in China. It was built in 1953 and from the off, it concentrated on aeronautic studies. By the time we arrived, the Universities website stated that "BUAA has grown into an open, multi-disciplined, research-oriented university of engineering science and technology with an emphasis on aeronautical and astronautically engineering. [...] BUAA, as a centre of both higher education and scientific research, has become one of the important bases for quality personnel education and scientific research in China[17]".

Beihang has been at the forefront of Chinese weapon technology for many years and the Americans who have worked there cannot (allegedly) get a job in government back home. We heard on the rumour mill that work on the campus involved research into stealth aircraft and the manufacturing of helicopters, which was where Beihang made its money.

It was not only home to students but lecturers and University staff also resided here. The Chinese way of doing things means that if you work somewhere, you must be given accommodation and even if they retire, they are allowed to stay. The retired teachers could often be seen milling around, normally getting in the way or exercising in the park.

The University was essentially a small town and all of the roads that criss-crossed the campus had their own names. The campus was a good deal larger than any I had seen at home and you could easily survive there without ever having to leave. In fact, it was so big and had so many buildings that it wouldn't be hard to imagine that there was a lost Roman Legion still marching around looking to get home. Even though we lived there for six months, there were many areas that we never set foot in and it was quite easy to get lost. There was a bank, post

---

[17] http://ev.buaa.edu.cn/

office and a pretty basic hotel (which was not recommended to us by anyone) as well as few other things:

Two Local Supermarkets - These were great and were not, as we had been lead to believe, much more expensive than Wal-Mart, as well as being a damn site closer. The first one we went into was called Your Goal, and was so new that according to the other teachers, it had not been there six months before hand. It was underground and judging by the size of the doors (which were massive and at least three foot thick), we could only theorise that this had been a bomb shelter in a previous life. Judging by the nature of some of the research that had been worked on at Beihang, this would be perfectly feasible. Your Goal had a bakery and was the only place on campus where we could buy fresh, Western style bread. The older, more knackered looking supermarket was called Chaoshifa and it reminded us of the Tesco Metro in our local high street. Not as nice as the newer, bigger one near by, but it did sell all the essentials as well as having a bit of character.

The Convenient Store - So called because even though it was not the nearest shop to us (it was over the road instead of in the basement of our building, which was also the home of the lift operators and a shop), but it was far and away the best and most convenient. We could have lived quite easily on what it sold, and one of the foreign teachers did just that. Not a day would go past (or so it seemed) when one or both of us would pay it a visit. It was always open when I got up in the morning and would sometimes still be open at 1am.

Campus Hospital - Life stopped at Beihang between 12:00 – 14:00, including health care. One of our colleagues needed to see a doctor and went after her class finished at 12pm to discover she couldn't have medical treatment at lunchtime so it was fortunate that she wasn't dying! We both tried to avoid the campus hospital during our stay, but we were not always successful.

The Local Gym - According to the campus map that we found in our room, there were allegedly a few of these dotted around the place. The only one we ever saw was directly opposite the Flying College. It was 'brand spanking' new and a fair old size. We were told that the 2008 Olympic weight lifting events would be held here, and whilst we were there, there were some international women's volleyball matches. Needless to say, we were not allowed to use it. In fact, it seemed that nobody was allowed to use it (apart from the volleyball players).

Lovers Lane - Or the park as it was more commonly known. This was in the middle of the campus and could be seen from outside of our apartment block. We walked through it to get to the Flying College and when we arrived, it looked like it had been neglected for a while. This was especially true of the lake that had hardly any water in it. When the weather improved, a massive team of gardeners appeared who would water and tend to it so that it turned into a beautiful green space that people would chill out in. They didn't like people sitting on the grass though.

This could have been due to the work that had been put into growing it in the first place, but it was more than likely down to the fact that it was the local dog population's toilet. In the morning, it was a common occurrence to see the old residents of the University practicing their Tai Chi. This was interesting to watch, especially when they used swords and I am not talking about fakes either, but real metal ones. The evening was the time of the day that the park became really popular, especially once the weather warmed up. It was very hard to find a seat because they had all been taken up by couples snogging. Privacy is at a premium here, so this was a perfect place to find some. Well, that and a cheap local hotel.

The park was surrounded by some mushroom shaped objects that during the two hour lunch period would play all sorts of music at almost noticeable levels. The more annoying thing about these was the fact that between 9:30pm and 10pm, happy birthday would be pumped out at a very loud volume. It was like listening to bad 'hold' music, but without the option of putting the phone down.

Nearly all of the trees in the park, and around the campus as a whole had what looked like white paint on them. We were told that this was not actually paint, but was designed to keep bugs from climbing up the trees and killing them. All of the trees that were planted along the roads were in a small bed of earth that seemed to be used as an outside toilet for animals and small children, so it was always recommended not to walk in them.

The Sports Pitches - There were loads of areas to try and keep fit if you fancied going outside and braving the almost ever present pollution. Sarah and Tana both started off trying to exercise on a regular basis, which meant Sarah would come back to the flat red in the face and ready to fall over from exhaustion. The college has some public running tracks and an assault course. The girls tried to use these, but when there were loads of students exercising there with matching tracksuits, the PE teachers didn't seem too pleased with sharing the facilities.

There were loads of basketball courts which were always full of students. As the ground was solid tarmac, it was not surprising that they were always getting injuries. There were a number of 7-a-side football pitches, which were just as busy as the basketball courts. As they were made of an artificial turf, injuries were almost non-existent. They also had a full size grass pitch, but it didn't seem to get a good deal of use. This could have been down to the fact that it cost 3000RMB to hire (about £215) which was almost my entire month's salary.

There were loads of random pieces of exercise equipment dotted all over campus. In fact, they seemed to be everywhere in China and could be used by anyone at anytime. Wherever we went, they were always painted blue and yellow. We did have a go on a few of them, but they didn't seem to have any resistance left in the mechanisms so they were actually of no use at all if you were using them to stay fit. It didn't stop them from being a popular hang out for the locals.

Eating Out - There was a wide selection of places to eat out on campus. Our favourite when we first arrived was Dining Hall 8. Our students told us that this was expensive (with 8RMB for a meal the average price), but we liked it and for no other reason than we thought it is very cheap. In fact, we thought that eating in any of the dining halls was so cheap that we very rarely cooked anything for ourselves. It also helped that it was open all day. Most of the food served was freshly cooked which was quite rare because not all of the dining halls did this. We did get bored of DH8 after a while and even though a couple of the other dining halls served food we liked (including No.5 which we had been told by Louk on our first night we were not allowed to use), we ended up going out of the campus to eat. There were a couple of proper restaurants as well, but these tended to be expensive so we didn't go to these very often.

Bike Sheds - They say there are nine million bicycles in Beijing, so there were a lot of these dotted around the campus. It is actually an understatement to say they were sheds as I have seen multi-story car parks that were smaller than these. Due to the amount of bikes in Beijing, having one stolen is a common occurrence and it is very rare to keep hold of one for very long. Buying a lock didn't help either. All it did was just slow the thieves down by about ten seconds. Most seem to have only one gear but people tended not to be going very fast on them anyway which is a good thing because there is a large probability of being hit. Anything more fancy on a bike than two wheels and a frame would be like having a big neon sign on it saying 'Steal me please'.

Tana bought a bike and she parked it downstairs. Needless to say, it was stolen not long afterwards but one of Sarah's students had the worst experience. He had bought an expensive bike, went to lunch and when he came back, the bike was gone. He had had it for less than two hours and hadn't even had a chance to ride it. The students had a saying; "You're not a real Beihang resident until you've had at least two bikes stolen."

Aircraft Museum - With Beihang's history in this field, it was not a surprise that they had this on campus. It was bizarre that this was next to the Flying College, and yet neither of us went into it, especially as we visited museums at every other opportunity. We could see some of the collection through the windows of one of the admin buildings we frequented. There were some classic planes and helicopters on display, but their rusting hulks gathering dirt and generally falling apart didn't make it seem all that worthwhile. The fact we had to pay when the students could get in for free was also a deciding factor in us not going in.

The Local Residents - We were normally allowed to get on with our business without any of the locals talking to us, but this wasn't always the case. Very early on in our life at Beihang, we met with one of the residents who Sarah so nicely called 'the village idiot'. The first encounter occurred in Dining Hall 8 when, uninvited he sat next to Tana and Sarah and proceeded to talk to them, but every other word was 'fuck'. He also tended to spit every time he spoke so by the end, both Sarah and Tana would put their arms over their plates to protect their food, in much the same way you would to stop someone looking at your work in an exam. We saw him quite a few times and always did our best to avoid him. I realised quite early on that he didn't seem to remember who we were even if you had spoken to him before, because I was able to pretend to be Norwegian or Dutch, said I couldn't understand English causing him to go away. This might seem a little unfair, but it was either that or get covered in a small waterfall of spittle every time he came close.

The Final Word - This must go to one of the funniest things we saw on campus, which was the secrecy department that was in the same building as the security department. This did not prove to be that hard to find either because they had rather conveniently put a big sign (in English as well as Chinese) on the side of the building telling everyone where it was! Obviously in the past, it had been so secret that it now needed to advertise.

Becoming Settled

The second week of teaching was when we began to settle into the routine that we more or less followed until the end the semester. I would go off teaching during the day and Sarah would spend most of the evenings doing likewise. We would normally spend lunch in either one of the dining halls, one of the restaurants outside of the west gate or (and this was the most common one), sitting in the flat watching a DVD. I also disposed of the goatee which did not return for the remainder of our trip, much to Sarah's joy!

The second week of teaching was also when things started to get a bit more interesting. The class that Sarah had had discipline problems with on her first night was still her most disruptive, so being the dutiful boyfriend; I thought I would help out. Before the class started, I simply went into the room and waited for the class to turn up. Once they were all there, I just got up and walked out. After the initial questions about who I was from the class, Sarah told them that I was her other half and that I had not been happy with their behaviour so far. After that, they were as good as gold. This was the first indication I had that just my physical presence was enough to put the fear of whatever God they believed in, into the students.

After this initial success, I thought I would turn up the heat on another of Sarah's students who was called Merry as he hadn't made the best impression on his new English teacher. In class, he kept complaining that he was bored and that he used to go around to his previous English teachers apartment to play computer games. He was also very disruptive in the classroom and Sarah was not having any success trying to control him. One night, he came into the dining hall we were eating in and after seeing Sarah, he made his way over and sat himself down at our table. Sarah subtly pointed out that this was the infamous Merry, so after introducing myself, I informed him that I never wanted to hear that he was misbehaving again. Needless to say, I never did and Sarah was most pleased with the outcome. Sarah also caught one of her students taking a picture of her backside with his mobile phone. Unfortunately for him, Sarah was a bit quick off the mark and confiscated it but was unable to work out if he had saved the picture or had deleted it (as he had promised). A quick search of the internet didn't reveal if it had ended up on a site or not.

I also had some problems with some of my student's and their mobile phones. This was only a week after telling them I never wanted to see or hear them in my class. Some people just like to learn the hard way, but at least they weren't taking pictures of my backside. After hearing two mobiles ring very loudly whilst I was giving a class, I confiscated them with the intention of bringing them back the next day. I gave them the impression that they would never get them back, as per my rules but it turned out that their mobiles meant more to them than just wires and microchips.

It turned out that their mobiles are their lives and when they lost one, it was like losing an arm or equivalent. One of the students whose phone I had confiscated had another one so he wasn't that bothered. As we had been led to believe from talking to the students that none of them were particularly well off, I found this one had to fathom, especially as the phones were quite new models and therefore, expensive. The other student was a different story altogether.

He was very upset that his phone had been taken and when the lesson finished he followed me out of the class. I was not keen to hand the phone back that day as it would be a good example to the other students to keep their phones off, hidden or nowhere near my classroom. Once I was outside, the student tried to grab my bag and was getting very irate about the whole thing. He was even started to shout at me, which was not meant to be a very Chinese thing to do. Shouting leads to confrontation and as I have said before, the Chinese are not great fans of this sort of thing. I finally lost patience and took him to the Dean where the student was given a dressing down Chinese style. News soon spread about this incident and phones became non-existent for the next few weeks. He also wrote me an apology, which was an interesting touch.

International Women's Day

Sarah, along with a couple of the other foreign female teachers was invited to go to the celebrations for International Women's Day although no-one had heard of it before. The way it was described sounded like it was going to be an official luncheon. However, the party was late (mainly due to Tana, who soon became notorious for her poor timekeeping) and problems with traffic (Beijing's roads could become very congested). They missed all of

53

the speeches (a good thing) and found out that it was only being held in the Banqueting Hall but there was absence of food (a bad thing).

The only food available was nibbles (also not a good thing – especially as it is quite hard eating pistachios with chopsticks!) and there wasn't much to go round either! It wasn't a total disaster though as Sarah managed to pocket the cute panda chopstick rest that was on her table. In her first lesson after this, Sarah discovered that the Chinese have a day for everything you could possibly think of. Unfortunately Teachers Day was in September so we would miss that and the presents associated with it. Bugger!

The Drifters

Even though I may not be the best player in the world, I do love kicking a football about and I was really keen to play some in China. During our induction week, the experienced teachers told me that their students loved to have a kick around with them and that mine would no doubt feel the same way. It would come as a shock when my students told me that they were not allowed to play football because it was against the rules of the college. I did try and find out on numerous occasions the reasons behind this and I could only find one story to why. This story involved a previous Flying College student had been injured by a falling goal (or gate depending on the story) and it was for that reason alone that they were banned. Shame that the same care did not extend to the basketball court and the multitude of injuries the students seemed to pick up playing on that.

Once I had their confidence, some of the students revealed that they would play the odd game when they should have been studying and at some ungodly hour on a Sunday morning. Another reason I didn't join them very often might have been down the fact that even though they always seemed happy for me to join them, they did tell me that I was a bit big and too powerful for them. I was quite impressed by some of their play and some would turn out to be very good players indeed.

Before I had even met the students though, I had already become a member of a football team, and all within two days of actually landing in the capital. A quick flick through the pages of the Beijing Lonely Planet listed an email address that anyone could write to asking for a game in one of the ex-pat leagues. The leagues Operations Manager emailed me back saying that he had sent my details to a team called the 'Beijing Drifters' and that a chap called Rupert, the teams manager would get in touch. He did say that if I didn't hear from him within the next week, I was to let him know as he would chase them up or find me an alternative team. He also said that if the Drifters didn't suit me I could get back in touch with him so he could find me another side.

I didn't have to wait long to receive an email from Rupert. He said that the team was currently placed third in the third division and that it was probably the most international of all the teams in Beijing with players from England, Ireland, Russia, Holland, Malaysia, China, Germany, Mexico, France, Spain, Africa and even Madagascar. He asked that if I was interested in playing with them, to send him some contact details (other than my email address) and he would send further details. He also wrote at the bottom of the email that the team was in desperate need of an injury free keeper. Knowing that my 11-a-side keeping skills are poor at the best of times, I hoped that they would have some space for me. As I only had the land line number to send, I sent that over with some information about myself.

Within five minutes of the email being sent, Rupert was on the phone talking to me about the team and even though I told him I was a striker, he replied they were in need of one of those as well. He had only put the tag line about the goal keeper because he was the first choice goalie, but due to work commitments and the fact that he had severely damaged his back during his time in the army, he couldn't always play. He said that the season had taken a break over the months of November to February due to the extreme cold and frozen pitches but hostilities would start again in the next couple of weeks. Impressed by his keenness to get me involved, I said I would be really interested in playing for the Drifters and told him to keep me informed of any up and coming fixtures, which didn't actually take that long.

5-a-side
My first experience of playing for the Drifters didn't really give me any clues as to what was to follow in the months to come. All communication about up and coming fixture would be via email, but Rupert's request for a goalie had gone unanswered. As he couldn't play himself due to his aforementioned work commitments, I said I would fill in as long as I had a run out in at least one game. Each team was in a group of four and would go through to the next round regardless of where they finished. Therefore, we would play a minimum of four games. We hammered the first team 8-0 as they were terrible. This did give us a false sense of greatness and the failings of the team were cruelly exposed in the next three games. Our one win meant that we finished third so we would meet a team that finished second in their group.

This turned out to a team made up completely of African players. Rupert informed me later that this team played in the 11-a-side league and some of their number were ex-international players that had come to China looking for a contract to finish their careers with. This was our best performance but it didn't stop us from being completely outplayed and we went down by three goals, which was not a bad result.

Christophe, a Frenchman with an Inspector Clouseau type accent was nice enough to offer me a lift back to Beihang. My description of the Universities location was a bit on the poor side so it was actually a good deal further away than I initially thought. It did give me a chance to talk to Christophe about life in Beijing and about how he had ended up here. He had worked in the hotel trade for about twenty years and was now in the process of overseeing the building of a brand new hotel, which would open in time for the Olympics. Christophe had been in Beijing for about five years and watched the city change beyond recognition. Areas that were once buildings were now parks and vice versa. High rise buildings had sprung up in place of the hutongs that once were the cities landscape and it was all in preparation for the 2008 Games. Christophe would be my lift to many a football match which save me from getting lost in the maze that is Beijing. His wit and calming influence on any game were always welcome, especially when we were on the end of a thumping.

Later on that night, I received a call from Rupert to see how I'd got on, but I think he was trying to find out if I would play again. He need not have had any fears on this because I only ever missed one session of five a side, which wasn't too bad considering there were some weekends where we were away or the amount of times I was ill.

Part 4 – The Shit Hits the Pan

<u>Illness</u>

We had all been warned in the orientation week that everyone is supposed to get this at least twice during a six month stay, and it doesn't matter what you do or how careful you are, you cannot avoid it (Sarah however proved to be the exception to the rule and she claims that she was the healthiest she has ever been for the six months we were in China). My bout of the dreaded Beijing Belly was not a pleasant experience and meant a couple of days lying around feeling sorry for myself along with plenty of visits to the toilet. It also felt like I had the flu as all of the joints in my body seemed to be hurting at the same time.

With my near constant use of the toilet, the damn thing became blocked within a day due to the amount of paper I had had to use and it stayed that way for the best part of a month. No amount of patience or use of a plunger would alleviate the problem. The thought of using dynamite did cross my mind but we could use the toilet in the other flat. It was fortunate that we had that because without it, we might have been in a bit of trouble. After a couple of days of use, we managed to block that one up as well. This turned out to be easier to unblock and we warned all of our guests to take it easy with the toilet paper when they came to visit.

After discreetly discussing our blockages with a couple of the long term teachers, this turned out to be not a unique problem. It seemed that that the Chinese pipe-work was not designed for Westerners use of toilet paper. We tried using less but when this didn't work, we invested in a bin to dispose of our waste paper, but having to dispose of this was never the nicest job. At least the smell didn't stand out too much against the general smell of the university, which on the hot days to come would be particular pungent. Whilst the blockage was in place, we were always waiting for a knock on the door from the one of our neighbours below to complain that their waste pipe had exploded into their toilet room. Thankfully, this never happened.

The only upside from this was that I looked a lot thinner than I had done for many a year, but I would not recommend this as a form of weight loss. We really couldn't put our finger on why I had become ill because I had eaten roughly the same food as everyone else and they had all been fine. After a couple of days, the worst of it had passed but it took me the best part of a week before I could face Chinese food again.

I wasn't best pleased that as I was just beginning to get over my illness, Louk dragged us out to some government agency to get our visas sorted out. I was feeling really weak and still a little sick but we didn't have to stay there for very long, which I was really glad about. Having not seen the outside world for a couple of days, I just wanted to go back home and crash out. We did have to leave our passports behind which neither of us was happy about, but Louk said that he would collect them in a week or so. Doug informed us that if we hadn't done this, we would have to leave the country which actually sounded like a good idea at this juncture. We had made a great effort and spent a good deal of money to get here so we thought we may as well stick it out.

The weather hadn't warmed up any either. This didn't stop the University from shutting the heating off. Neither of us was particularly happy about this either, but at least we had brought some winter thermals to keep us warm, though an Eskimo outfit would have gone down better. Teaching in a room that was so cold that I had to wear gloves and at least three layers of clothes was not my idea of a good time.

On a lighter note, we had our first visitor. Jill, who had been on our induction week, came up for a couple of days. She and Sarah went to Beihai Park, although most sites of interest in the park were being refurbished for the Olympics and they couldn't get near them. This turned out to be a regular occurrence when we started to visit the sights of Beijing as so much of what we would like to have seen was covered in scaffolding.

* * * * *

<u>11-a-side</u>
  Game 10 - Drifters (1) v Beijing Celtic B (6) –
Even though I had been laid up on the sofa and not eaten
very much for the days preceding this game, I said that I
would definitely be able to play. Before travelling to the
ground for an 11-a-side game, we would meet at the
Club Football Bar[18], located conveniently not that far from
an Underground Station. A couple of the players had cars
which always doubled up as team buses. This was the
first time I had met Rupert and he was very welcoming of
not only me, but all the other new players that had
turned up. Rupert explained to me that the Drifters had
always had a problem with getting sufficient numbers to
play because most of their regulars were business men
that might be dragged away from Beijing at a moments
notice, even at the weekend.
  Christophe gave me and a few others a lift to a
ground that was at the end of some of the bumpiest
roads I have been on. I was sure that an all-terrain
vehicle would have been better suited to this than
Christophe's 'family car'. It was also one of the poorest
areas I ever went to throughout our entire stay and most
probably a snap shot of what Beijing was like in the era
before China became the sweatshop of the world. The
roads nearer to the complex were considerably better,
but this was because it was once used as a training area
by the Chinese National football team. It was easy to see
that the pitches were no longer in use for this purpose. I
only ever saw two pitches (even though there could have
been more). The first had grass so long that it was hard
to see your feet and the ball would run sluggishly as
though it was a muddy pitch. I had played on pitches with
grass as long as this before, but only at rugby.

---

[18] The Club Football bar was the only bar in Beijing I would regularly go to,
not only because we would meet there before matches but because it was
the best place to watch live football. The walls were covered in football
memorabilia from around the world including photos, shirts and scarves
donated by the patrons trying to leave their own mark. It would not be
uncommon for every television in the place to be showing different game
from loads of countries around the world, even though I never saw a Chinese
game on the box. Their only concession to local players was a National Team
photo behind the bar.

The other was so lacking in grass that when the wind picked up (and the wind was particularly strong in this game), we were blinded by the dust. We all joked that the only thing missing was tumbleweed. I hadn't played on grass for a few years and I knew that I was going to struggle a bit on the uneven surface. Rupert said to the 'newbies' that the rules in the 11-a-side league were as the FIFA rule book except for one major difference; rolling subs. This would prove to be very handy, especially for the heavy smokers and less fit members of the team.

We had about sixteen players in total and we even had a young Korean guy who said he would play in goal. He really looked the part as well and insisted on wearing shorts whilst between the sticks, which was brave considering how cold it was. As is my experience (and no doubt that of many other players), there is a big difference between looking and actually being the part. Unfortunately for this guy, he most definitely wasn't the part. He flapped at crosses and showed that he wouldn't have been able to catch a cold. Rupert substituted him at half time and he never turned up for another game.

As the Ref called us to start, I thought that it would be the same as back home where you stroll on at your leisure and get into your position, but not here. Both teams (led by their respective captains) would walk behind the Ref onto the pitch and line up very much like teams in the Champions League would. Then there was the obligatory coin toss, the winning captain would choose ends, the whistle would blow and everyone would walk off to their positions. I thought that this would be a one off but it happened in every single 11-a-side game. Thankfully, the 5-a-side didn't bother with formalities like this.

We were thumped. We deserved to lose, but the main difference between the teams was their centre forward. He didn't look like much and was a little overweight, but he knew how to score which is something we were lacking. I played most of the game on the left wing, but I did get to have a go up front as well. It was mentioned in the match report that I had an excellent game, even though I only remember flattening some bloke in a shoulder to shoulder challenge, being blinded by the dust and hitting the bar with a 35-yard free kick. It didn't go in either but just cannoned off the bar and was cleared. This was the biggest defeat of the season, and we were informed by Rupert that the last time the Drifters were beaten as comprehensively as this, they went on an unbeaten run of seven games. Judging by this performance, it was difficult to predict any such run happening in the near future.

Class Things in Class #1

Our students were a never ending source of information, entertainment and on the odd occasion, frustration.

1) I was so annoyed with one of my classes that I told them that if they did not improve and stop sleeping in class, I would fail them all. I also took the digital camera into class to take photos of them playing cards and sleeping threatening to show them to the Dean. This seemed to do the trick because there was suddenly a dramatic increase in attendance and effort.

2) One of Sarah's students was giving a presentation to the rest of the class and Sarah asked him to stop speaking in Chinese. The rest of the class started to wet themselves laughing because it turned out that he was actually talking in English, but it was so poor Sarah couldn't understand a word of it.

3) One of Sarah's students told her that she was the strictest foreign teacher they have ever had but that she was a lot more organised than the last one. Sarah replied it was probably because she was older than the last teacher and not fresh out of university. The student said he thought it was because she had worked in Human Resources! Oh how quickly they learn!!!!

4) My Class 9 were definitely the weakest of all the classes I taught, so I thought it would be a good time to whip them into shape. I told the class that I had been speaking to Dean Tang about

them (which was actually a lie) and he said that I could fail any or all of them if I felt that they didn't make the grade (which was the truth). Cue best class with these guys and good effort by them for the rest of term and who said lying was wrong. I was only following Doug's tip of being strict to begin with and then chilling out, honest.

5) One of the views the students had were that western girls were 'easy' and were all quite surprised when I said I only had the one girlfriend. My reply was to ask them which country in the world has the largest population to which they all replied 'China'. All I could say to that was 'and Western girls are easy are they?' No reply.

Little Trouble In Big China

The weather had begun to improve, and quite dramatically by mid March which meant that only after a couple of weeks of the heating being turned off, we didn't miss it. It is not quite T-Shirt weather, but there was no longer any need to wrap up like an arctic explorer to go anywhere.

The improvement in the weather meant that we both began to notice that the level of pollution had also started to rise. We thought how it would be nice when we get home to see the stars in the sky, because at night there was always a layer of smog in the air. I read on the internet that less than 1% of the 500 Chinese cities have clean air; respiratory disease is China's leading cause of death. You don't need to smoke in China; the atmosphere does all the damage for you.

I had a real craving for some western food, and more specifically a burger. I put this down to all of the Chinese food I had and the Beijing Belly. Doug suggested a restaurant and off we went for what was by far and away the most expensive meal we had paid for since getting to Beijing. 58RMB[19] for a small burger and some

---

[19] Compared to back home, this was actually quite cheap for this sort of meal but in China, this was a lot.

rather poor chips was almost three times as much as any previous meal, and was the worst value for money.

The salad bar may have been 'all you can eat', but that was quite poor as well. However, I was quite happy just to be eating something again. What was even more annoying is that we found that we could have bought a much nice burger for a fraction of the price at Lush in Wudaokou!

5-a-side

The first season of 5-a-side was played on some pitches near to the Lido hotel area. Lots of rich business men and tourists stayed here which meant that there were a lot of prostitutes plying their trade. Due to this, the competition rules were adjusted slightly. The rule book stated that no players were allowed to bring prostitutes to the ground. Allegedly, this had happened so much in previous seasons that the league had felt it necessary to tell players not to do it. Rupert said that he had confidence in the Drifters not to break this rule because those of us who were married (or had girlfriends) wouldn't do so on moral grounds and English teachers wouldn't do so due to financial reasons. That was me covered on both counts then!

For 5-a-side games, I tended to meet Christophe at the Underground station near Club Football and after the matches had finished, I would go back to Beihang in a taxi. As we were playing in the 3rd Division, our games were on Thursday nights with the games kicking off at either 8pm or 9pm. There were two games per evening. The pitches were a little longer than the equivalent ones back home and had goals very similar to those found on a hockey pitch. The rules were pretty simple (which helped); the goalie was not allowed to pick up a back pass even though he could come out of his area, no scoring in the oppositions goal from your own half and most important of all, you could kick the ball over head height. This was really handy as none of us were the most skilful of players.

Game 1 - Drifters (4) v Bouncing Beavers (1) - In our first game of the evening, we played a very edgy first half which saw us leading 1-0 at the break. The
64

second half was a bit different though and after five minutes of magical pass and movement (which had been severely lacking in the 11-a-side game), we had gone 4-0 up. I think we achieved this by spending the first half lobbing aimless balls in the Beavers penalty area so that they weren't ready for our complete change in style during the second. The Beavers did manage to pull one back late on, (which gave Rupert, who was playing goal this evening, something to moan about) but I would put this down to us saving ourselves for the next game. Well, to be honest, we were all knackered.

     Game 2 - Drifters (2) v Devils (3) - I didn't know this until after the game but the Drifters had never beaten the Devils (who were a team of Swiss ex-pats) and it was a record that was not broken on this occasion either. The first half finished at one goal a piece but this was down more to the fact that their strikers spent most of their time kicking the ball straight at Rupert. We had made a couple of chances and the second half could have gone either way. It went the way of the Swiss, thanks in no small part to Rupert who threw the ball out straight to the feet of the Swiss striker. We pinned them down in their own half for what remained of the game but we just couldn't find a way through their goalkeeper to tie up the scores. It was after the Devil's game that Rupert informed me that I had become a true Drifter. Rupert had launched a hopeless ball down the pitch, which was easily cut out by the oppositions defence. I turned around and exclaimed "What the fuck was that?" This, it turns out, is the sort of language that Rupert understood.

Chinese Bureaucracy

     We were called in to a meeting with Dean Tang on a Thursday afternoon. In fact, the only time we were ever called into a meeting with the Dean was on a Thursday afternoon, which was really annoying for me because that was the only afternoon I had free each week. Everyone else thought it was great because they actually got to miss lectures. Anyway, I digress. Once again, Amanda was there acting as interpreter which was a little strange as we were sure that the Dean's English was actually better than hers. We were all given new contracts that we were expected to sign there and then. Sarah and Tana had other ideas and wanted to take them home to look at the in greater detail. Sarah was very keen to do this, especially as her HR head was on and she does get a little suspicious when things like this happen. When we examined them, they did seem to be similar to the contracts we had signed at home, except these had the missing appendices which were full of items that we were not happy about. Later, we spoke to William about our contracts and the things we were not happy with, but it was clear that they were not going to change anything and he just said that we shouldn't worry about the clauses we were worried about because we could ignore them. It did raise the questions that if they weren't important, why were they in there in the first place?

<u>Angus Comes to Town and more Illness</u>
Yes, after only just recovering from Beijing Belly, I contracted Conjunctivitis or 'Pink Eye' as the Americans kept calling it. This once again meant more time laying around feeling sorry for myself. This was terrible timing as the first of our visitors from back home decided to come over and see us, my cousin Angus.

He managed to find his way to Beihang from the airport and without being ripped off either which was a positive sign. He even managed to get to the North Gate of the Uni, but once inside he didn't bother to read the directions I'd sent him and he got lost. Through pure luck, he managed to find his way to the State Administration of Foreign Experts Affairs (SAFEA), the department that dealt with all things relating to the foreign teachers where one the staff rang me to let me Angus was with them. After going to collect him, Doug and I decided we needed to work hard to keep him up for as long as possible, so we took him to the now legendary Astray. After lunch, we took him down to the Lido district so he could do some shopping. Angus didn't hang around and bought enough bootleg DVD's to last his entire visit. In the evening, we took him to Lush for some food and beer, but he gave up the ghost at around nine, which wasn't bad going.

The Sites, the Sounds and Smell of Beijing #1

The second day of his visit was also the first time the Flying College organised a trip for us, and they had said that it was not a problem for Angus to join us. William and Mr. G had been assigned to look after us and along the way; we picked up a Chinese lady who called herself Cindy. William had stocked up the mini-bus with bread rolls and water. Tana told us that she called the croissants we were eating crescent rolls so we had many hours of entertainment 'taking the Mickey' out of her. This did seem to be a regular occurrence from this point because Tana was so American with her use of the English language that even Doug stuck his oar in from time to time.

Tiananmen Square - When we arrived at Tiananmen Square, we headed for the Gate of Heavenly Peace. This is now the entrance to the Forbidden City and is famous for the portrait of Chairman Mao that adorns it. This is the same picture that had paint filled eggs thrown at it during the Democracy protests of 1989. According to William, the picture is painted in such a way that wherever you stand, Mao's eyes can see you but all I could think about were 'those' lyrics to the Beatles song 'Revolution'. It was decided that someone should take a picture of all of us in the Square, and seeing how I really do not like my picture being taken, I decided that I would take it.

As everyone lined up, unbeknownst to me a group of military looking types were marching in my direction. I say military looking types because nearly every job seems to have a military looking uniform, even if they have nothing to do with the armed services or police, so it did get a little confusing. According to the others, the military types kept marching towards me and it looked as though they were going to march into me until the very last moment when one of them shouted an order and they went around. It was at this point that I actually noticed them and they all had a grin on their faces.

The Forbidden City[20] - The first building we saw was under scaffolding and we were not allowed anywhere near it. A Health and Safety officer from the UK might well have had a heart attack if he saw the way these guys were hanging off of the scaffolding. It was like the famous pictures taken of workers on the Empire State Building in 1920's. The first courtyard was having parts of its paving torn up. It seemed that the only way to keep the original paving stones in good condition was to dig them up and replace them with brand new ones. Due to this work, it made the place look like a massive movie set and I was quite upset when I saw this. I believe that if you go to look at a historical site, it really defeats the object if it looks as though it has just been built. This was not the only place in China that I felt this. We spent most of the morning wandering around the Forbidden City, and although we knew it was going to be big, nothing really prepared us for the enormity of the place.

We didn't have much of a chance to look at the City in great detail because almost as soon as we arrived, William was telling us all to hurry up as we were going to be late for the next part of the day. One of the few places we were allowed to spend anytime was the Royal Gardens. We were told that this was the only place in the Royal Palace to have trees in it. This was to minimise the areas where an assassin could hide and kill the Emperor or any members of his Royal Court. This was also the place where the Emperor would choose the Royal Concubines from the best looking girls in the Empire. It's good to be the Emperor! The other memorable thing was the sight of a Starbucks that had been put in one of the older buildings. I thought this had gone? For a Communist country, the almighty dollar still seems to be the be all and end all.

Food - Once we left the City, we had to sit around for about half an hour waiting for the mini bus to fight its way through the traffic. This didn't go down too well with anyone especially after the way we had been rushed along. We were then taken for a massive Chinese style lunch where we finally had some Beijing Duck.

---

[20] The Forbidden City was built between 1406 & 1420 during the mid-Ming dynasty and was the home of twenty-four Emperors until 1911, and the fall of Imperial China.

Lovely! Our Chinese hosts also ordered us a fish dish, which involved bringing the still living fish in a bucket, very much like a lobster is brought to a consumer in a Western restaurant. We thought the fish was dead until it started thrashing about and almost knocking the bucket over. That was quite a surprise but the Chinese didn't even bat an eyelid. After lunch, we were rushed off to our next destination.

Temple of Heaven - The Temple of Heaven[21] was like an oasis of calm compared to the rest of Beijing. The thing we really noticed about the place was just how quiet and peaceful it was. Walking around, all could you hear was the breeze. No car horns, space to walk around in and not that many people coming up to you trying to sell us things (especially after we got past the entrance!). The entrance itself was full of entertainers, musicians and groups of people singing pro-Chinese songs. Some were even dressed in royal style clothing and were trying to charge 5RMB for people to take their picture. Stuff that! They should have been paying us because the noise they made with their instruments made cats fighting sound tuneful.

Angus seemed to be learning the unwritten rules of China pretty quickly and completely ignored this sign by taking a picture and then walking off. The Temple complex was full of interesting things to see and unlike the Forbidden City, William was not so keen for us to hurry up all of the time. The main walkway had a special pathway running down the middle of it that used to be reserved for the Emperor to walk on. These days, it seemed that anyone could take a stroll on it, so we all made sure we took the opportunity to do so. We visited the Echo Wall where you can allegedly stand at one end of it and start talking, a person standing at any other part of it will be able to hear you clearly. However, when we tried to do this, a screaming child (or someone playing a Yoko Ono record, we are not quite sure) had had the same idea and that was all we could hear.

---

[21] The construction of the Temple of Heaven began in 1420 and was built to some very religious specifications. It was considered a very sacred site and the Emperor himself would perform major ceremonies there.

We also saw for the first time, the latest fashion for children that are just beginning to walk around and these were trousers with a slit in the seat. This was evidently designed to allow these children to do their 'business' at anytime and place they chose. Nappies, as it turned out, were not sold in Chinese shops so we would have to be mindful of any local asking us to hold their baby whilst taking a photo[22]. The child might have left us with an unwanted present. One of the children we saw with particular trousers was sliding down a slope on his backside so all of us agreed that we wouldn't walk up this bit ourselves fearing what we might find on our shoes. We were able to experience the resonating stone whilst at the Temple, which was bit weird. We had been warned by the other teachers that had been here before us about this and that there was always a massive queue to get on it. However, we were a bit lucky here and managed to all have a go as there didn't seem to be anyone else around. It is a round stone set in the ground. Once someone stood on it and spoke, you could hear your voice echo around you and go through your body.

The people you were talking to would only hear your normal voice though. All very clever but it did beg the question, why? Why not or because they could are the only two answers I can think of. Inside the grounds of the Temple was the Divine Music Administration. This turned out to be a music school, but for some reason they gave it this rather snazzy name. We were able to sit in the main practice room for the musicians that would have once attended this school during the Imperial days and watch traditional Chinese instruments being played in their natural environment. Connected to the practice room, a museum had been added about Chinese music.

---

[22] Nappies were not the only product that we found wasn't for sale. No matter how hard we looked, we could never find any deodorant, and had to ask our visitors from back home to bring with them fresh supplies of the stuff. This lack of anti-perspirants meant that there was always a smell of stale sweat about the place which became more noticeable when taking a journey on the underground or a bus. Sarah was quick to point out that the Flying College absolutely reaked of the body odour of young men whoes testoterone levels were high at the best of times. I must admit that I didn't myself, but that might be down to the fact that I am use to being in changing rooms where that sort of smell is prevelant anyway!

They had used the buildings that were already there and filled them with instruments and the best bit was you could actually play them as they did not have any signs up or glass in the way to stop you. We did make a bit of a racket.

Shopping & More Food - William had promised us a shopping trip so he took us to the Silk Market. This was quite an experience because it was the first time we had really negotiated on prices. We had some help from our Chinese hosts who kept telling the sellers off for trying to charge us too much for things. We finally found some wall decorations for the flat, even though the seller did haggle quite hard on the price. Angus took to the market like a duck to concrete. We tried to teach him a few of the basic rules of bartering in a Chinese market. Even one that is so obviously geared to the tourist market:

1) Don't appear too keen
2) Question the quality of the product
3) When a price is given, always give a price a lot lower and work your way to some middle ground.

Unfortunately, he ignored all of them but he always seemed happy with what he had bought and the price he had paid so we gave up in the end letting him get on with it.

To finish the day off, we were then taken out for yet another meal, but by this time we were keen to go to home because we were all tired from quite a long day. Angus was especially tired because he was suffering from Jet Lag and kept falling asleep at the table. We did have the strangest food we'd eaten since being in Beijing; Ducks feet. These were smothered in mustard and some unidentified spices and it tasted rather rubbery. Needless to say, we all found this a bit much but the Chinese seemed to find our attempts to eat them quite amusing. This would not be the last time this would happen either.

To follow this up, the Flying College said that they would arrange a trip to the Great Wall and a weekend trip to Xi'an, which meant that we would not have to organise it ourselves, which was just the way we like it. Unfortunately, this turned out to be the only day I would be able to spend some quality time with Angus. His visit didn't stop me from playing for The Drifters. Priorities and all that!

11-a-side

Game 11 - Drifters (2) v Mafia FC (3) - Another game, and another new player. He was a young Chinese student who liked to be called Jimmy. We weren't sure how serious we should take his playing ability because he turned up in a car full of his friends, who turned to be his fan club. Mafia FC, as you would expect with a team name like this, were mostly made up of Italian ex-pats so a couple of days before the game, I found a web site listing Italian profanities on it that I thought would come in useful. I wish I had spent some time actually learning some, instead of just trying to be funny. Rupert said that he would not be able to attend this game and his only advice was not to laugh too much when the opposition would roll around on the ground crying for half the game.

It would be nice to write that the Italian reputation for being a bunch of divers that complain about everything, cheat unremorsefully, hit the ground clutching their face from the slightest of touches and whining about any and all decisions that don't go their way would be unfounded. However, this was definitely not the case and to a man, they lived down to their reputation spending every moment doing all the things listed above as well as taking every opportunity to kick any Drifter remorselessly. I did get fed up of all the play acting after about ten minutes and as soon as an Italian hit the ground in my vicinity, I would do exactly the same. This achieved its desired result of winding up the opposition, but I was a bit dismayed when my team mates asked me to calm it down a bit.

The performance was vast improvement on the week before and in the first half, Jimmy showed us that he was a class act terrorising the Italian defence and scoring our goals. We had controlled vast periods of the game but in the second half, the Italians marked Jimmy out for some special attention and we reverted to pumping the ball up front in the hope that he would run onto it and score unlike the first when we had played some intelligent passing moves.

As I was walking off the pitch, I was quite surprised when one of the Italians came up to apologise to me for kicking me so blatantly. I was not so surprised when another member of their team came up and asked me why I had spent so much time mocking their side with all of my play acting. I would have loved to turn around and say that it was because they were a load of cheats who deserved to be thrown out of the league, but the old rugby player in me kicked in and said that it should be left on the pitch and we should all go out for a beer. Thankfully, he didn't take me up on this but at least he walked away without badgering me further.

The Drifters

After playing for a couple of weeks, I learned how cosmopolitan the team was nationality wise and how many characters there were (Apologies to anyone who played in the Drifters with me that has not had a mention).

Rupert (English) – Our glorious leader, he worked teaching best practice in business skills, having started out in China as an English teacher. Like many of the Drifters, he was not known for his patience or lack of restraint and some of the members of the team took his example a little literally, including me it must be said.

Markus (German) – His day job was at Volkswagen. He once told us a story that the Chinese government had asked for the resistance on the horn to be lessened so that it would be easy to press (as if they needed any help). By far the oldest player in the team, but he had the stamina of a much younger man and was a class player. In his first game for the club at the 5-a-side competition, he modestly said he didn't really have a position of choice and then proceeded to run rings around the opposition in an attacking midfield role.

Adam (Australian) – An English teacher. Rupert noted that the ball might get past him on occasions, but rarely does an opposition player get to follow it. Said he couldn't play in defence and then proceeded to play blinders in that position in nearly every Drifter game he played. A great bloke and it was shame that injury kept him out of the team for most of the 11-a-side games, but the second season of 5-a-side as well.

Richard (Chinese) – We might have been playing in an ex-pats league, but that didn't mean that we didn't extend the hand of friendship to any Chinese player that was willing to pull on a Drifter shirt. Richard played at the back and could always be relied on to put in a couple of big tackles every game.

Arakawa (Japanese) – This guy worked bloody hard at whatever position he played in. A tough tackler, he never gave up on any cause, which did lead to the odd goal here and there. He was prone to the odd lapse in concentration, but considering he would normally come to football straight from working a twelve hour day, we forgave him. There was a rumour that after one game where he was the direct cause of an opponent's goal, he emailed the whole team to apologise. A bit over the top you might think, but that was the sort of guy he was. To prevent this from happening during my tenure, the whole team would tell him after any mistake he made that it was alright just in case he was a Samurai in disguise and would commit hara-kiri!

Matthias (German) – He had a reputation for coming off the bench, doing a mazy run and then going on to the sidelines for a smoke before repeating the whole thing five minutes later. When the mood took him, which was quite often, as the second 5-a-side season went on he showed that once he had put down his oxygen mask, he would score loads of quality goals. He was one of, if not the most gifted members of the team and a pleasure to play with.

Stuart (Irish) – An English teacher, and a true Celtic warrior. He reminded me a little bit of Mark Hughes in his playing days. It wasn't only because he scored loads of crucial goals, but off the pitch he was a mild mannered chap. He suffered from one of the worse cases of white line fever I have ever seen. He turned berating the ref into an art form and would normally have to be substituted at least once a game to prevent him from being sent off. Due to his fiery nature on the pitch, he was normally selected to be captain and did so in a way very similar to myself. He shouted, a lot!

Paul (English) – Another English teacher who was based in Tianjin, an hours train journey from Beijing and therefore he was only available to play at the weekends. He said he could play as either a keeper or centre forward and became a real asset to the team. Like Stuart, he suffered from a heavy dose of white line fever but off of the pitch, he was a chilled out as you can be. A nice guy to-boot. (No pun intended!)

Albert (Spanish) – Not gifted with height but he made up for this by being tenacious in whatever position he was playing in. We did nickname him the Duracell Bunny because he always seemed to have endless energy. We didn't always see eye to eye (and this will be covered in due course), but we always kissed (not literally) and made up.

Paschalis (Greek) – A work mate of Markus who in a moment of madness decided that the Drifters were the team for him. Rupert was a little concerned that he did not look like a natural Drifter player as he was annoying good looking and clearly fit. Markus also told us that he had played at quite a high level of football in Germany and it showed. It was a shame that he only played in the last six games of the 5-a-side before I went home because he was a touch of class.

Kelvin (Chinese) – When he played (which was not as often as anyone would have liked due to his work commitments), he stayed at the back tackling anything and everything that moved.

Robison (Malagasy) - Older than God, but looked twenty years younger than most of the people in the team! A natural play-maker in the team and a tough tackler, it was shame he didn't play that many games for the Drifters during my tenure. When he was on the pitch, it was no coincidence that our attacks looked a lot more organised in their approach. He would also play traditional Madagascan music in some of the bars in Beijing which we would go and watch after 5-a-side, as long as we had not been beaten that night.

Azat (Russian) - Would always drive himself to the ground (wherever it may be) and emerge from his car with a fag in his mouth, wearing his big lairy shades. He challenged Matthias and Rupert for the title of heaviest smoker in the team, but nicotine withdrawal added an extra snap to his tackling in midfield.

Ru (Scottish) – Another English teacher but with cultured footballing brain. He was as tall as Peter Crouch and at least once a game, there would be an individual moment of footballing class. He never managed to make it down to the 5-a-side nights, which was a real loss.

Bansoon (Chinese) – Like Adam, claimed that his best position was in midfield, but proceeded to play so well in defence that he played himself into that position for the rest of the season.

Amine (Belgian) – A doctor for Médicine sans Frontière, he would miss the odd game due to the fact he was in deepest darkest China doing his best to cure the country of its illnesses. A midfield dynamo, he would always begin any sentence with "Hey guys" and have a big smile on his face. He would set up and score loads of goals for both the Drifter sides and when he didn't play, there was a hole in the team.

Pablo (Portuguese) – Never played in the 5-a-sides, but could normally be counted on for the odd goal in the 11-a-side. They were never 'tap-ins' either and they tended to be scored after a mazy run leaving at least a couple of players on their backside in his wake.

Sjoerd (Dutch) – He didn't play that many games after my arrival, but when he did, he played out wide where his measured crossing would normally go to waste due to the failings of our forwards (which was me most of the time). It was a shame that he had such a big falling out with Rupert.

Jimmy (Chinese) – The rumour was that he had played for a Chinese professional team. He would become known as the 'Jimmy-nator' after scoring a hatful of goals, but disappeared as quickly as he had arrived. Rupert did get the occasional email from Jimmy stating how much he would like to play for the team again, but it turned out that he was in a band and that took priority.

He was obviously a guy who liked an audience.

<u>5-a-side</u>
> *Game 3 - Drifters (9) v Barbarians 2 (2)*
> *Game 4 - Drifters (1) v Newbies (6)* - I actually
didn't play in either of these games because I was
suffering from conjunctivitis. Apart from the thumping
win and crushing defeat, Rupert (who was preparing to
give a business lecture on "Conflict Resolution") ended up
having such a massive argument with Sjoerd that the
Dutchmen only played a couple of games after this. A bit
of a shame really but nobody said that playing for the
Drifters was ever an easy experience.

<u>Bright Lights, Big City</u>
I still didn't know that I was beginning to suffer
from conjunctivitis. I struggled on with my classes
thinking that it was just something stuck in my eye that
just wouldn't go away and it most probably didn't help
that I couldn't help rubbing it. It got so pink that my
students even began to notice it and one of them was
good enough to take me to the hospital on campus to
have it examined. I told the Doctor that it felt like
something was stuck in my eye. The doctor didn't really
examine me at any length, but said that I had something
in it, which I was sure I had said only a moment before.
She gave me four different eye drops for it, which did
seem a bit excessive. These didn't seem to be doing me
any good and Sarah took the time to look up the active
ingredients on the Internet as they were handily written
in English on the packaging.

It turned out that some of them had been
banned in the West and one could actually damage the
eye. After finding this out, the drops were placed into a
cupboard and forgotten about. This experience gave me
supreme confidence in the Chinese health system. After
we had related this to Doug, he told us that the one and
only time he had visited the campus hospital when he
had also been suffering from an eye problem of his own,
they had given him eardrops. Nice. The campus hospital
was exceedingly cheap, even compared to the one just up
the road from the University but this really was a case of
you get what you pay for.

By the middle of the week, my eye was getting so pink that even the students at the back of the class could see it and I was finding it difficult to concentrate during class. After finishing for the day I went to bed for a lie down that would last the rest of the afternoon as well as most of the next day. Angus didn't let my illness nor Sarah's unavailability get in the way of his holiday and decided to check out some of the local landmarks by himself. It was because of these solo visits that Angus became the by word for what not to do in China. He had evidently not been listening to our advice in the Silk Market because when he went to other markets during his stay, he was ripped off left right and centre. It wasn't only in markets that he fell for some of the underhand way the Chinese used to fleece the unwary traveller of their money:

1) *The Great Wall at Badaling* – This is nearest bit of the Great Wall to Beijing, and therefore is the most geared up for the tourist. It is still an hour's drive away but it is possible to catch public transport there, which is what Angus did. Having negotiated this quite successfully, he stepped off of the bus and was accosted by a taxi driver. The cabbie said that he would take Angus to the entrance for only, and I stress the only, 30RMB. The driver then proceeded to drive the five or so meters from the bus stop to the Wall's entrance and told him to get out. What we found unbelievable was that Angus was more than happy to pay up.

2) *The Tea Shop* – Having stepped out for a massage, but I must point out, not one that finished with the so-called 'happy ending', Angus decided to go for a spot of lunch. Picking one of the higher end tea shops that we would never have dared go in for fear of bankrupting ourselves, Angus was asked by one of the waitresses serving him if he would like to take his beverage in a private room. After being led upstairs, he proceeded to drink his one-cup of tea and then asked for the bill having enjoyed

what he described as a very picturesque setting. When the bill arrived, it came to 200RMB. I almost fainted when he told me that he had quite willingly paid it.

We might not have been in China for long, but even we knew that large amounts of money were leaving Angus's pocket, even by British prices. When it came to sampling some of Beijing's nightlife, Angus was in luck. Ray was roughly the same age as Angus, interested in going out to meet members of the opposite sex and most importantly, was not ill. He would take Angus out for the odd evening out including a visit to the local KTV, or Karaoke bar. It seemed that these were as popular in China as they are in Japan. It didn't seem to matter to Angus that we didn't spend too much time together as he looked to be having a good time even if he was allowing himself to be ripped off a lot of the time.

Tractor
I might not have been at my sprightly best, but I did want to spend some time with Angus because he had travelled quite a long way to see me so I suggested that we visit a restaurant we had been introduced to a few weeks before. It was called 'Tractor' and it specialised in Russian food[23]. We would end up taking all of our visitors here because the food was great and the beer was extremely cheap.

It was a bit of a strange place because from the outside it didn't actually look like a restaurant. It didn't have any signage, the door was a huge wooden thing that didn't look very welcoming and it wasn't until you looked in the windows that you could see what it was.

For a restaurant the beer was exceedingly cheap at 5RMB a pint for the local brew. It also served a selection of beers imported from Russia, which were a good deal more expensive as well as a rather interesting

---

[23] There were actually two restaurants of this name in Beijing and both of them were located quite conveniently near an underground station. One was based on the main thoroughfare and was geared towards the tourist as it was more expensive even though it didn't do anything too different from the one we frequented.

selection of spirits. The most intriguing of which was the snake vodka. It was housed in a massive jar that was on display on the front counter and yes; it did have real snakes in it. I was never brave enough to try this, and I am not the biggest fan of vodka either. It was also possible to receive your starter after you had eaten your main course.

They would also stagger the delivery of the food so someone could have already finished their meal before another person had actually received theirs. I only ever ordered the same main course on every visit, the legendary steak wrapped in bacon.

Even though I ordered the same thing every time didn't mean I would get the same thing every time. I would never know what 'veg' would be brought out on the plate and it was impossible to tell if I was going to receive either mashed potatoes or chips. These little mishaps just added to the experience and everyone loved a visit to 'Tractor'.

11-a-side
Game 12 - Drifters (4) v Never Stop (1) - I may have missed the 5-a-side game during the week, but I felt well enough by it's end to join the Drifters for some football. I most probably shouldn't have gone because I still had a massive pain in the side of my head but I was fed up with moping around the apartment. When I turned up at Club Football, everyone commented on my eye and I thought I was in for some expert advice from Amine. He took one look at it and said "You better see a doctor about that". Thanks. The infection was going though, but China was not proving to be beneficial to my health. I had five bouts of Diarrhoea as well as the 'Pink Eye'.

Never Stop were made up of young, fit and athletic Koreans who before the game kicked off got themselves into a huddle and did a sort of battle cry to get them in the mood. On this occasion, it didn't help them even though they tried it again at the beginning of the second half. We were by far and away the better team on the day. Rupert once again stood on the sideline because we had a brand new keeper in the shape of Paul. Not only did he look the part, but he was the part as well.

So much so in fact, that Rupert felt he could continue with his 'true calling'; to watch over everyone's coats and bags! It didn't stop Paul from letting in a soft goal though.

In fact, apart from his one and only cock-up (which was followed by twenty minutes of saying a word that sounded remarkably similar to duck whilst banging his head against the post), he almost brought a tear to Rupert's' eye. Not only was he aggressive toward the opposition to the point of aneurism, but also to his own team as the defence dared to only jog out when they should have been running. His command of Korean swear words came in handy, especially when one of them put in a late challenge on him. The icing on the cake was when Rupert discovered that he and Paul came from the same city back in Britain!

Jimmy turned up with his hangers on and gave another star performance but everyone in the team contributed to this fine victory. Jimmy proceeded to score a memorable hat-trick, made all the more so by the fact that each one of his celebrations would not have looked out of place in a 'Frankie Goes to Hollywood' video!

The whole team put in so many big tackles that it would have been impossible to keep a tally and the central midfielders took control of the game breaking down many an opposition attack before they really became dangerous. We were actually lucky to have eleven players for the whole game as Stuart put in one of his lunges that resulted in a yellow card. The throbbing vein on his head did little to quell our fears that this could, and most probably would, turn into a red by the end of the game.

I played out wide in this game and the only memorable thing I did during the first 88 minutes was to run into the box with a Korean defender hanging on to me by wrapping his arm around my waist. The ref' didn't even give a free kick; disgraceful!

My contribution changed dramatically in the 89th minute when I broke into the box trying to pick up a loose ball with their goal keeper running towards me. It is a well known fact that an oil tanker takes 10 miles to go from full speed to full stop and as of this day, everyone knew that my breaking system was equally as quick. The goalkeeper saved my shot brilliantly, but somehow ended up head butting my knee with his teeth. Cue five minutes of a Korean rolling around on the ground in agony.

Rupert said that it had been like watching a fly hitting the windscreen of a car. I was amazed that none of his team mates came up to harass me or the ref' show me a card, even though it had been an accidental clash. We played out the last couple of minutes and I made a point of shaking hands with the goalie at the end of the game, but he looked in severe discomfort. The guys joked that he was suffering from multiple broken bones and some internal bleeding, but they all went to find out how badly he had been hurt. Not because they were concerned for him but we were due to play the same team in only two weeks time.

The Sites, Sounds and Smell of Beijing #2

Beijing Capital Museum - Angus flew back home having said that he had had a great time, even though his wallet was considerably lighter than when he'd arrived. His tales and photos of the places he had visited made us realise that we really should make more of an effort to see some. With an improvement in the weather and the fact that I was going to be relatively illness free for a while (even though my eye would stay a nice shade of pink for a while longer), we thought we make up for some lost time. After a look at the Beijing Lonely Planet, we made a beeline to one of the Capital Museums (of which there seem to be four). It was a very new building and we could tell this by the fact that it was not covered in a layer of dust and the walls didn't have loads of cracks in them. The building looked huge from the outside, but once we went inside, we realised that there is very little to actually see.

This is because it has been designed to be an open plan building which did seem to me to be a bit of waste of space. There was a lot to enjoy, even though we didn't know what most of it was about as the majority of the signs were in Chinese. We did avoid the exhibition on ancient stationery and other study utensils, because we wanted to avoid the long queue, or was it because we were sure there were more interesting things to see, like paint drying for instance! They did have quite an extensive book shop in the basement which did have a selection of titles in English. Doug had told me about a book called 'Mao, Man not God' that he said was an unintentional comedy classic. We didn't see it here, but I did see the autobiography of the last Emperor. A pretty good read but it did become quite difficult in the final chapters when he was quite clearly being brainwashed by the Communists[24].

'Destroy'

It was around this time that we noticed a red symbol daubed on the front of nearly all of the buildings out of the North and West Gates. The symbol, which looked like this 拆 means 'demolish'. Like the red marks used during the Black Death, these buildings were to be destroyed for no other reason than they will not look that nice when all of the visitors to the Olympics arrive in 2008. With the stadium and Olympic tower just up the road, this area may well be visited but God knows why. With all of the sites of historical interest and all of the major shopping districts located in the centre of the city, why anyone would want to pay a visit the area around Beihang is beyond me.

As the government is trying to put its best face on, this means that all of the businesses will have to go somewhere else or fold because all of the properties are rented from the government. One of the shop owners said some not so flattering comments about the government to us. Well, she actually said that she hated the government for what they were doing and this was quite a revelation. None of us expected to hear a Chinese National being so critical of the Government, especially to some foreigners!

---

[24] Puyi Aisin-Gioro, the Last Emperor of China and later the puppet Ruler of the Japanese ruled state of Manchukuo (or Manchuria) was captured by the Soviets at the end of the Second World War and given to the Chinese communists after their victory in the civil war against the Kumintang. He would spend ten years in prison where he was 're-educated' until his release when he became a gardener a the Beijing Botanical Gardens. The book is called 'From Emperor to Citizen' and is well worth a read.

The destruction did not take long to start either. The first shops were closed and demolished within a week of the first appearance of the red symbol. The workmen would work a pretty standard day but once they had downed tools, the scavengers would move in hunting in the ruins for any bits of metal or other substances they could recycle for money. We saw the odd security guard posted around the demolition sites to cut this practise out, but it didn't seem to make a blind bit of difference.

These scavengers would always ride up on the three wheeled work-bikes,[25] filling them up with anything and everything that was worth something. This would include the metal that had been embedded in the concrete walls, cardboard and even the empty plastic bottles the workmen had drunk out of. We never found out where this scrap ended up, but it must have paid well enough because there was never a shortage of people doing it.

All of the closures meant that all the shops and restaurants we had just started getting use to were beginning to disappear, though some of them we able to stay open until we left. I did feel sorry for the shop owner who had opened up a week or so after we had arrived to see it shut down by the government only a month later. It did seem to be a bit random as to which buildings were to be demolished next. Apart from the fact that we now had to make an effort to buy our bootleg CD's/DVD's (because Ivy's was one of the first to go), it turned out that the majority of people who made their livelihoods in these premises not only worked there, but it was also their homes. For all the supposed progress that China has been going through of late, taking away people's means of supporting themselves as well as their homes was a bit draconian.

---

[25] These curious vehicles were everywhere and it was very rare to see one that was loaded to overflowing with stuff. The only times I ever saw empty one was after a beer delivery at the Convenient Store and when someone was sleeping on one. The all seemed to have been hand built but whatever material had been used in their construction must have been tough because the weights on the back axles must have been tremendous. It would be common to see someone sitting on the piles of stuff hitching a ride. Needless to say, the driver never seemed to peddle them very fast.

Learning the Lingo

      With some of my free time taken up with the Drifters, Sarah thought she should find an outside interest. She decided she would take professional Chinese lessons. After a month long search, Sarah finally found a language school whose classes were flexible enough to fit around her classes back at Beihang. The only downside was the teacher, who didn't speak any English so the learning process was a little random. Most of the students seemed to be Korean but there is the odd western face in the crowd and they would occasionally go out for lunches together. When Sarah didn't turn up for a class, some of her classmates would ring her up to see if she was okay and to check that she would be turning up for the next class, which was nice. Sarah did have a great deal of empathy with her own students after doing this for a couple of weeks.

      It was during one of Sarah's Chinese lessons that she saw a different take of celebrating someone's birthday with a cake. It may sound quite harmless, but then again, this is China. After discovering that it was one of the students' birthdays, the teacher went out and bought a birthday cake. Once everyone was back in the room, the whole class proceeded to sing happy birthday in Spanish, English, Korean, Russian and Mandarin. After this, the teacher shoved her hand into the cake, pulled out a wad of it and smeared it into the birthdays girls face. The Korean's followed suit and began throwing cake all over the place. It turned out that it is the traditional in not only China, but also Korea, to throw cake about on someone's birthday. The rest of the class were surprised when Sarah admitted that this tradition doesn't occur in the West. The class admitted afterwards that they would normally buy two cakes. One for throwing, the other for eating.

      I never saw this but our own students seemed to have their particular way of celebrating a birthday. This involved the birthday boy being picked up by his four limbs and then his legs were straddled over an open door. He was then moved up and down in a way that looked quite painful, especially as the doors had handles and catches. A variation on this involved using a tree. I was glad that I didn't tell my students when it was my birthday because even though I was convinced that they would not be able to pick me up, I didn't want them to have had the opportunity to put this to the test

5-a-side

Rupert had told us that he would not be able to play due to some business commitments, so Stuart volunteered to take over the captain's armband. This meant little change in the decibel levels, but with an Irish brogue instead of one from the north of England. In this spirit of volunteering, I put my name forward to go in goal stating that I found playing in the smaller goals a lot easier than the 11-a-side variety. Rupert took this to mean that I thought 5-a-side goalkeeping was easy, but Christophe (who had seen me play in goal before) was confident that I would do a good job. The two matches were billed as the Beijing Derby. Our opponents and the Drifters were the only two teams in the 11-a-side league to use Beijing in their team names and the two clubs had a long history (for this league anyway) of playing against each other. How the opposition managed to field two teams in this league astounded me considering we only just managed to field one.

Game 5 - Drifters (4) v Athletico Beijing White (3) - As soon as the game kicked off, it felt as though the team had taken Rupert's words to heart and decided that I needed a good work out for my first game in goal. There seemed to be a general consensus from the team that they were all strikers, which left a gaping hole in defence allowing the opposition to pepper me with shots. Luckily for me, the oppositions shooting was not the best and they mostly kicked it straight at me and I did my best to make my physical presence felt for anyone who got too close. We managed to sneak a couple of goals before half time but I had been unable to keep a clean sheet so we went into the interval all square. I had not seen Stuart give a team talk before, and the language was very similar to the one he used during the game; full of expletives but strangely to the point. I was quite surprised when half way through the rant, he turned to me and asked for me to 'help him out', but all I could come up with was that we needed to have some people defending.

When the whistle blew for the second half, the whole team started playing a good deal better and we overpowered the opposition by scoring two very good goals. The only problem with the second half was that I had neglected to read up on the rules of the league and unwittingly picked up a pack pass. Cue despair from my team mates and the Ref pointing at the spot. I did redeem myself by not only saving the penalty, but the follow up shot as well. My team mates all congratulated me on my reflexes but later they joked that I had only given the penalty away because their defending had been so good that I was no longer the centre of attention that I had been in the first half and I wanted to get back into the spotlight. I was unable to keep a clean sheet for the remainder of the half but I only conceded one, so three points in the bag.

Game 6 - Drifters (5) v Athletico Beijing Red (2) - We really picked up our game for the second leg of our Athletico derby and it was a shame that Rupert was not there to see his recurring wet dream realised where the Drifters passed smoothly, calmly and effortlessly that we were 3-0 up at half time. It was so smooth that Stuart didn't have a vein threatening to pop out the side of his head when the whistle went. We were all nice and relaxed and hoping that there that would be more of the same, but as this is the Drifters, nothing ever works out the way you'd expect it to.

Christophe, who up until this point had had a very good game thought that the proceedings needed a bit of spicing up and 'accidentally' lobbed me to give Athletico a goal. All of our good work was instantly thrown out of the window. Five minutes of stress, a few colourful words of abuse and our passing game fell apart. Our defending, striking and any resemblance to any footballer was also lost. Athletico scored another one and looked like squaring things up.

Our world had turned upside down so much that the Ref asked Stuart to calm Christophe down! It is at moments like this that you need your Captain to step up to the plate and get things back on track. Stuart managed to get a hold of the ball and dribbled through the opposition, rounded the keeper and scored a tight angle. With confidence restored (even if the calmness was still conspicuous by its absence) Arakawa, who was being shouted at by all of his team mates (including me!) to pass the ball completed the scoring and Athletico's heart went, as well as silencing his team mates. Six points out of six and the team were very pleased by their nights work.

To celebrate, those who could went to a British styled pub called The Goose and Duck for some beers and chips. Robinson was there playing a gig so our exploits got a mention from the only man in the pub with a microphone, much to our delight. It would have been nice to have a shower before we went to the pub as we all hummed a bit, but no one complained so that made it alright. Our smell was no doubt disguised by the heavy stench of tobacco that permeated through the air.

Drink

Baijiu - Baijiu literally translates into English as 'white alcohol' and can be considered to be China's national drink. It is poured out at meals and normally accompanied by a shout of 'Gambai', an equivalent of cheers. Every one around the table (especially the men) is expected to down their drink, which is then re-filled even if you did not completely finish it. The glass is about half the size of a shot glass but it doesn't make the stuff any less lethal. Doug said that it gets its distinctive taste by it being filtered through horse dung, which may, or may not be, true! Even though this sounds bizarre, even by Chinese standards, it would not surprise me because it really does taste like shit! Many of our colleagues had been given this drink as a way of testing their mettle but many of the teachers we met that experienced this, found that they could drink all the Chinese under the table with ease!

The first time I tasted it was on the last night of the induction week and I vowed never to drink it again unless it couldn't be avoided. Whenever we were offered it, I would calmly decline and I would always be asked what I would like to drink instead. This could have been considered by some to be a loss of face, but as I didn't care at all about this and most of the Chinese people I ever spent time with seemed to be a little wary of me, I would always get to drink exactly what I wanted. Sarah and whoever else was with me at these times would normally thank me for this.

Some of the other teachers told us about their attempts to avoid drinking it themselves when they were out with the staff of their respective colleges. My personal favourite was Andrew who after his glass was filled would exclaim "What's that over there!" and then pointed in the opposite direction to himself. When everyone had turned their heads to look at what he was pointing at, he would throw the drink over his shoulder. Class! Doug also told us of the time that one of the previous teachers was a bit of a drinker and when absolutely hammered one night, had been persuaded (by Doug) to snort it, which duly happened.

Neither snorting nor drinking it is recommended though and anyone caught making it should be sent to prison for crimes against humanity. It is also said to burn with a rather fetching blue flame and it does have other uses including engine cleaner, red wine stain remover, diamond etcher and Room 101 torture. Since we've been back, Sarah has discovered that you can actually buy it in a Chinese supermarket in London's Soho, for considerably more than we would have paid for it in Beijing.

Chinese Beer - None of the small shops on Campus sold any foreign beer, so we had to make do with the local brew. The Convenient Store was the place where we would purchase most of our lager. This was also the place where we learned you can buy a 640ml bottle of beer for 2RMB (14 pence) and take the empty back for a reimbursement of 0.5RMB (not many pence at all). Therefore, for every four bottles bought and drunk, you could get one free! Much cheapness all round, even though we did discover that this could be done at nearly all of the small shops on campus.

Tsingdao was the beer we drank the most of during our stay, even though when we were out we would try any other brand if it was available, just to have something different. Chinese beer was always drinkable (if a little on the watery side, but after a while, it became almost palatable), but it did become a little bland after a while. We could never be sure where the beer that we purchased at the Convenient Store was actually from, because when we had Tsingdao at the brewery, it did not taste anything like the stuff we were used to. We thought it best not too ask to many questions and the sight of one of the tricycles making its way onto Campus loaded with beer was always most welcome.

Shui Jiu - Shui Jiu roughly translates as Watery Wine. It tasted more like sugar water and it was only available in certain kinds of restaurants. This was probably a good thing because I could not taste the alcohol, and would most probably have fallen over after only a few glasses. It reminded me bit of Gripe Water.

Diet Coke - Finding Diet Coke (well, diet soft drinks in general) was a rarity. Sonia told us that she had not seen it once in the place she was teaching in. After this, we started to take notice of places where we saw it for sale, and when we did see it, it could be up to 3RMB more expensive in restaurants and hotels than the full fat variety. There does not seem to be any rhyme or reason as to why this is the case, but Doug theorised that not that many people drink them so it is a bit more of a luxury item. Diet Pepsi was the only other brand of diet soft drink we saw for sale.

Rules of the Flying College
One of the first things that we noticed during the first few weeks at the Flying College was there seemed to be quite a lot of rules that the students had to abide to. Fair enough you would think, but the College did not at any time tell us what these rules actually were and this did dampen my early attempts to get to know the students better. Questions about them playing football and having girlfriends would be greeted with blank looks before I was informed that they were not allowed to play the former or have the latter. In one class, I found the rule book lying on a desk but it was all in Chinese, so I asked my students to translate it for me in class whilst another one wrote them down.

One of the students informed me that these rules were written by a military man and they weren't fair because none of them were in the armed forces. This man turned out to be Lao Ding and of him, more after. They did make for interesting listening and I have included a list of some of the more interesting ones below.

I must point out that these rules have been edited because nearly all of them had "If this rule is broken, the student will be punished" at the end of every sentence. Nice!

1) Students are not allowed to have girlfriends.
2) All students must act as gentlemen when they are outside of college grounds (In other words, no going out drinking, visiting karaoke bars or having anything resembling a good time).
3) Students are not allowed to smoke or drink in and outside of college.
4) Students are not allowed movies or magazines of a sexual nature.
5) Students are not allowed to play football (Okay, this one I knew but I still couldn't figure the rationale` behind this rule because I knew that the Dean and William both enjoyed playing football.).
6) Students are not allowed to have long hair and must cut their hair on a regular basis. They were not allowed to have their hair too short either.
7) Every student must speak Mandarin. Local dialects are not allowed (I was informed later that Cantonese was the first language of some of my students so not only did they have to learn Mandarin, they were learning English as well).
8) Students are not allowed to do anything that does not bear any relation to their studies (I was glad that breathing was essential).
9) Students are not allowed to ride bicycles at anytime (Evidently, a previous student had been killed riding a bicycle in the past. I did wonder if one of them was killed whilst walking from his

dorm to the College, would they be banned from walking as well).

10) If a student is not in the dormitory at 10:30, you must tell an instructor immediately (The curfew was 10:30pm, which did lead to some problems when some of my students wanted to come and play for the Drifters at 5-a-side. 10:30 was also the time when the power in the dormitory would be shut off). This explained the amount of phone chargers lying on the classroom floors that I would nearly trip over every time I walked in.

11) Students are not allowed to fight with each other (but evidently, anyone else is fine).

12) If the electricity is off, students must not move around (Going to the toilet is therefore a bit of an issue).

13) All students must be awake by 6:30am everyday (except Sunday) and must report every morning to the running track in their sports clothes (also except Sunday). Students who do not turn up for training on time will be punished and must complete their daily exercise unless they are given permission not to do so.

14) If you do not obey No.9, you will be in trouble (Having a rule just to point out that a previous rule must be obeyed is a bit over the top methinks).

15) All students must eat in the Flying Colleges dining hall (This was a constant gripe for the students as they felt that the food was 'not delicious', as they would so eloquently put it. Any reference to food would utilise the word delicious, be it nice or horrible).

16) Students are not allowed to talk or waste their food whilst in the dining hall. When students are in the dining hall, they can only eat.

17) Students must love themselves (this is what it really said). If a student does not like the food, they must not argue with the cook (A truly bizarre rule this one and showing that customer services was something the Flying College was reluctant to introduce).

18) Students must ensure that the classroom and the communal areas around the classroom are always clean (There then followed 23 rules about cleaning that just seemed like a nightmare to go through, so these were ignored).

This is only a choice selection as the rule book was about 50 pages long and I couldn't be bothered to listen to anymore after a couple of lessons. I got the impression that the students were quite keen to stop this exercise as well. Not only because they were fed up with these rules, but I think that they were quite keen that I shouldn't know them so they could get away with certain things. They would learn that I wouldn't follow the Colleges line on rules.

I found these rules a bit over the top and so did all of the other foreign teachers I told about it so I thought I would turn it on its head for a while. In one of the following lessons, I asked each class to tell me what they would change about the Flying College if they were in charge. Most of what I got back was what I expected including:

1) More free time (completely understandable as they tended to be in the College from 8am until 10pm everyday whether they had classes or not)
2) Being allowed to eat wherever they wanted to.
3) To keep the power on in the dormitories after 10:30pm.
4) No curfew at 10:30pm.
5) To change some of the Chinese teachers, who they claimed cared not for the students and what they were doing.
6) To have ex-pilots as instructors (I thought they were anyway, but evidently they are not!)
7) To be allowed to have girlfriends and play football.
8) To train air stewardesses at the college because, as one group put it, they would make the male students more inclined to stay awake during the day.

Tea (I'm sure I've mentioned that they picked their own names), in Class 9 who was beginning to reveal himself to be the class comic came up with the best set of rules by far. His were:

1) Getting out of bed during the day would be forbidden.
2) Going to bed before 10pm is forbidden.
3) Students are not allowed to fight in uniform (having so much testosterone in such a confined space did lead to many a spat).
4) If you lose a fight, you will be punished.
5) You will be punished if you did not have a girlfriend.
6) You will be punished if you have an ugly haircut.
7) Smoking is allowed but not in the washroom. It turned out that this is the place where the smokers would go in the hope of avoiding detection from the Flying College staff. It did mean that all of the freshly hand washed clothes, (as the College did not supply them with access to a washing machine), would smell of cigarette smoke so they would get into trouble regardless of if they smoked or not.
8) If you ask a girl for her phone number and she says no, do not tell her you are from the Flying College so she will not be put off if one of your friends asks the same thing later.

This was hilarious and Tea ended with top marks for his work as well as good deal of respect for me. The ability to tell jokes in a foreign language is something to be admired.

Watching Chinese TV
The University had supplied every foreign teacher with a reasonably sized television. A quick flick through revealed loads of channels but there was only one was in English, the laughable CCTV-9. CCTV (or as it is formally known, China Central Television) one of the many state run TV networks in China, and as you would

expect, it does not have any editorial independence from government.

There were two channels we could get sport on, which was great because there would be loads of games from the English Premiership. It was also useful to watch the World Cup when that started and I am sure that during the Czech Republic game against the USA, I could hear a massive cheer go around the campus whenever the Czech's scored.

The only English language channel was the aforementioned CCTV-9. The programming we tended to see was on world and Chinese news, Chinese language programmes and travel documentaries. It was supposedly set up for those English speakers outside of China to learn more about the country but from what I have read, it has not been reaching its target audience. It would seem that its most ardent viewers are the native Chinese trying to improve their English.

This failure is without doubt down to all of the programming being dreadful, with editorial bias in nearly everything we saw. The best example I can give was during the 2006 Winter Olympics. Everything focused on the Chinese competitors and no other countries participants even got a mention. This became a real pain as I would have liked to have known who was actually picking up the medals other than the Chinese. It was as though no one else was participating. After the games had finished, there was a review programme of the whole shebang with the Italian Ambassador as a special guest. I was sure I could see him squirming in his chair as the only questions he was asked concerned the Chinese competitors and not one was about his own country. Italy might not have had the best Olympics but it would have been nice to hear something about it.

Jiang Heping, the director of CCTV-9 admits that the channel is not un-biased. On the issue of bias he says it is the goal of CCTV-9 "to voice a Chinese perspective on world affairs and to break the western voice's monopoly on the news. Our opinions on the world are quite different from those of CNN and the BBC. We are taking great efforts to minimise the tone of propaganda, to balance our reports, and to be objective. But we definitely won't be reporting as much negative domestic news as the western media.[26]" It was little wonder that most of the foreign teachers had an extensive DVD collection and we gave up trying to watch it after a couple of weeks!

We couldn't escape from CCTV though, because there were two TV's in Dining Hall 8 and these would normally have some sports coverage on it. If it wasn't football or basketball, it tended to be Chinese achievements in world sporting competitions (such as the Olympics), but there were only so many games of Table Tennis you can watch before wanting to shoot the screen with a large gun.

Dashan - Not only is CCTV 9 the home of rubbish English language television, it is also the home of Dashan (or Mark Rowswell as his parents named him), a Canadian who has become a major celebrity in China due to his ability to speak Mandarin like a native. He first came to my attention in an article in That's Beijing[27]. Dashan translates into English as Big Mountain and it can be argued that he is the most famous Westerner in China (this statement does not include Westerners who have stayed in the West). I must admit that I had never heard of the man before I came to China.

When I asked Doug about Dashan, he started to spit blood claiming that he hated him. Seeing as Doug is normally so cool about everything, this was most unexpected but after asking a couple of other people the same thing, it turned out they had the same view on the subject. Dashan it would seem was not popular amongst the ex-pats community. Once he had calmed down from his earlier statement, Doug revealed that the main reason for his dislike of Dashan was the smugness of the man.

One thing was for certain after I became aware of who he was, I saw Dashan's face on adverts all over

---

[26] http://en.wikipedia.org/wiki/CCTV_International

[27] That's Beijing was a free monthly English language magazine that we would try to pick up when we were out and about. It was a great way of finding out about restaurants, nightclubs, sport and other recreational activities in the city. It would also have the odd tit bit of information including articles on workers jobs (this is how I found out how much the lift girls earned) and interviews with foreign celebrities.

China, be they on the television or in the shops. The man, it seemed, was everywhere and Doug was right, he looked very smug.

Chinese Social Customs

Hoping that we wouldn't be caught out by the different social customs we were expecting in China, Sarah had bought a book detailing these potential pitfalls and how we could avoid them. I may have been slack learning the language, but I did read this. Granted it was on the plane on the way over, but it was only small and killed about an hour so that was good. Most of these concepts were covered in the induction week, where it was explained that the older generation put more stock in these traditions than those following them. After spending so much time in the company of my students, I would say that this is correct.

Respect - The book stated that the Chinese were very proud of its country's long history and past achievements. With this long history comes an equally long tradition for doing things and even though Mao tried to sweep out the old and bring in the new with the Cultural Revolution[28], old habits die hard. Respect for ones elders and people in positions of authority was still common and we could expect our students to respect us, not only because we were older than them but also because we were their teachers. Therefore, they would refer to us by our job title and not by our name. This indeed happened and it was quite weird to begin with, but once my students got to know me I found that in class they would use the title, but outside of it they would use my name. If introducing me to someone that didn't know me (normally their illegal girlfriends), they would say "This is Ross. He is my English Teacher".

---

[28] The Cultural Revolution was launched by Mao in 1966 to gain the political initiative he had lost in previous years due to his inept leadership of China. The effects of this period in Chinese history were devastating. Countless artefacts from Chinese past were destroyed and the education system ground to a halt. Intellectuals were sent to labour camps and anyone who questioned the thoughts of Mao could expect to be arrested. This was a dark period in China's history.

Gift Giving – The book mentioned that the Chinese consider gifts as an important way to show courtesy, especially to one's hosts. We therefore thought that buying some nice western style chocolate would go down a treat. This did backfire on us a little bit as the Chinese do not have a tradition for sweet things so we didn't hand all of it out, even though the ones we did give out were graciously received.

Mianzi (Face) – I have already mentioned the concept of losing/gaining face but without explanation. Maintaining 'Face' in China was one of the things the book emphasized as being very important, and it was something you didn't want to lose. 'Face' could be lost by demeaning a person, especially in public by shouting, insulting embarrassing or shaming them. This did lead to problems though. I had read in one of the guide books an article about the Aviation Museum, which was based a good few miles out of Beijing, but there was allegedly a bus in the centre of Beijing that would take us to the entrance. The museum promised much, especially Chairman Mao's private plane. Being a good Communist and man of the people, he also had his own private train that had been purpose built for him in East Germany, but we never found out where this was on display.

The forces of darkness (or the fear the Chinese have of losing face) conspired against us and we never made it. When we arrived at the bus stop, we couldn't find any reference to the bus we needed to catch. When we asked some of the locals if this was the right place, they all replied yes. Doug pointed out that they would have said this even if it was the wrong place as they didn't want to lose face by showing their fellow countrymen that they didn't know the answer. 'Face' has no doubt led to the fact that the Chinese language doesn't really have a word for 'No' in it.

Numbers – The number 4 is considered unlucky, which did have its advantages. The price of a Mobile Phone Sim card depended on the reference number the manufacture had printed on it. The more 4's it had, the cheaper it was. It was even possible to barter these down by even more as none of the locals would buy them. 4 is considered unlucky because in Chinese, the word sound is similar to one used for 'death'. Any number containing a four is also considered unlucky. It wouldn't surprise me to find out that this was the reason we were given accommodation in Building 114 and on the 14th level. The number 8 though is the other side of the coin as it sounds similar to the word for 'fortune'. Therefore, mobile Sim cards with loads of 8's on it would sell for a very high price. There are other numbers that have meanings in China but these were the only two that affected us during our trip.

Guanxi (Trust) - Throughout their history, this has been the glue that has held Chinese society together. It is all about building up connections to get what you want by doing favours for others in the hope that when they have something you need, you would be able to get them to repay the favour. This concept came into business a lot, and Rupert used to complain about it on a regular basis. He always found it annoying because the way the Chinese wouldn't necessarily buy the best product or service, but to go with the client they felt they could trust the most. A series of meetings with a potential Chinese client would mean spending hours just trying to gain their trust before you even had a chance to sell your product. Rupert always seemed to find this very frustrating. Someone without any connections would therefore find making a substantial living in China a struggle.

Part 5 - **From Chopin To The Drifters**

11-a-side

Game 13 - Drifters (2) v Beida Korea (1) - Beida Korea, a team of young, fit Koreans students who had yet to suffer from the effects of smoking and drinking over a number of years to ravage their youthful bodies. They were fast, they were skilful, they had been playing together for about two years and they came into this game unbeaten. The Beijing Drifters were none of these things. Our strengths were an ability to swear in multiple languages and fight with each other for no obvious reason. No two Drifters teams were ever the same and like the French Rugby team, you never knew which team was actually going to turn up. Like 'Never Stop', this Korean team started the game (and the second half) by having a group hug and a shout before proceeding to cheat all the way through the game. They have obviously been watching too much top flight Italian football. One even kicked me in the back of the leg, but the ref decided in his infinite wisdom to give a free kick against me!

We started without any of the war chants, but we were in a positive mood and I had thought I would break my duck and score a goal for the team. In the first 20 minutes, I hit every part of the Beida goal except the one that counts including shots where it would have been easier to score. Corner flags and the sun were more likely to be hit by me in this sort of form. In fact, that is not strictly true as I did managed to put the ball in the net from a corner but it was disallowed for a push on the player in front of me. Considering the guy ran into me and fell over because he made dwarves look tall, I thought that the decision was a bit harsh. Richard did his best for Chinese/Korean diplomatic relations by smacking down the opposition winger.

There is no disgrace in being booked for a challenge that wouldn't have looked out of place in a Bruce Lee movie. It took about half an hour for the first trademark Stuart moment. He made a rather robust tackle and when the referee blew for a free kick, Stuart let loose a barrage of abuse cursing the referee, his wife, his sister and many other minor relatives, in language that would make the late Bernard Manning blush. He only calmed down slightly on discovering that the referee had in fact awarded the free kick to the Drifters.

Our positive start didn't last though and the Koreans took the lead, some what against the run of play but this wasn't going to be the Drifter team that had played against the Celtics a few weeks before. That, and the fact that Stuart looked as though he was going kill someone if we didn't start scoring! One of footballs great clichés is that scoring just before the break is good for your confidence and not the opposition's. We duly scored just before the ref blew for half time with Pablo breaking through three tackles and bundling the ball into the net. Not only did the confidence flow back, but the vein on the side of Stuarts head throbbed a little slower.

The second half belonged completely to the Drifters and was the best concerted passage of football we had played up until this point. Our tackling clearly rattled the Beida attack to the extent that they ended up pumping high balls into the box which were easily mopped up by Adam and Christophe. Mid way through the half, we scored the goal that our play so richly deserved. Pablo took advantage of some poor defending and from the penalty spot; he looked to be letting loose an absolute rocket. However, he miscued it and fired it limply straight at the keeper. The goalie seemed to be shocked that anyone could shoot so badly and after failing three times to keep hold of the ball, he palmed it into his own net.

The many different nationalities and the different ways of pronouncing words in English was really noticeable in this game. In one of our many attacks, Arakawa shouted 'Sappori' which did sound brilliant. We all thought that this was some sort of battle cry and meant that we should really go for the throat of the Koreans. Rupert was all ready to adopt it as an official Drifter battle cry only to discover that we had all misheard the English word 'support'.

As things were running smoothly, it was time for a trademark Drifter implosion. Albert had been hacked down by one of the Beida defenders and had raised himself from the ground with fire pouring from his eyes. I felt that he was going to deck the defender and get himself sent off so I grabbed him in such as way that he couldn't get away. I was most surprised when he turned on me and started to give me a hard time. The Beida supporters on the sideline were shocked into silence as Albert and I started scrapping. The Referee, clearly worried that any action on his part might bring Stuart's wrath down on the remaining members of his family, stayed well out of it. Rupert said afterwards that from his position on the sidelines, it looked like a ventriloquist scrapping with his puppet! We calmed down enough to finish the game but there were still sparks in the air as we trouped off at the final whistle.

There was still time for another Drifter (or two) to loose the plot. Stuart, who must have felt a little left out of the handbag swinging, decided that he needed an argument of his own. With five minutes to play, Rupert substituted Pablo; Stuart decided that it was time for a lively debate on the merits of such an action. What Stuart didn't know though was that Pablo had told Rupert at half time that he needed to leave early, and by leaving the pitch with only five minutes left, he had stayed on the pitch longer than he had planned to. After this exchange, Rupert was keen to point out that his parents were actually married before he was born.

With the final whistle came scenes of celebration from not only the Drifters but a couple of Athletico players (who were currently lying in second) that had come along to watch. This was also the game when I realised that I truly become a Drifter. I was quick to temper, argued with the ref and generally behaved as my own worst enemy. It was great!

Spring Was Upon Us

The weather may have started to get warmer, but it was also beginning to get a little wilder. The winds began to blow and when we woke up one morning, everything was covered in a layer of dust from the Gobi desert, which is not that far away from Beijing and supposedly getting closer with each passing year. The Lonely Planet mentioned that there had been a massive tree planting program implemented in the last few years to cut down the amount of dust coming in from the desert. Doug commented that it had been relatively effective because the storms were not as severe as they were when he had first been in China. In one of his first ever classes at Beihang, only one student turned up for a class due to a massive dust storm that was ravaging the campus. With the rise in temperature came a rise in pollution. Over the weekend of the 8th and 9th April, one of the Drifters told us that Beijing had the lowest air quality on the planet. We could tell how bad it was because we had difficulty seeing the buildings on the other side of the park through the smog and haze. We had read that respiratory disease is a big killer in China and we were beginning to see why.

The Sites, the Sounds and Smell of Beijing #3

The Drum and Bell Towers - With the warmer weather came an increased desire to get out of the apartment and see the sights. Our first ports of call were the Bell and Drum Towers which were really interesting. These towers were used in the days before the invention of the wrist watch as a way of telling the citizens of the city the time (These seemed to be a real Chinese feature as we also saw a Drum Tower in Xi'an when we visited there). The drums are still beaten at regular times today, but this seems to be for the benefit of any tourists that just happen to be around (like us). These were now such a tourist trap that the ground floor levels have been converted into a tea house and restaurant respectively. There was actually very little space left for the information panels that had been erected in the Towers as most of the space had been taken up by souvenir shops.

Visiting these towers was an excellent place to see the changing face of China at first hand. These towers were in one of the few remaining areas of Beijing where you could see Hutongs. The Towers used to be the tallest buildings in Beijing at three stories, but no longer. Standing at the top of the Tower, all you can see in the distance were skyscrapers, which is a pity because it is destroying the traditional face of the city. Also visible from the Towers were the destruction the government had wrought on its on people in pursuit of the almighty dollar. All of the Hutongs south of the Drum Tower had been demolished, no doubt displacing the people who had most probably lived there for generations. Occasionally someone would find a TV report from the outside world about this and would email it around. If true, this is absolutely disgraceful.

Ethnic Minorities Park - This was just up the road from Beihang and directly opposite the still under construction Olympic Stadium. Until recently, it was allegedly called the Racist Park and even though the English around the place left a lot to be desired, at least someone told them that this was a mistake and even more bizarrely, somebody actually listened. It was a shame that we couldn't get a picture of the sign before the name change for our collection. The park itself was designed to show the homes and lifestyles of all of the 56 different nationalities (or ethnic groups to everyone else in the world) that make up China. This may soon become a museum to these people because I suspect their ways of life are being slowly eroded by the modern world and the encroachment of the Han Chinese, by far and away the largest ethnic body in China[29].

The Friendship Store - Doug also took us on a visit to a piece of Chinese shopping history, The Friendship Store which was the first store in Beijing to sell goods to foreigners. At one point, Westerners were not allowed to shop in the same places as the Chinese or use the money that the Chinese were given. Foreigners had their own money, and this was the only shop that this 'special' money could be spent in. As it was such a landmark and still existed even though China has become a consumer heaven, we thought we would pay it a visit. The shop itself was full of fantastic pieces of jade, wall hangings and other Chinese related goods, but the prices were sky high. The only defence for these extortionate prices was that could almost guarantee that if the sign said it was jade, then it was jade. Something that could not be guaranteed at the markets we usually shopped at. An interesting experience, but due to the prices I got the

---

[29] The Han Chinese make up over 90% of the total Chinese population.

impression that we would never be walking through its doors again, which did turn out to be the case.

5-a-side
        It felt a bit like 'after the Lord Mayor's show' with our next 5-a-side games and the weather didn't help matters much. Not only was it the first day I had seen rain since we had arrived in Beijing, but to top it off, it was bloody cold. This didn't put me in the best of moods for the matches and maybe that showed in my performances, even though the rest of the team said that I played well.
        Game 7 - Drifters (2) v British School Accies (3) - After my heroics the week before, I turned up with my goalkeeping gear knowing that if Rupert was absent, I would end up in goal. Our first opponents were well known to most of my team mates as some of them had played against and for the Drifters in the past. I had heard mention of one of their players being a bit good and this was the first time I had the pleasure of seeing him in the flesh.
        He was affectionately known as Little Dave and he was the best foreign player I saw in China. He had a nice touch, great skill and what was even more annoying was that he was such a nice guy. He was always complementary of an opposition player but he was definitely the difference between the two teams. We had taken a two goal lead early on but he won the game for the Accies almost single handedly by scoring three amazing goals that I had little or no chance of stopping. However much it hurts, you can only respect a player for some of the things Dave pulled out the hat.
        Being this good didn't make him popular with everyone. Rupert told me a story that Dave was asked to play in a foreigner's representative team against a Chinese select in some sort of exhibition match. He completely out played the opposition and the foreigners were quite a few goals in front at the break. This did not go down well with the Chinese who, in an 'Escape to Victory' moment, demanded that Dave be removed before the second half began because this might have been a 'friendly' and the result didn't matter as long as

the Chinese won, but this wasn't going to happen with Dave still on the pitch. Needless to say, Dave didn't leave the field and the foreigner's won by a massive score.

Game 8 - Drifters (1) v Bouncing Beavers (5)- Either we had become worse, or the Beavers had improved dramatically. We had plenty of opportunities to score loads of goals and we all thought that we made enough chances to actually win, but in the end we were thumped. After the six points we had picked up last week, this was a disappointment and left a bitter taste in the mouth. The only highlights were that Christophe was so disappointed with it all that he wrote the match report in French and Albert and I didn't end up smacking each other (well, this was a highlight for me as I was getting a little fed up of arguing with people shorter than me).

Chinese Roads

For a country famous for the amount of bicycles on the road, it was amazing how many privately owned vehicles there were. According to Doug, it had only been in that last couple of years that the ban on privately ownership of a motor vehicle was lifted. Obviously all of the ones that Chairman Mao and his Communist Party cronies had used were not his own, but belonged to the 'people', who would no doubt never have been allowed to use them. There were still a lot of bikes on the road but the people who rode them really were dicing with death because some of the driving we saw was a little on the dangerous side (more on this later). Apart from these, taxis were the most prominent type of car on the road.

Taxis really were our lifeblood during our time in China. There always seemed to be plenty of taxis about, apart from when it rained, which was not very often. The longest I had to wait for one was an hour, but that was a very rainy evening and at a time when the restaurants were closing so everyone was doing the same thing. The average wait was about five minutes because there were just so many of the damn things driving around all of the time, sometimes I would have about half a dozen all tripping over each other trying to get my business.

When we first got to China, there were three different prices that the taxis would charge. They were

1.20, 1.60 or 2.00 RMB per kilometre. I only ever got in one 1.20 because they were a bit like hen's teeth as they were being phased out. These and the 1.60 really were a case of 'you got what you paid for'. They were dirty (to such an extent that I put my clothes in the wash after having been in one) and not the most looked after cars I had ever seen. The dirt seemed to be the one thing keeping them together. The 2.00 were all brand new and sometimes it was worth getting just to sit in a nice, clean-ish car. During our stay, and in a moment of pure genius, the Beijing government decided that all the taxis should be the same price at 2.00. After this, we would only get the nicer looking cabs. The guys in the once cheaper cabs must be thanking the government about that one because the only reason to get one through choice had gone!

Taxis charged by the distance they travelled and not the amount of time you are in them (unless you are in some serious traffic and even then they go up very slowly)[30]. London cabbies could learn a thing or two from this! Like their British counter parts, they also liked to strike up a random conversation if they figured out that you understood what they are saying. On one journey, Doug spent the majority of the time responding to the drivers comments about the poor skills of women drivers. It seems that some subjects are just universal.

The drivers could also be quite belligerent sometimes, mostly it seemed when it concerned the air-conditioning. With the soon to arrive over powering hot weather, it was nice to step into a cooler environment which a taxi could offer. However, there were occasions when the driver would simply refuse to turn it on, even with the threat of you getting out if they didn't. Sometimes, you just had to leave a taxi to find one that

---

[30] As with a lot things in China, the taxi drivers you could barter with. No one knew who had discovered this, but it was possible to ask a taxi driver if he would take a fare without putting it on the clock. As most taxi's cruised the streets looking for a fare, it was easy for the driver to get away with this. It was useful to know how much the journey would normally cost because then the price given to the driver could be less. If the driver could be persuaded to do this, it was of benefit to both parties. The driver made 100% of the fare and the passengers would reach their destination for less money than they normally have paid.

would turn on the A/C just to cool down from the ever present heat. It might have been an expensive way to cool down, but it did the trick none the less.

One other thing is that because the cars drive on the right, the left side passenger door does not open. Due to the dangers of even going near a Chinese road, this is most probably a good thing.

Some of the Drifters had their own cars and were happy to drive around on China's roads, but all I could think was that they were braver than they looked as this really was taking your life in their hands. All the rules of the road that would apply back home were simply ignored. In one particular incident we were all off to grab some pizza from a well known American chain, so well known in fact that we'd never heard of it. I was tempted to name it but they no doubt have some lawyers sitting around waiting to sue someone for any negative remarks. As usual the American's definition of great pizza and ours were on two completely different planets.

Anyway, there were too many of us for one cab so we split into two. I went in the first and Sarah in the second. The taxis seemed to take two different routes and Sarah's group arrived first, which was amazing, considering that on the main road their driver didn't seem to feel it was necessary to slow down when the car in front had put his brakes on! It was not surprising therefore that the taxi ploughed into the back of the other car! The taxi driver got out, as did the driver of the car in front (in the middle of a four lane road!) leaving the rather bewildered passengers debating whether they should wait and witness the dispute or get out on the dangerously busy highway and try and flag another taxi down, obviously without paying for the first one.

After a little deliberation they all got out and tried to flag down another cab. At which point their taxi driver panicked at the thought of losing his fare, came running back to the cab and herded them all back in! Rather shocked at being in the crash they refused to pay the full fare and negotiated a cheaper deal. However the real turn up for the books, was the fact that the cab I was in still arrived <u>after</u> theirs, despite the fact that they'd had time to have a crash and sit on the highway for 10 minutes going nowhere!

It was also during our many taxi journeys that we learned that the white lines on the road are merely a suggestion (if that!) as to where the lanes in the road start and finish. Most of the drivers on the road tended to ignore these, trying to cram their cars into the smallest gap possible, so that they could get to their destination or the hospital, even quicker! This lack of common sense on the road would lead to other mishaps, some of which could be life threatening. At home, when a motorist hears a siren from a police car or an ambulance, they tend move to the sides of the road to let them through. Not so in China. No one gets out of the way, and sometimes they even speed up, as if fearful that they may lose their place, as wherever they are going is far more important than obstructing the paths of justice or denying a patient the life saving treatment they may so desperately need!

Pedestrians didn't have an easy time of it either. Crossing the road would be best described as a real life game of 'Frogger'. There were traffic lights and signals to tell the traffic when to stop, but this meant absolutely nothing. The lights may have gone red for the traffic, but didn't mean anyone had to pay attention to them. Cars, and more often than not, bikes would still drive through regardless of the fact that someone might be crossing the road on foot.

On some of the bigger cross-roads, there were men on the corners (in uniform of course) who would aid you in crossing the road. This would involve them blowing their whistle when the green man lit up and would use a different signal with their whistle when the red man was on to warn you that it is too dangerous to cross. Even though they are standing there, it didn't stop traffic from going through the red lights trying to run you over. The Green Cross Code Man should make an effort to come out to China at some point, especially if he also brought his Darth Vader costume!

11-a-side
        Game 14 - Drifters (3) v Never Stop (2) - We were playing on a different pitch for this game in another

area of Beijing. It was a small sports stadium with a running track around the pitch and a stand (a novel experience for, me having only ever played on the local park back home). The major difference between this pitch and the one we had played on before was that this was Astroturf. I was quite glad to be playing on this because the grass pitches we had played on before had been a nightmare for me. With an almost non-existent touch at the best of times, playing on a very bumpy pitch had not been beneficial to my game. We were all very keen for a victory to continue our winning run, and there was an added incentive that it was Christophes birthday with drinks promised after the game, regardless of the result! The beer was bound to taste sweeter with three points in the bag. Just before kick off the Koreans did their now obligatory huddled yell and I noticed that their goalkeeper was the same one I had flattened a couple of weeks before.

We instantly went on the attack and it only took five minutes for the Drifters to take the lead. Two of the Never Stop defenders went for the same ball and proceeded to run into each other much like Alan Hansen and Willie Miller did when playing for Scotland against the USSR in the 1982 World Cup. Finding the two defenders on the floor and nothing but air between me and the keeper, I ran as fast as I could towards the goal. Showing some pace that surprised all of my team mates, I ran into the box and thundered the ball into the bottom corner. Cue some Alan Shearer-esque celebrations, putting one hand up in the air as I was running away from goal whilst my team mates went wild! As we were the Drifters though, our celebrations were short lived and the curse of poor defending did for us again. And within a couple of minutes of taking the lead, the Koreans were level. This was the cue for Paul to turn red and shout a lot at the defence.

This was definitely the kick up the backside we needed and after that setback, we put their defence under a lot of pressure but couldn't quite score a second. After about 20 minutes of this, Markus made a great run from midfield but as he was just about to enter the Korean area, I took the ball off of him. I still cannot think why I did this but it mattered not because me, crossing in front of Markus confused the defence and I was able to smack the ball with such ferocity that even though I kicked it directly at the keeper, he wasn't fast enough to stop it. Cue more celebrations but my time on the pitch was about to come to an end, at least until half time anyway. I went for a header against one of the Korean midfielders but I can't remember anything after that until I hit the floor in absolute agony. I was face down on the pitch and even though I could hear the voices of my team mates asking me if I was okay, all I could think to do was to move my fingers and toes to see if everything was working. Luckily they were but I walked off the pitch spitting blood as I seemed to have bitten into my lip.

I proceeded to watch the rest of the half from the sidelines as the team battled to maintain our lead, but with only a couple of minutes to go until the break, the Koreans equalised. My heart sank and Paul started to shout out another barrage of expletives. Rupert, (from the sidelines) and Stuart, (from the centre circle) proceeded to do the same. The whistle went and the team trooped off and Rupert gave us the right speech and the right time to raise our spirits. Feeling much better for the break, inspired by Ruperts speech and looking to score a hat trick, I said I was ready to come back onto the pitch.

The game was in the balance for the whole of the second half with both teams going for the win and producing heroics in defence to stop the other from scoring. With only ten minutes left and Rupert's blood pressure going up as the Koreans seem to be the more likely to score, Adam made a great tackle and burst into midfield. Seeing me unmarked, he played a defence splitting pass onto my run. Gathering the ball, I reached the edge of the box and seeing the Korean defence closing in, I toe punted the ball as hard as I could. Any football coach would no doubt tell you that doing this is so wrong and that only very young children do it, but I didn't care as the ball crashed into the net. More Shearer-esque celebrations and the Koreans looking dejected, wondering how some out of condition and 'slightly' overweight Westerner beat them for pace, not once, but twice!

The Drifters shut up shop and with Stuart playing a more defensive midfield position to break up any Korean attacks (and any bones in the process) we hung on for another win. We walked off of the pitch with a massive sense of relief. Everyone looked overjoyed with the result, especially Chirstophe who said that this was the perfect birthday present and that everyone was invited to join him at Club Football for beers. Not everyone came along (which was a shame) but those who did, piled into the club and took over the free pool table that was situated in the back. It was the perfect way to finish off the day, and Christophe even brought along his family to join us including his two very young daughters. Being Christophe's children, they seemed to only speak French which was fortunate really. Stuart continued where he left off on the football pitch and turned the air a little blue, even after Rupert had asked him to keep it as clean as possible. Stuart failed dismally much to everyone else's amusement. Christophe left early but on his way out (and to no one else's knowledge) had paid for everyone's food and drink. We all left full of cheer but we never did this again which was shame because underneath all of the agro, the Drifters were a great bunch of lads.

Class Things in Class #2
1) I felt that I was doing too much talking during my classes, so I asked my students to talk about what they thought was one of Man's great inventions. What I didn't expect was, not one, but two students decided to talk about condoms. One of the students had even produced a PowerPoint presentation to illustrate what he was talking about. It did make a refreshing change from listening to talks about planes, computers and cars though!
2) I took a map of China into class to ask the students where Sarah and I should pay a visit to whilst in China. Most of the suggestions involved the students telling me about their home

provinces. One of the ideas was completely bonkers, involving going across China to Tibet and then making a tour of the western provinces. When I asked the student how long it would take to get to Tibet by train, he replied that it would take about 44 hours. No wonder the class started laughing when he had made the suggestion in the first place. The one that really stood out was taking a trip to Inner Mongolia with the opportunity of riding horses and camping under the stars.

3) Both Sarah and I had become fed up with students sleeping in class so we started to administer some punishments to the ones we caught. Sarah's involved her students buying her chocolate, and mine had to buy me a small bottle of Coke. I wanted to make it beer (and not only because it was cheaper than Coke!), but the students could get into real trouble if they were caught bringing any in. Some of the students complained that I couldn't administer these fines, but they stopped their whinging as soon as I threatened them with a visit to the Dean instead. Sarah's students were just as annoyed by this, but it didn't stop them from sleeping. Sarah ended up with so much chocolate that she stopped punishing them in this way because there was a danger that there wouldn't be enough room in the fridge for beer!

Nights on the Town

As we were spending more time in the company of Ray and Rob, we thought we would organise a night out in the centre of town. I had shown myself to be a reliable 'chappie,' and even trustworthy enough to look after the Drifter's kit bag, so Rupert had given me a Gold Card for a bar in town called The Den which would give me a discount on drinks. As none of the group had been here before and as I had this card, it was here that we decided to go.

The evening did not get off to the best of starts because the bar said that my card was out of date! After saying that we would all leave, they changed their tune pretty quickly so we sat down. The place was overpriced and definitely designed for ex-pats with well paid jobs. The real highlight of the evening was when Ray had one of the local ladies of the night (who frequented the place) come over to our table. She got bored with our company because she realised pretty quickly that none of us were going to use her services, or even buy her a drink, so she wandered off to find someone who was a bit more susceptible to her charms!

Ray also joined us (hookers not included this time) when the SAFEA organised a trip for us to go to the Friendship Hotel to watch a specially organised classical concert. Tana also decided to come along but Doug, who had experienced trips like this before, decided to stay at home and do something less boring instead. We left an hour before the concert started because we were travelling through rush hour traffic. However, the traffic was non-existent and we arrived so early that we went window-shopping to kill time. However, Tana found all of the shoe departments and we were all quite worried that we wouldn't be back in time.

When we finally sat down for the music, the night didn't get off to the most interesting of starts because the conductor spent over half an hour introducing nearly every instrument to the audience. He did this with a female interpreter which was such a waste of time particularly when she got something wrong and he corrected her, in English! What is it with older Chinese men employing younger women to act as their translators when they are better English speakers than the person speaking on their behalf? As Dean Tang kept using Amanda to do his translating during meetings, we were beginning to get the impression that this was the way things were done around here!

The room itself was ridiculously warm and the music was so soothing that I fell asleep during one of the pieces, only to be woken when the percussionist crashed her cymbals. The second half of the show had a couple of guest performers. One was a Belgian French horn player who hit so many bum notes, that it was hard to keep a straight face. The second was an opera singer and we thought that this would be the end of the concert but even though the fat lady had sung, it just seemed to go on forever, even after she'd left the stage.

I also hung out with four of my students, who had been asking me to join them for dinner since we had arrived. I managed to get an invite for Sarah, and Tana came along as she had nothing else to do. We went to a restaurant that served food from their home province and they asked us what we liked and ordered accordingly. This was no doubt kudos for them, but they were great company and it was nice to spend some time with my students outside of the classroom. I was quite surprised and a little embarrassed when they paid for all of us. We all decided we would return the favour at a later date, preferably a meal where a knife and fork had to be used!

5-a-side

Game 9 - Drifters (2) v British School Accies (1) - After beating us the week before, the Accies turned up with a few different players, no doubt hoping to beat us more convincingly. Once again, they had Little Dave but the 'newbies' included a version of me (tall, bald and pretty solid) and some midfielder, who I'd been told could dribble the ball all day and get rid of his own shadow. I liked the way my team mates were trying to install some confidence in me as I was playing in goal again. Stuart wasn't able to play, and because the guys knew I could shout a bit, I was given the job of captain for the evening.

After what I hoped was a stirring speech, the team played like men possessed tackling everything for the entire first half. If one of the opposition players did get through, their shooting angles were made so tight that I didn't have too much work to save the ball. With Stuart absent and me in goal, Amine stepped up to be the Drifters player that exploded after what could only be described a horrendous tackle. Christophe joked that after very nearly punching the Accies player that had almost cut him in half, he should emigrate to the UK as that sort of aggression is not normally associated with the mainland European Drifters. Amine took this to heart, taking up Stuart's mantle by cursing and swearing excessively. This did the trick though because with some classic counter attacking, we managed to nick a goal putting us in the lead just before the break.

Everyone had worked really hard to get this lead and we all knew that we would have to work doubly hard to win this game. For the whole of the second half, we were under constant pressure. The Accies managed to equalise after throwing everything at us and I feared that this game would go the same way as the week before, but Albert had other ideas. Having put in a new set of Duracell batteries during the break, he stole the ball and with all the Accies outfield players on the attack, he ran on unhindered into their half to score. Cue renewed concentration and the will to win. The relief on everyone's face when the final whistle went was obvious for all to see. They were a tough team to play and even tougher to beat, but they were all gracious in defeat. We were very pleased with our nights work, but our next game was to be against the team top of the league, which just happened to be unbeaten.

Game 10 - Drifters (0) v Newbies (3) - We were very tired from the first match and it really showed as the Newbies, who were a lot younger and more organised rang rings around us. The guys tried very hard and I had my work cut out to keep the score down, but we never looked like we were going to get a result out of this game. We took some consolation from the game because the Newbies scored two very early goals but we managed to keep them out for nearly the remainder of the match until they slotted in their third right at the death. During that time, we even had some shots of our own and this was a defeat not to be ashamed of. We played as well against the highly mobile and skilled Newbies team as we did in the first match.

As a footnote to this game, Christophe made me laugh at the beginning of the second half by calling out to the team "Come on Drifters, let's be brave". The sentence was meant to inspire but the way he said 'brave' reminded me of Inspector Clouseau. Being Christophe, he took it in his stride and was in no way offended that I laughed at his accent. There was also a bit of a love in between me and Albert because when we were asked who should be man of the match, we both talked about each others performance in glowing terms. Everyone else had a good laugh at this, which was better than the 'slanging' match a couple of weeks back.

A few of us decided that we should have a drink so we went to a restaurant just up the road from the ground. It was the weirdest restaurant I have ever been to as the theme of the place seemed to be that of a prison. The waiters wore guard uniforms (including metal helmets) and the women looked a bit like Nazi Stormtroopers! The walls were black, grey and white and the atmosphere was very subdued. The beer was still wet though and laughingly overpriced.

Bootlegs and Bootlegging
It did not take us very long to realize that China is the bootlegging capital of the world. DVD's, CD's, computer games, clothing, designer goods etc were freely available at any of the markets that were dotted around the place. The DVD shops were something to be experienced. They were chock full of the latest releases, including films that had only just come out in the cinema. Granted, these tended to have been recorded in the cinema itself with a handheld camera but they were still available.

Both 'The De Vinci Code' and 'Pirate of the Caribbean: Dead Man's Chest' were both available to buy from even the street vendors, which actually turned out to be useful as both of the films were banned by the Chinese authorities. Well, 'Pirates of the Caribbean' was definitely banned (we cannot be sure why even though the implied cannibalism could have been the reason) but 'The De Vinci Code' was taken off at the cinema after two weeks even though it was still playing to full houses. The official reason was that it was time for another film to have a cinematic run.

Bootleg DVD's would cost anywhere from 10RMB (£0.70 approx) for a single disc film to at least 600RMB (£40 approx) for a multi disc box set. These box sets were great. They included all the series of a particular show and as long as they had already been released on DVD in America, they were an exact copy. I even bought one set where the show had been copied directly from digital television and the quality was still superb. In terms of quality and the value for money, they were 'a must have'.

The official products were considerable more expensive (a single disc would put you back at least 25RMB or approximately £1.70). Bootleg DVD's even came in two types, DVD5 and DVD9. Allegedly the DVD9's were of better quality and tended to have the special features, as long as the original had been a single disc in the first place. It tended only to be the official versions that had the second disc's, but not always. Bootleg CD's were the same, but these could also be a little random. I bought a Tanya Donelly album and it came with a free poster of Angus Young from AC/DC with it!

The bootleg shops that we frequented the most, (especially after Ivy's was closed down) were near the Lido. This had the biggest and best DVD shops we saw in our whole time out in China as well as more besides. As there were quite a few hotels near the Lido, this was the area where lots of the Westerners who visited the country (that were not backpackers or staying on the cheap) would end up, especially as it was on the road to the airport. It had a large tourist market (very different from the local ones), numerous beggars, the aforementioned prostitutes and golf shops.

Doug had told us that when he first came to Beijing, this area had a lot more DVD shops but the government had closed some of them down after pressure from Western businesses who would not pour money into the country unless something was done about the bootleggers. I was witness to a massive police raid on these shops on one of my visits, but they didn't permanently shut the shops down. The rumour was that they knew who to pay in the police/government (delete as appropriate) so they could continue trading.

Another way of seeing bootleg films or listening to music was to download them from the internet. My students were the first people I met in China who openly admitted to downloading whatever they wanted to from the internet. Most of them had laptops or MP3 phones so they were always downloading music or films to enjoy in the small amount of free time they had. As the majority did not have that much money in the first place, they would only use the free download sites. I was given the odd web address to try and download stuff but there was nothing on any of these sites that really took my fancy.

It turned out that nearly all of the foreign teachers on our floor were on a download frenzy which was the reason why everything took so long to download. By the end of our time there, the download speed had improved dramatically but by this stage, my hard drive was straining under the number of downloads I had and if we'd stayed any longer, I would have had to invest in some more memory.

11-a-side

Game 15 - Drifters (0) v Athletico Beijing (4) - Back on the Astroturf but the less said about this game the better, especially as Rupert had billed it as the one he most wanted win. The Drifters had had a good record against Athletico in the 5-a-side game but with 11-a-side, our record was poor and he wanted this to change. Sending out the call for as many players as possible did the trick because we had 21 people turn up, but this became a curse as we had too many. This was also the one game I shouldn't have turned up for because I was once again suffering from a bit of the Beijing Belly.

I felt ill and I didn't have any energy. These two combined meant I played so badly that I spent more time on the sidelines than on the pitch. Due to the number of Drifter's we didn't have time to gel as a team before players were substituted. As a result, our performance was stilted. Little Dave was playing and he tore our defence apart. Their defence was solid and we never came close to winning the midfield battle. Our unbeaten streak had ended and everyone looked as ill as I felt when they walked off, especially Paul the goalie, who had had a torrid time against Little Dave. Having played in goal against him myself, I knew how he felt.

* * * * *

Chinese Hospitals

China doesn't have any free health care, but we do in Britain. Which one is the communist country I hear you ask? Well, not China, that's for sure but I digress. Whenever any of our students went to hospital (which was often and could be for things as trivial as the common cold or a broken fingernail[31]), they would have to pay for any treatment they received. Hospitals also seem to be based along the same lines as anything else in China. The more you pay, the better the service you would receive. As has been said before, the on campus hospital was a bit of a joke and even the students said it was a waste of time, but they didn't have that much of a choice in where they went for treatment. There was a series of foreign hospitals dotted around the place and you really did pay for what you got. The treatment, care and even the building itself were top notch, but you paid through the nose for it. Needless to say, we never went to one of these and I think it would have had to have been a real emergency to get us to go.

We both paid visits to a hospital that was just outside of the University, though I was the only one who went there for any sort of treatment. Every time I went, the same things sprung to mind:

1) Before even entering the hospital, I would have to queue in an outside building to register and pay a deposit. I never found out why we had to do this, but you wouldn't be seen by anyone without the deposit slip. At least you were able to claim it back after you had finished.
2) There was absolutely no privacy. I would be sitting with a consultant and random people would keep walking in and out to ask questions or to start queuing. Queuing outside of the room was apparently a no no. Maybe they feared that

---

[31] It seemed that the less able the Class, the more excuses they would have to go to hospital and they would have to have a friend take them there because they were incapable of going there themselves. I had kept a register and between mid April and the beginning of June, I did not have a full class in Class 9 who on overall ability, were by far and away my least able class.

the Doctor would disappear if they didn't stand in the room to keep an eye on them.

3) Before receiving any treatment, I would have to pay for it in advance. This would mean standing in a massive queue before going back to the Doctor to be examined. If I was prescribed anything, I would have to queue up somewhere else to get it.

4) There would always be people just sitting in rooms attached to intravenous drips. We had been warned in our induction week that this was one of the favoured ways of treating anything. I was glad I never had one of these stuck in my arm because I am not a great fan of needles and none of the hospitals I went into looked very clean.

The Underground City

I visited this on my own after hearing about it from Angus as well some of the other foreign teachers that had ventured to it in the past. Construction started in 1969 when the relations between China and the Soviet Union deteriorated to such a degree that they almost went to war with one another. The works continued on the Underground City for the next ten years and were built to protect against a possible nuclear attack. Like so many other things it has now become a tourist attraction, but God knows why? It is series of tunnels covered with random pictures of military hardware, mostly American and dating from World War II onwards.

The tour group were asked not to take pictures and it was easy to comply. There was nothing to see except empty and damp tunnels. One of the guys did ask the reason for not being allowed to take any pictures, and he was brushed off with the answer "It is a military instillation". The place was so high tech that the air ducts led up to the surface with minimal air filtration systems, or that was how it looked anyway. I was even sure that I could hear the sound of an underground train as we walked through. The tunnels themselves were only eight meters underground, and proved to be quite useless for the purpose they had been built for by a study made some years after the construction had finished. Another great Mao idea that turned out to be utterly useless, which seems to be the general theme with most things Mao related.

The end of the tour was just bonkers, as they had a silk producing centre showing the group how the stuff was made. As usual, this turned out to be yet another tourist trap because after the demonstration, the tour guide asked the group how much we thought the silk would cost to buy. No one answered except for one guy who fell into the trap and said he would like to know. Cue the guide taking the man to one side to show him all of the wares that were available.

All I could think of was that silk production would have been an essential practice after a nuclear war. Surely producing food would have been more beneficial to the general population, but as this didn't seem to be a major consideration during peace time. God knows how many millions of Chinese would have starved to death if there had been a nuclear war!

5-a-side

Game 11 - Drifters (3) v Athletico White (1) - Playing the sort of football that Rupert only saw in a wet dream, this was the best team performance I had seen from my vantage point in goal. Once again, I was made Captain as Stuart and Rupert were not available so when picking the team, Albert mentioned that he would like to play as a defender as this was actually his natural position. Matthias started on the left, Adam on the right and Bansoon up front. From the beginning there was a good deal of passing, running off of the ball and only one (that I could remember anyway) suicidal piece of defending. Anyway, as was the Drifter way, we had loads of possession, loads of shots but we couldn't kill off the opposition and we went into half time only one nil up. It was scored by Matthias low into the far corner. He had spent nearly the whole of the game tackling someone and then skinning the next guy with his skill. He deserved more but it wasn't to be.

The second half started much the same with the attack making a valuable contribution up front by harrying the opposition into giving the ball away. It was after one of these attacks that Adam put the ball through the defenders legs and shot in our second goal. I was even having dreams of keeping a clean sheet, but reality intervened! We were caught on the counter and their striker placed the ball under my diving hand, but Matthias had a little bit of magic left in him and scored our third. Special mention must go to Albert who was a revelation as a defender and won so many headers that the opposition congratulated him on his performance. Not bad considering he was about a foot shorter than every other player on the pitch!

Game 12 - Drifters (2) v Barbarians 2 (2)

Albert had made a guest appearance for the Barbarians 2 the week before, so we were hoping for some inside information on how they were going to play. We had absolutely annihilated these guys when we had played them before so we felt that we were up for another six points, but either:

1) we were over confident
2) knackered
3) they played above themselves

or a combination of all three meant that we really struggled to get anywhere in this game. The match started much the same as the one before it and we crafted an excellent goal. Every player in the team ran into the space, confused their defence and Bansoon shot low at goal. The ball hit the post and then hit their goalie on the backside before creeping in like an express snail with their goalkeeper scrabbling across the ground in an attempt to stop it. In football, it doesn't matter how they go in because they all count. It was after this positive start that we fell apart and let the opposition run the game.

As the half wore on, we found ourselves defending more and more. Albert continued to be a revelation at the back and Adam pulled off a brilliant tackle sliding in from behind the Barbarian player with perfect timing to save a certain goal. He also showed some great reactions because I was sliding across the ground to try and win the ball myself but instead almost took his head off. The Barbarians managed to score an equalizer and as the half time whistle blew, we all walked off feeling that we were lucky to have finished all square.

After some stern words from Albert at the break, we rallied and played a lot better, but the Barbarians managed to score a second on the break. What made it more annoying was that it was a carbon copy of their first goal. They put a copious amount of passes together in the midfield and then slotted through to the runner who found himself in space. Adam proved what a good defender he was by clearing the ball in front of goal more times that I can remember.

Unfortunately it tended to be the oppositions goal! Albert who's Duracell's were working overtime kept things solid at the back and Matthias looked dangerous every time he got the ball continued to press the opposition. Matthias managed to hit the post late on in the game and it looked as though our chance to equalise had gone. However, after another good piece of tackling, Matthias ran down the right and put the ball across the face of the goal. Adam managed to stick a boot out and we scored. The Barbarians lost heart and we looked the more likely to win, but the clock was against us and it finished a draw. We were happy that we had four points from a possible six and only the second unbeaten night that season but it really should have been a maximum haul as the opposition were two of the weakest in the league.

Avoiding the Deposit

The Flying College was a hive of activity as they were expecting a visit from some important dignitaries. It was a bit obvious something was going on as all of my students turned up in their full uniform which I had never seen before. The other clues were that the college was clean and the downstairs toilet didn't smell (in fact, the downstairs toilet didn't smell, it absolutely stank and on particularly bad days, it would make the whole reception area stink as well. Not the most pleasant of greetings when walking into work it must be said). When I mentioned this to the students, they joked that it smelt as bad as it did because Dean Tang used it. As soon as the visitors had concluded their inspection, things returned to normal. Well, as normal as they do out there.

This was also the first time we were asked by William if we would stay on for the next semester. Even though at this early stage we had decided to go home once the contract was up, we gave the diplomatic answer and said that we would think about it. We were trying to avoid talking to William as he kept reminding us that we had not paid our deposit. As luck would have it, every time he did so()it was near the end of the month, so we could always plead poverty!

We did feel that we were going to have to plead poverty more than once, as Mrs. Lu was her usual helpful self. As it was the end of the month, I was quite keen to get my money so I could do some touristy things, so I went and asked for it. The only answer I got was the same as I got last month which was 'Maybe'. Even at this early stage, it was becoming a bit tired of all this. I told Sarah this and when she went in later, she managed to get hers. I was quite infuriated by this but I received mine later that same day. It did make me wonder why I couldn't have got it in the first place. We soon figured out the process we would have to go through to get paid. We had to ask Mrs. Lu for our wages three times because on the third, we would get our money. What made this even more annoying is that none of the other teachers had to go through this rigmarole. Their departments actually come looking for them to pay them their money.

The Voice of Beihang

SAFEA were keen to talk to me as they wanted me to do a voice over for the Universities promotional film. This film was to be sent all over the world to anyone that fancied studying at Beihang. What was really weird about it, was I was told that I had been asked to do this because I had come highly recommended. As I have never done anything like this before, I was left guessing where this recommendation had come from. I was not that keen to begin with as we had been warned not to do anything like this for free, but after they waved a large sum of money under my nose, I thought it would have been rude to say no!

It transpired that I would have to work for my money. SAFEA had already produced a script, but they wanted me to re-write because they thought that it sounded too Chinese. It was easy to see why because it used the same archaic style of English that my students were also prone to using. A couple of re-writes later and the SAFEA rep who was co-ordinating this finally said that they were happy to proceed to the recording stage. The recording took place in an area of the University I had never been to before. It was quite an old, austere looking place with massive wooden doors.

The studio was through a maze of corridors and up a few flights of stairs. The equipment looked very modern, but the recording booth had not been soundproofed properly so I could hear the engineer talking to me through the glass without the help of headphones. It only took a couple of takes before I was told that they were happy with the results and I went home. The fee was most welcome and I was given a couple of copies of the DVD to take home with me.

After telling everyone about my voice over work, Ray asked me if I fancied doing a 30 minute show for the campus radio. I was very keen to do this and spent forever trying to work out what songs I was going to play. I thought I would be doing the show on my own, so I selected about 25 minutes worth of music and thought about some interesting things I wanted to say about them. It didn't turn out that way as I was interviewed by a Chinese student asking me about the songs and why I had selected them[32]. I was glad that the show was only being broadcast over the park mushrooms as I thought it was dreadful and no one would actually hear it.

---

[32] The songs I chose to play were Good Vibrations – The Beach Boys, Like a Rolling Stone – Bob Dylan, 25 Miles – Edwin Starr, Gimmie Shelter – Rolling Stones, Take Me to the River – Al Green, Race with the Devil – Gene Vincent & the Blue Caps and last but not least, Get Down and Get With It – Slade. I dread to think what it sounded like as it ended up being unscripted. I just remember that every time I mentioned a song, I said that it was fantastic and great to drive to.

Work Begins on Building 114

You might remember that I have mentioned that the building we were in was in need of some repair work. Well, actually a lot of work was needed. Fair do's to the college as they pulled their collectives fingers out and started work on it, but in their infinite wisdom, they would start the work very early in the morning. The alarm clock was dispensed with on these mornings! When I looked at the work, I couldn't fathom what they were doing. They had drilled massive holes into the wall; sometimes even into the massive cracks that already existed. They had then place metal brackets over the cracks, but they had only used one pin so we couldn't work out how these pins were going to hold the wall together. The only thing I thought the builders had succeeded in doing was to create a lot of mess, and a layer of dust that quickly transferred itself to our flat floor. I cannot be sure if this is related, but we had three power cuts at this point and always at night, which played havoc with everyone's downloading.

As there was nothing much else to do other than sleep, these power cuts were a cue for a good proportion of the teachers to socialise. People would stand in the corridor with an assortment of candles and torches, looking out across the Beijing skyline to see that buildings just outside of the University still had power. On one of these occasions, so many people appeared in the corridor that we had an impromptu party in one of the teacher's rooms which was one of the few occasions we would talk at any length to teachers other than Ray, Doug or Tana. It was quite interesting what they would say as well.

One of the favourite topics of conversation were the rumours that they had heard on the grapevine regarding the Government. The most interesting ones for me were:

1) China has a large number of state executions and some are allegedly timed so that the deceased organs can reserved for a rich westerner who had come over for a cheap transplant.

2) China doesn't have its own AWACS system (A category of planes carrying big, rotating radar discs for use in surveillance during military operations), but due to the number of spies it has around the world, it had allegedly managed to obtain some information regarding it. The experimental plane they had built to test their AWACS system had crashed with all of China's experts in this field on it, killing them all. The reason that they were on the plane when they could easily have monitored the experiment on the ground was because they didn't want the USA to intercept the radio transmissions. Back to square one then boys!

Another topic of conversation were the things their Chinese students had said to them. These included:

1) The gap between the richest and the poorest people is now the biggest in the world (and I thought that this was a communist country?).
2) The Chinese do not understand the idea of volunteering for anything. None of them saw the benefit of giving free English lessons to the poorest of children because that might put them on an equal footing with the people who can afford to have the education.
3) The students were very keen to talk about the recent invasion of Iraq and used it as evidence for American imperialism, but they did agree that the first Iraq conflict was justified because of their unlawful invasion of Kuwait. When it was pointed out that Iraq claimed Kuwait was one of its provinces was the reason why it invaded in 1990 and had threatened to before this date. The students would all say that this was a disgrace, but when it was pointed out that this was the same view that their government had for Taiwan, they quickly changed their tune and say that was justified because the island had once been part of the motherland. None of them could see that they thought it was wrong for one

country was okay for them[33] and this was one of Andrew's favourite arguments against the official government line that his students would repeat to him during classes. No one had admitted to even mentioning Tibet!

4) The students were very critical of the Japanese. A few of them had read reports that the Japanese had changed their history books to deny that there were any human rights crimes during their occupation of Nanjing. They found this denial very upsetting, but they wouldn't accept that their government would ever change the truth.

5) Genghis Khan was Chinese and not a Mongol. There was a rumour that an old teacher had been pulled in front of the Head of the University because he had said Genghis Khan was in no way. shape or form Chinese to his class. Just an example of changing history to make it show as though Chinese had never been invaded or conquered by a foreign power.

6) Mao was a great man. Without him, modern China would not exist. (Everyone in the room laughed at this one).

7) The USA was evil, intent of conquering the world. This didn't stop the majority of everybody's students, watching American films, the NBA or trying to have the best American accent.

Another topic of conversation revolved around spies and spying. The statistic bandied about was that 1 in every 10 teachers in China was actually a spy, using education as a cover. We knew about 20, so statistically there should have been at least 2 spies. We would spend hours trying to wind each other up trying to work out who the spy was (if there was one). We would normally pick

---

[33] When I heard this argument in one of my own classes, I didn't have the heart to bring it to their attention that Japan and Portugal had also owned Taiwan at points in its history and so would their claims to retake it because they owned it in the past would be a justified as their own claim.

on Ray because he looked a bit Chinese (well, more than anyone else that is) but he would say it was Tana saying that her dizzy blonde persona was just an act to lull us into a false sense of security. This rumbled on for months and never stopped being an entertaining subject to talk about.

Food

We went to China with the intention of going native; that is only eating and cooking local food. We had been used to having the 'same old same old' from the local Chinese take away in the UK, but there was only one Chinese dish we had during our entire stay that we had had back at home and that was Beijing Duck. It turned out that the food that tends to be served back in the UK is the southern based Cantonese style. The cooking ourselves part fell by the wayside pretty quickly when we figured out that it was just as cheap to go to the Campus canteens.

The college was surrounded by restaurants and we did do our best to eat in as many as we could. Doug, Ray and Mark were normally on hand to help us out with the menu, because as this was not a tourist area, few of them had menus in English. Mark had explained to us that before he was able to recognise Chinese symbols, he would walk into a restaurant and just pick random things from the menu. The trick was to remember the ones he liked, or at least the ones that didn't make him throw up!

One of our favourite restaurants in Beijing was outside of the North Gate and was lovingly called Ashtray. No one could tell us why because it had been known by this name to the English teaching community for such a long time that anyone who knew its origins had left China years before even Doug turned up. It was here that we had a soup that was served in such a way that it had the Ying Yang symbol on top of it. We also had fruit in caramelised stuff that when left to cool, would become as hard as concrete and impossible to eat. The caramelised coating was so hot when it was initially served that they supplied a container of water to dunk the food in to cool it down before putting it in your mouth. I have a feeling though that someone stupid enough to put it in their

130

mouth before cooling it down and then have the cheek to sue in a 'Stella Awards[34]' tribute. It must be said that China does have the right idea when treating idiots with the contempt they deserve.

They also did a nice line in fruit salad, served in thin runny yoghurt style dressing. This was lovely but my favourite dish was this thin fried bread that had sultanas in it. This stuff was really addictive, and it got to the point that when we went out for dinner, two portions would have to be ordered. One for me and one for everybody else! It was a sad day when Ashtray closed down for refurbishment because it didn't re-open again before we left.

We would also frequent restaurants outside the West Gate. The majority were the Muslim style from the West of China and some of the dishes we tucked into the most were:

Chuanr (or kebab) – This consisted of small pieces of meat (either plain or covered in spices) placed on skewers and roasted on a charcoal grill. I could never be sure exactly what the meat was, but we were told that it tended to be mutton. Everyone loved a bit of chuanr, except me. I think it was because the others tended to like them spicy (spicy food is not for me) or that whenever I did have one that wasn't spicy, I found it difficult to find the meat in with all of the chunks of fat! They were cheap though and readily available. It was so popular that some of our colleagues were keen to stage a chuanr eating competition.

Dapanji (Big Plate of Chicken) – This really did say exactly what it was. It consisted of a massive dish with large lumps of a whole chicken (and yes, we did find a beak in one portion we ordered), loads of big noodles, potatoes and peppers cooked in a curry type sauce. Nice.

---

[34] The Stella Awards are named after Stella Liebeck who spilled a cup of McDonalds' coffee over her lap, burning herself. She successfully sued McDonalds for not labelling their coffee as being served 'hot' and was awarded $2.9 million in damages which were subsequently reduced by the judge to $640,000. The Stella Award was originated to celebrate this event and is subsequently awarded to people who have taken out lawsuits due to their own stupidity.

Jing Jiang Rousi - As well as the fruit salad and the sultana bread this was possibly the most frequently ordered dish when I was present. I am not the most experimental person when it comes to food, so when I find something I like, I tend to stick with it to the detriment of everything else. Jing Jiang Rousi was strips of pork in a dark sauce (similar to the one with duck), served with little flat squares of tofu. In fact it was very similar to the Beijing Duck, just without the duck.

The way to eat Jing Jiang Rousi was to carefully pick up a tofu square (the size of a small hankie) and first lay it over your bowl of rice. You would then place strips of pork in the middle of the square. Once this was done you would somehow, with chopsticks, wrap the tofu square around the strips of pork and shove it in your mouth. Sarah was never able to do this without using her fingers but I managed to become extremely adept at doing it all smoothly with chopsticks with no spillage. Doug and Ray gave me the honorary title of 'Chopstick Master' for achieving this feat.

Gongbao Jiding - This was an extremely popular dish, mainly because if you didn't know what to order in a restaurant they would always point to this on their menu because it is a popular dish amongst westerners. Sarah particularly enjoyed this dish but I wasn't so keen. It varied from place to place in degrees of spiciness. Some restaurants took it upon themselves to save us from the heat by removing the spice whilst others clearly took great pleasure in making it as spicy as possible. Tana and Sarah searched high and wide for the best Gongbao Jiding and in conclusion discovered much to their delight, the best place was just outside the Universities West Gate.

Gongbao Jiding - Peanuts, chicken, peppers and chilli peppers. Disgusting as far as I was concerned but everyone else seemed to like it.

Yuxiang Rousi (Fish Flavoured Pork) – Bamboo, peppers, black wood fungus, peppers, ginger, more spices and, oh yes, some port. Fish? Nowhere to be seen. To my taste buds, it didn't even taste of fish.

We also tried loads of other dishes that we can hardly remember the names of. There were plenty of vegetarian dishes such as 'Buddha's Five Earthly Pleasures', which wasn't much help when we wanted to know what was actually in it. The vegetarian options were all well and good, but all the food was fried in animal fat. It was very difficult to find anything that wasn't actually fried. There was also a rib dish that came in a lovely sauce and was cooked in such a way that you were given a plastic glove to eat it with because it was so messy. The taste was great though.

The one other thing that really sticks in the memory from eating outside of the West Gate was the smell. It was foul because the unused food had either been left on the road side to rot or poured into the drains and it only got worse the warmer the weather became. It would not be uncommon to walk past the restaurants on our way to the Underground or Wal-Mart. The general smell of pollution that hung over Beijing was bad enough but this topped that[35].

Snack foods - There were a few really popular snack foods that could all be got from little stalls anywhere and everywhere in Beijing. The first was pineapple on a stick, which later became melon on a stick! All across town there would be old guys with carts carefully slicing up melons or pineapples and pushing the quarter onto a stick so that you could eat it like an ice lolly. We would also see sweet potatoes and corn being cooked in what seemed to be old oil drums, which looked less than hygienic. Only Tana was brave enough to eat any of these though, and she never learned her lesson because she normally threw most of it away for tasting disgusting.

A snack we did enjoy was Jian Bing. These were great fun to watch being made. It was like a giant crepe filled with plum sauce, giant crisp bread, more spring onion and if you really wanted it, a dodgy looking sausage – we never went for the sausage. The trick to consuming these was to not eat them too soon after they

---

[35] Even though we eventually became inured to the smell of the place, it permeated into everything we owned. This became only too apparent when we returned home and we spent our entire first week washing all our clothes just to get rid of the stench!

had been made as you would burn your tongue but not to leave it too late as the crispy layer would go soggy. There was a definite art to eating these!

Our favourite snack was something we called Chinese pizza because we never found out its real name. It has a very small pizza like base with slightly spicy meat spread across it and it became our number one take away snack. It was absolutely delicious but we did wonder how much damage it was doing to our insides. It was always served in a paper bag and if left for long enough, the bag would become almost see through with the amount of oil and grease. I could just hear my arteries hardening up as I was eating it. It was a little hot for my tastes so if I had the chance, I would cover it in tomato ketchup to cool it down.

Not only did we experience some of what China had to offer, but we branched out into other nationalities.

Russian Food – Always sampled at Tractor but it was affectionately known to all as 'The Russian'. On one visit there, I had trouble remembering how to use a knife and fork, very embarrassing.

Korean Food – We tried out a couple of Korean places and the food was also very nice, but you did have to cook everything yourself. Unlike the Chinese method of using a fondue style fat dipping system, you would cook it over a charcoal, or even a coal base which did leave a distinctive taste in the mouth. I would love to be able to say what we had, but it was hard enough trying to remember the names of the Chinese dishes we would have on a regular basis. Like other non-Chinese restaurants, Korean food was a bit on the pricey side.

Western Food – All of the Western fast food chains are considered to be a higher end meal because they tend to be three times more expensive than a bog standard Chinese restaurant. This is a complete contrast from home. They are always packed as well. In the beginning I would only frequent them on special occasions or after one of my many bouts of food poisoning. The longer we were there, the more I would tuck into a KFC[36]. The downside was, and this is without

---

[36] My consumption of KFC became a bit of a joke to our friends back home

exception, that they were expensive. This even included fast food establishments such as KFC and McDonalds. The impression was that just because it was Western, it had to be expensive.

KFC is actually the king of the fast food market in China and wherever we went, Colonel Sanders face would be there to great us. It seemed that I was making a tour of KFC's in China because whenever we stepped off of the train, there was always one either inside of just outside of the station. It was always good to have one of their syrupy cokes to wake myself up as well as having some breakfast before planning our next move. It was also the perfect place to keep cool when the weather was a bit on the warm side as they were all fitted with air-conditioning. There is an urban legend that states that when KFC introduced their 'Finger Lickin' Good' slogan in China, it was mistranslated as 'eat your fingers off.' It didn't seem to have affected their sales much!

We spent a lot of time trying to find a good pizza restaurant. This proved to be a lot harder than we thought. Cheese was an alien concept to China until recently, and so they have not perfected the making of it yet. Hutong Pizza was about as good as it got, and the rest were just plain bad. There was a Chinese restaurant chain that specialised in their attempt at pizza and it did have a couple of things going for it. All you could eat and drink, which included beer. Sweet! However, it did have a couple of things not going for it; the food and the drink. Historically, the Chinese have not had cheese so the pizza didn't taste all that great. The beer was a bit watery but these were minor grumbles as I went a couple of time and I always enjoyed it.

5-a-side

As Christophe couldn't play because he was taking his family on a holiday, I had to make my own way to football. After getting directions from Rupert, I realised it was near the Lido Hotel and the western supermarket

---

who said I should have called this trip 'Ross eats KFC and had diarrhoea for six months'. These two had absolutely no connection to each other though, allegedly.

we frequented on occasion. As I wasn't sure how long it would take me to get to the ground, I thought I would leave Beihang with plenty of time to spare. If I was really early, I thought it would be a good time to look in all of the bootleg DVD shops, if they were actually open. The last time I had been in the area, they were all being raided by the police.

The first shop I walked into didn't seem to have any DVD's for sale except some really old black and white movies that no-one would be interested in buying. As I was about to walk out, a member of the shop staff walked up and handed me a piece of paper. The paper had written on it "Due to police crack downs on the sale of non-copywrited items, we have placed our DVD's out the back. If you are interested in seeing them, please nod your head". After being impressed by the level of English of the person who had written this statement, I nodded my head. I was shown through a metal door similar to the one we had on the apartment in Beihang to be confronted with the largest selection of DVD's I had seen in Beijing. They had exactly what I wanted, but I did wonder why the DVD's were out the back when all of the counterfeit CD's were still openly on sale.

Whilst walking down to the football pitches, I was accosted by one of the local prostitutes. After beating a hasty retreat (remembering the rules of the league where no prostitutes were allowed at fixtures!), I made a beeline for the pitch. When I arrived at the ground, I told Rupert what had happened and he went on to explain that in the three years he had been living in Beijing that had never happened to him. He found it even more annoying because I had been wearing my dirty football kit and he always turned up to the ground in a business suit. I was all ready to take up my usual place in goal when Rupert informed me that he had not turned up to watch, but to play. I was looking forward to playing out on pitch, but I told the rest of the team that I had been dropped from the goal keeping duties. It was also the last night of this 5-a-side league and our position in mid-table was assured so we were essentially playing for pride.

Game 13 - Drifters (0) v Devils (1) - This was a very close game and if points were awarded for shots on

goal then
we would have romped home. However, they are not and
so we didn't. This was not the most frenetic 5-a-side
match I have ever played in and it seemed to be played
more as a training game than anything else. Nothing
much happened in the first half and it ended 0-0. Rupert
spent the half time team talk pointing out that it was very
quiet (especially for a Drifters team) and that we needed
to pass the ball around a bit more. We dutifully started
off the second half with significantly more passing and
Amine stepped up to the Drifter stereotype and dutifully
threw his toys out of the pram for a while.

As we were lacking any other French speakers in
the team, Amine got the chance to practice throwing
tantrums in English. Stuart took on the midfield general
role against the Swiss but instead of covering every part
of the pitch he stood around out of the action, telling
others what to do in a loud voice. We had a really good
second half but the Swiss goalie, always tough to beat at
the best of times was having a great game and we just
couldn't get the ball past him. Unfortunately, our goalie
was not having as solid a game and we conceded a goal
at the final whistle. Arakawa accepted responsibility for
the goal and immediately substituted himself. A few
Premiership footballers could take note from this act. The
final whistle went and we trudged off the pitch as the
Swiss had proved to be our 'nemesis' once again.

Game 14 - Drifters (7) v Athletico Red (1) - The
last game of the season was against one of our Athletico
rivals and Rupert pointed out afterwards that it was an
absolute pleasure to watch goal after goal flying past
their keeper. He also admitted that even though he had
very little to do during the game, when he was called
upon to actually do something he got it wrong and
Athletico scored their only goal of the night. Our
lackadaisical play from the first game was still apparent in
the first half of this one as well and we found it hard to
get out of first gear. Arakawa was running everywhere at
top speed trying to erase the memories of the first game,
shooting at every opportunity and was rewarded with the
only goal of the first half for his trouble. It was a text
book Arakawa goal to boot. He took on a few opposition

players, got himself into a tricky angle from goal and then unleashed a rocket.

After a few choice words of wisdom from Rupert at half time, we really stepped on the gas and blew Athletico off the pitch. It might have helped that Stuart moved up from his usual midfield role to stand on the opposition's goal line, talk to their goalkeeper (who was actually a friend of his) and only paused occasionally to tap in a goal here and there. Albert proved to Rupert what a good defender he was (and wondered why he had never mentioned it to him before) covering about five miles in the second half. Amine, who had run out of English expletives from the first game, contented himself with around 100 mazy forward runs and a couple of goals. For myself, I managed to score a couple of goals and was very pleased with my overall performance. The only bad news from the night was that Adam made so many tackles that his knee gave up the ghost and he had to be carried off the pitch and into a taxi to take him home. This injury stopped him from playing for the Drifters for the remainder of my time in Beijing. This was a real loss not only because he was an asset to the team, but he was a nice guy too.

5-a-side Table (1st Season)
Position/Team

	P	W	D	L	F	A	Pts
01. Newbies	14	12	1	1	46	14	37
02. Bouncing Beavers	14	11	1	2	60	32	34
03. Devils	14	9	0	5	47	29	27
04. DRIFTERS	14	7	1	6	42	34	22
05. British School Accies	14	5	1	8	43	48	16
06. Athletico Red	14	3	1	10	31	52	10
07. Barbarians 2	14	3	1	10	27	56	10
08. Athletico White	14	1	0	13	32	65	3

Chinese Football

I didn't really know that much about Chinese football before setting foot in the country. I knew that the national team had played in the 2002 World Cup Finals (their one and so far, only appearance), a couple of their players had played for Crystal Palace in the late 1990's with one of them (Sun Jihai) now playing at Manchester City and a few of Europe's bigger clubs would go on summer tour to China. With the massive potential market ready to be exploited, it was not a surprise really.

With this in mind, I thought that one of the better ways of breaking the ice with students would be to talk about football and get them to talk about their local teams as I had spoken about mine in my introductory talk. Having had a look on my football management game to get idea of team names and the colours of the strips, I thought my research would put me in good stead. I could not have been more wrong. Out of almost 120 students, only one of them had any interest in their local team.

They didn't care much for the national side either. "I don't follow them because the team is rubbish" was the usual response. They were only interested in South American or European national and club sides. I had even seen one of my students wearing a Japanese strip, which considering history between the two countries was a real surprise. He did make me laugh though, because when I asked him why he was wearing that particular shirt, he tried to cover over the badge even though I, and everyone else in the room had seen it!

It seemed as though all of the tours from these big clubs over the years had done the trick. My students supported Manchester United, AC Milan, Real Madrid, Bayern Munich, Brazil, England, Holland, Italy, France, in fact anyone as long as they were not Chinese. They had all heard of Sun Jihai and he was considered a bit of a hero as he was good enough to play in a foreign country, but they couldn't tell me of any other Chinese players playing abroad. They couldn't even tell me that much about any of the players in China.

After raising the subject of football in nearly every lesson at some point, some information about my students view on the game became a little clearer. Even though they didn't have a lot of time for the Japanese due to the events of World War Two, they did have respect for the national team saying it was one of, if not the best team in Asia. The other Asian team they respected was South Korea. I did find out that this was down to the fact that since the first match between South Korea and China in 1950, China have yet to beat them which had lead to something the Sino journalists call 'Korea-phobia'.

They would also mention Dalian Shide, whom Dean Tang said were an excellent team. They are considered to be the Manchester United of Chinese football. They have been by far and away the most successful team in China since the formation of the modern league system in the mid 1990's. No one supported them though, not even the guys who came from Dalian.

Things might be about to change though with clubs using a number of strategy's to increase their profile in the Far East. One way is to sign one of the more high profile players, like Manchester United with Dong Fangzhuo who has only played for the club when they have toured China. To be fair to both the club and the player, there has been some work permit problems that has caused this problem. An example of how this has been successful was with one the Koreans who played the odd game for the Drifters. He would turn up in his Man Utd strip and he only supported them because the Korean footballer Park Ji-Sung played for them. Before that, he had followed PSV Eindhoven as that was the club Park had played for before Man Utd.

Other avenues into China are the ones both Real Madrid and Glasgow Rangers (to name but two) have made, which are to have coaching and management contracts in place. They no doubt feel that having some sort of presence in the world's most populous country would be of financial benefit to them.

Another is the one Sheffield United have taken and that is buying a controlling interest in one of the Chinese league clubs. Chengdu's football team, whose moniker has already been changed from Five Bulls to Blades (the nickname of Sheffield United) is the one they have invested in and have even taken one of their players to England. Real Madrid has also followed this route when they bought into Beijing Gu'oan. Only time will tell on this.

<u>Preparing for May Week</u>

With May Week rapidly approaching, we were beginning to think about where we would like to spend our week off. We were also receiving a lot of emails from some of the people from our orientation week who were coming to Beijing and wanting to catch up with us. Some of the girls got in early and asked if they could stay in our spare room, which was not a problem. What was a problem was actually getting out of Beijing.

As for ourselves, we had planned to go to Dalian, which is on China's northern coast. However. Lu Ying (from SAFEA) came from Dalian and said it was really boring. She couldn't understand why we would want to spend more than a couple of days there as there wasn't that much to do. She also said that if we were to visit Dalian when she was there, we would be able to stay with her family. As we like things cheap, (free is even better of course!) we knocked this one on the head and vowed to go there when she was in town. Having a quick look through the Lonely Planet, we thought we would go to Nanjing, the sight of one of the great atrocities of the Second World War[37]. It was after trying to get train tickets that we were reminded that China is not the most tourist friendly of places.

Every time we tried to go somewhere, we couldn't get tickets; they were too expensive or only available for places we didn't want to see. Sarah even spent time trudging down to the main Beijing Railway station to try and buy tickets there. Doug had told us that there was a special foreigner's ticket office at Beijing Railway station so we would only have to queue with other foreigners and all the station staff at that counter would speak English.

Tana decided to go as well to offer any assistance she could as her Mandarin was slightly better than Sarah's. When they arrived, they had to queue to get into the station itself which was a real pain. There were loads of beggars circulating the station and they

---

[37] To find out more on this subject, read 'The Rape of Nanking: The Forgotten Holocaust of World War II' by Iris Chang. An excellent, but disturbing read!

kept coming up to us and tugging at their sleeves and begging for money. Tana was getting quite freaked out by it as they all seemed to make a beeline for her.

Once inside the station it wasn't obvious where the ticket office for foreigners was, so after wandering all over the place Tana kept stopping people and asking in her best Chinese where it was. Eventually, someone was able to point them in the right direction. Sarah decided to try and do the talking without Tana's help to test what little Chinese she had learnt. She only got as far as asking in her best Mandarin "do you speak English?" The reply she got was (in Mandarin) "Your Chinese is fine, we can speak in Chinese". Sarah didn't actually understand this response and Tana had to translate.

After staring blankly at each other for a while as Sarah desperately tried to form the right Mandarin words in her mind that she needed to use, she gave up and shoved the letter at the ticket seller that her student had prepared in case something like this occurred. After communicating through a series of grunts, hand gestures and the odd intervention by Tana, it transpired that the tickets we wanted were all sold out. Sarah wanted to ask for alternative trains and times etc but the seller was clearly not going to be of any help and for some strange reason blatantly refused to speak English, which isn't what you expect from the foreign ticket office designated for non-mandarin speakers.

After this line of enquiry failed to get us anywhere, Sarah even enlisted the help of one of her students to get some tickets. He was successful but they were off the black-market and the hike in price was too high for our meagre budget. In the end, Sarah was getting far too stressed out by the whole thing so we knocked it on the head and decided to visit some of the sights in and around Beijing we had not yet visited. With Doug and Tana both staying in the capital and a load of people from our induction week in Shanghai coming to town that we were both keen to catch up with, we were not going to be short of company.

Class Things in Class #3

1) Sarah and I also felt that our students kept saying the word 'maybe' whenever they were asked anything, or just started to speak. In an attempt to stop this, I would write the person's name on the board when they said it, but I did get caught myself saying it a couple of times which got the whole class laughing. I did catch out one of my students though. Falcon Lee was a bit of a cocksure chap, and his English was superb, but I did feel that his application to work was lacking. I asked him which month came after April and what animal produces honey.

2) Answering both questions only to see his name written on the board not only got a lot of laughs, but I think it also got his respect because after this he was not so stand offish to me. I said that his English was so good that if his career as a pilot didn't work out, he should become a translator even though he felt that he was not good enough. After this period, I was sure that China is one of the last countries in the world where you can totally humiliate your students without fear or reprisals. I was close on a couple of occasions to testing this theory out by having a dunce's cap made up, but instead of a big 'D', I would put a 'W' on it for wukwei[38].

3) In my last lesson before May Week, I really couldn't be bothered to do any teaching. I was going to get the students to talk about what they were going to do with their time off but then we had a power cut. I decided that the room was

---

[38] I was told that Wukwei means turtle, but can also be used as an insult the nearest equivalent in English would be to call someone an idiot. The reasoning being that Turtles are quite long lived and even though the Chinese respect their elders, if you are as long lived as a Turtle there is the possibility that your brain will not be as good as that of a younger man. My students had given this title to one of my predecessors leading him to believe that it was a term of endearment. Doug eventually told him the real meaning and they even tried the same trick on me, but by the time they did, I already knew what it meant. As part of this sentence 'Nide muchin shr ega da wukwei', it becomes one of the biggest insults in Mandarin. It means 'Your father is a big turtle'. To be thought of as someone who comes from a turtle egg is particularly insulting because a turtle does not know its mother as turtles are promiscuous!

too dark to teach in and so we went outside. This was one of the nicest days we experienced in China. It was warm without being too hot and there was a lovely blue sky. The students were all happy to be going outside and we sat in the park. Things were going very well until some old bloke came over and had a go at us for sitting on the grass. I chose to ignore him because he didn't actually talk to me directly, but my students informed me that he was the head of the whole of Beihang University. Oh well, you live and learn!

4) After a month of teaching, I got into the habit during the first lecture of the week of asking the students if they had a nice weekend and enquire as to what they had got up to. I clicked pretty quickly early on that when the other students said that one of their friends had stayed in a hotel, it was because they were in the company of a young lady. With seven male and six females students to a room (in separate blocks of course), the chances of getting some privacy were very always a little on the slim side. Booking into the cheapest hotel out of campus was the only way for them to get some quality time with their girlfriends. Asking if a student had stayed in a hotel would always get a round of laughter from the rest of the class as well the embarrassment of the person asked. Most would reply that they were a good man and would never do such a thing, but it was always obvious to everyone in the room that they were lying. As this line of conversation would always lead to the same result, I started to ask what the students would be getting up to at the weekend in the last lecture of the week. Hotels would always be top of the banter list and once again, those accused of using them would always strenuously deny any such behaviour. In the end, any excuse to mention hotels and the use would enter into any and every lecture. This was a very handy piece of information to have as it broke down some of

the barriers with the students as it showed them that I had a genuine interest in their lives.

Part 6 – May Week

May Week is one of three so called 'Golden Weeks' (the other two are in January, or February depending on the year and October). These 'Golden Weeks' are a new concept having only been introduced in 2000 where the government had the bright idea that there should be times when the Chinese could travel around the country spending time with their families and seeing the many sights China has to offer. Needless to say, these weeks have become renowned for the whole of China seems to be on the move.

There were rumours that the weekend before May Week would be treated like a couple of weekdays which we didn't like the sound of at all, especially with all of the things we were beginning to plan. Only one of my class monitors asked me if we were going to have lessons on the weekend, but my reply was that as I had not been asked, there wouldn't be any. They should enjoy their time off, because I knew I would, which led to smiles all round even though none of them were allowed to leave Beijing. We felt that this was a bit mean, but as some of them lived almost a two day journey away by train, we could see why the college had imposed this rule on them.

Day 1 - Flush with cash from my voiceover work that was now burning a sizable hole in my pocket, Doug took me to the computer market so I could buy an mp3 player. The computer market was not a market in the traditional sense. It was only a couple of miles away from Beihang and it was located on the bottom floors of three massive skyscrapers. On every one of my visits, it was always unbearably hot, due no doubt to the masses of computer equipment and monitor screens that were continually on. Taking a bottle of water was a requirement of any visit. It was possible to lose ones bearings due to its size, which meant that is could be quite tricky trying to find exactly what you came into buy.

Having researched some models on the web, I was surprised that the prices in the market were not too dissimilar from those I would have paid if I had bought them in the UK, especially when you consider that most of the stuff sold in the market had been manufactured in

China in the first place. After three months, I was surprised that certain aspects of life in China still perplexed me!

What this market did have in common with the other ones I had frequented since I had arrived, was that it was full of independent sellers operating from small stalls. The big differences were:

1) All of the products were the genuine article. Bootleg products were conspicuous by their absence.
2) Bartering really didn't reduce the price by much, if at all.

We eventually found what I was after, and Doug managed to get me a little bit of a reduction off of the final price but it still made a serious dent into my bank roll!

After arriving back at Beihang, both Hannah and Sonia (from the induction week) were in our room enjoying a cup of tea with Sarah. A couple of hours later, Ali, another of the inductees, also arrived so I took them for a quick tour of the campus which they all agreed was much nicer than either of their own. Ali was very happy to be away from Chongqing and especially glad to be away from another of the foreign teachers she worked with.

She then proceeded to tell us some horror stories about him swearing in class to students, being drunk more often than not around campus and not being nice to anyone at all. She also said that he had tried to get a rock band together with some of the students, but they hated him so much that they tried to practise as many times as they could without raising his suspicions that they were doing so behind his back. All in all, he made her life in Chongching a misery and so she was very happy to be with people whose company she enjoyed. She said that she had been looking forward to this trip for weeks.

As there were more of our induction week colleagues staying in the centre of Beijing, we had organised for everyone to go to Tractor (why we didn't ask for commission from the restaurant for the amount of business we took I will never know!) Whilst we were waiting for the girls, Mrs. Lu rang us? We were both a little apprehensive about this as we were afraid she was going to ask us to work over May Week. I tried to have a conversation with her, but due to our poor knowledge of each other languages, she passed the phone to Dean Tang. The Dean asked us if we would like to join him and all of the other Flying College staff for dinner tomorrow and as he said it would be paid for by the college, we thought it would have been rude to refuse.

As we made our way into town, we had our first experience of how busy Beijing gets during May Week. We saw the queue for Xizhimen underground station stretch from the platform, up two flights of steps and all the way back to the road. However, this was not the only way in so we walked around to the other entrance to find that there wasn't a queue. In fact, apart from us, no one was using this entrance. There seems to be a general lack common sense in China, a statement that every foreign resident I spoke to agreed with. Once we arrived at the nearest underground station to the restaurant, we were met by Caroline and Laura. It was great to see them all again and catch up with all of their adventures. As usual, the food in Tractor was great.

To finish the night off, we went to The Den and even though I was able to produce my discount card, we had to threaten leaving before they would knock some money off of the exorbitant prices. Ray came along, as well as Rupert from the Drifters. A great night all round, but on reflection, Sarah and I realised that was most probably the first time we have been out for a drink together since our leaving Britain drink in February.

Day 2 - After a nice lie in (which is always a good idea), I said that I would help Ali book her train ticket to Xi'an, her next destination before returning to Chongching. I didn't rate her chances, considering the difficulty we'd had trying to get tickets anywhere for ourselves. As luck would have it, we ran into one of my students who took us to a travel agents we had not heard of before just outside of the University. He managed to arrange the whole thing which made me think that I should get my students to do this for me all the time.

We left the girls to their own devices as we had a lunch appointment to keep. We met up with the Dean but for a dreadful moment, we thought it was just the two of us, Tana, the Dean and the Colleges Communist Party representative, whom the Dean told us didn't speak any English. However, the rest of the staff didn't take long to turn up. Sara had said she was preparing to visit friends in another part of China, and didn't fancy joining us as she had done it too many times before. She did warn us that it was not a good idea to sit next to Mrs. Lu as she would be continually pile food onto your plate which you would be expected to eat.

We were taken to one of the nicer restaurants on campus. Dean Tang sat with us and this was the first time we have really been able to speak to him. The Dean the ordered all of the food and he told us the Chinese and English names for everything. Sarah and Tana duly made notes of the ones they liked best for future reference. I had drawn the short straw and sat next to Mrs. Lu, but she was having a restrained day as she didn't put too much food on my plate.

All the food was described as delicious and very good for us in some way. This got a bit boring after the tenth time of telling. There was so much food we were all felt stuffed when we unwittingly fell into a Chinese hospitality trap because Emily asked us if we liked spicy food. I said no but Sarah and Tana said that they did thinking that they were making conversation. The Dean took this as an opportunity to order a massive plate of spicy food. Both Tana and Sarah made a brave attempt to eat some even though no one else around the table was having any.

The Dean apologised for not organising trips to the Great Wall and Xi'an that he had promised us, but he said that he now had more time on his hands and he would do his best to rectify this. Not long after we returned to the apartment, one of the College staff rang us to say they have organised a bus to take us to the Great Wall in a couple of day's time. We spent the rest of the day lying on the sofa unable to move due to the weight of food we had eaten. We were so stuffed that when the girls rang us to say that they were going for Tappas, we had to decline.

Day 3 - Instead of visiting one of the major tourist sights of Beijing, we decided we would go somewhere off the beaten track hoping that the crowds would be somewhere else. We were a little apprehensive about our day out because we were going without Doug who we had come to rely for translation and direction. We had decided to head to the South West of the city to the Marco Polo Bridge[39], or Lugou Qiao as the locals call it. The underground didn't stretch that far but we thought we would get as far as we could and then take a cab. The underground was more packed than normal and the lack of anti-perspirant from the locals was nearly over powering. Apart from this, the journey was quite straightforward and our taxi driver dropped us off in the walled town of Wanping.

Wanping was built to act as a defensive position in case of an attack on Beijing. This was a beautiful little place and it gave an idea of what Beijing may have look like in the Imperial age, just on a much smaller scale as it had not been spoiled by any modern buildings that had been built there. There weren't any skyscrapers, the hutongs hadn't been replaced with apartment blocks, the town walls were still in one piece and there were few motorised vehicles. The only modern building we saw was the Memorial Hall of the War of Resistance against Japan, but this didn't seem to be out of place and this was one of the reasons I had wanted to come here. It was around Wanping that the famous Marco Polo Bridge incident occurred on 7th July 1937. The Japanese were in control of much of the area around Wanping and decided that on this day, they would occupy a nearby railway junction. The Japanese and Chinese soldiers exchanged fire and this was all the Japanese needed to attack and occupy Beijing. This was the beginning of the full-scale war

---

[39] The bridge is known by this name in the West due to the praise it received in the writings of Marco Polo, who's book 'Il Milione' ('The Million' or as it is better known, 'The Travels of Marco Polo) detailed his travels along the Silk Road to China.

between these two countries that would last until Japan's defeat in 1945.

The Memorial Hall was very interesting, but there wasn't one caption written in English. Luckily I had read up on this subject having spent a good deal of the previous week researching Nanjing in preparation for our non-visit there. It was full of brilliant images and artefacts including some of the Japanese torture devices. The one that really stuck in the memory was a metal cage designed to be rolled down a hill with a captive inside it. This would have been bad enough were it not for the fact that the cage was full of spikes. This must have been excruciating and I doubt whether many people would have come out of this alive. There was also the famous picture purported to show two Japanese soldiers that had had a competition to see which one of them could behead 100 Chinese prisoners first.

After completing our tour of the museum, we made our way out of Wanping to the Marco Polo Bridge itself. Dating from the late 1100's, it crosses the Yongding River which looked as though water hadn't been along its course in many a year. Greenery was growing out of the riverbed and there were derelict hulks of boats on what was once a river bed. The bridge has along its length almost 500 stone lions that legend has it move positions during the night and they were carved to look different from one another. The bridge no longer acts as the only way over the river and has become just another tourist attraction.

Next to Wanping is the 'Memorial Garden of the War of Resistance against Japan'. It was a very sombre place that from a distance seemed to be full of stone columns. It was only when we got nearer to them that we saw that they were carved with scenes of Chinese people and their struggles against the Japanese. After this, we decided to make our way back to Beihang.

We thought we would make a go of catching the bus, but we didn't recognise any of the characters for any of the destinations listed. Luckily, a street cleaner had heard our conversation and came over to help. Her English was very good and we wondered why she was not putting this to good use instead of cleaning the sides of the roads. The bus journey seemed to take an age and by the time we got back, it was dinnertime. The girls had were also back from their daily excursion and so we went to Ashtray. It was here that Ali proceeded to tell everyone? how clean she thought the restaurant was, because she had yet to see a rat running around it! I am so glad that we hadn't ended up in Chongqing.

Day 4 - Another day and another trip. Along with Tana and Doug, we decided that we would go to the Fragrant Hills Park and the Reclining Buddha. The Reclining Buddha was one of the few places in the Beijing area that Doug hadn't been. However, we left a little late in the morning and the one bus that would take us to both of these places was absolutely packed, and so was the next one and the one after that as well. We changed tack and took a couple of other buses to get to the Fragrant Hills but they were all pretty packed and seats were as rare as duck's teeth!

We were quite lucky that we were all able to get onto this bus because it was heaving and we were all hanging on for dear life to what ever we could find. Tana found it all very exciting but all I could think off was the Weird Al Yankovich song 'Another One Rides the Bus'. At one stage when even more people tried to get on, the driver started to shout at me in Chinese to move (translation provided by Doug) but there was absolutely nowhere I could go, so I just shouted back and made a frustrated hand gesture at him. Most of the Chinese in the bus found this quite amusing.

Due to traffic, our lateness in getting up and the enormous crowds out for the day, we decided against the Reclining Buddha and said we would go there another time. Doug didn't mind too much as some of his friends had been there and all they said was there was statue of a Buddha lying on its side. The title gave that one away really and in the end, we never got there.

The park was built in 1186 during the Jin Dynasty and was continually added to down the centuries until the mid-1800 when it was damaged by British and French troops during the Second Opium War[40]. The site

---

[40] The Second Opium War was fought between 1856 and 1860 between the

was used as a base by the Communists before they marched into Beijing at the end of the Civil War and since 1949, there has been an extensive restoration programme. It was a very picturesque place and it was nice that we had come to see it in the spring when the flowers had just all come into bloom. The park was full of hills and to see some of the views the park offers, we needed to get to the top of one. Doug had been here before on more than one occasion and had taken both methods of reaching the top which were walking or taking the cable car.

Doug recommended the cable car because the walk was a lot longer than it seemed from where we were standing. It didn't look that far but we had learned to take Doug's advice on such matters, and even though Tana was very keen to walk, we refused and so she joined us in taking the easy way up. As a compromise though, we said that we would walk down. We were very pleased that we had taken Doug's advice because at ground level, it looked as though there was only one hill to climb to reach the top.

This turned out to be deceptive as the first hill obscured all the other, slightly taller hills that lay behind it. When we came to the end of the cable car run at the top of the last hill, we all turned around to look at the view, which no doubt would have been amazing if there had not been so much pollution in the air. We would quite clearly see all of the stairs that Tana had been so eager to climb and my legs were particularly pleased that they hadn't had to walk up them.

We didn't stay very long at the top. There wasn't much to see (because there was a lot of pollution in the air that day) or do (except buy something from one of the obligatory naff souvenir sellers), so we started the long walk down. It was very easy to walk off of the beaten paths not knowing where we would end up and as this was once the playground of the Emperors, there were loads of buildings hidden within the trees.

Most were in ruins but there were signs in English telling us what they were. Nearly every single one

allied Anglo-French forces and the Chinese.

of the plaques mentioned that the allied British and French armies had destroyed these buildings and the destruction wrought by foreign powers during the decline of Imperial China is still a thorny issue. This was not the only place we saw plaques of this nature and it did give the impression that the Chinese liked taking our money but that didn't mean they were going to like us for it.

About half way down, Doug twisted his ankle quite badly but he was able to stagger on, which was fortunate because it may have been a problem getting him to the bottom if we had had to carry him. We saw a cave mentioned on one of the signposts and Tana got very excited at the prospect of sitting somewhere she thought the Emperors used to contemplate the world. However, when we got there, we found that the entrance was about one foot high and had bars across it to stop people from getting in. The look on Tana's face of total disappointment was an absolute picture. As Doug had seen the cave before and was well aware of what to expect, he knew that Tana would be disappointed so he took a picture of that precise moment she saw it so we could enjoy it whenever we felt like it. The journey back to Beihang was more straightforward as we were able to get the direct bus, but it was still as busy as the journey out which must have been hell for Doug as he was unable to rest his ankle.

More of the Shanghai induction group had arrived and were staying at a hostel near Tiananmen Square. The girls told us that a visit to the nearby Qianmen Quanjude Roast Duck Restaurant had been organised. Doug had been there before and warned us that the food was not very good, the service was equally poor and it was very expensive. The only thing going for it was that it was one of the few restaurants that had survived through the Communist era and many visiting dignitaries had been taken there. It was easy to see who had been there as their pictures adorned the walls. We decided against going but said we would meet everyone for a drink afterwards.

Our journey took us a little longer than expected because for some strange reason, the Tiananmen underground station was closed. Ali, Hannah and Sonia said that the restaurant was very expensive so they had not been able to afford much on the menu and were a little annoyed by the groups' choice. After forking out an extortionate amount of money for what one of the party said was "a horribly greasy duck", we ploughed back to the hostel which had a small bar where the beer was cold, cheap and in plentiful supply. It was great to have caught up with so many of the people we had spent time with in Shanghai.

Day 5 - Finally, we were going to Changcheng, the wall of 10,000 Li[41] Wall or in English, the Great Wall of China. None of the Flying College staff decided to come with us but they had volunteered two first year students to accompany us instead. One of the students was in Sarah's class 4 so they chatted for most of the journey and his level of English surprised her, as it was much better than anything he had so far said in any of her lessons. Rather strangely he thought that there was too much English conversation in her lessons, but that was the whole point of Sarah being here.

Obviously he hadn't been paying much attention when the 'oral English' had been put on his lesson timetable. He had hoped that the lessons would be more about the culture of the West than any kind of exercise in helping the students practice their spoken English. Sarah was quite chuffed that he thought there was too much conversation because she had been worried up that there hadn't been the opportunity for the students to practice their spoken English, so in a strange way his comments were very reassuring. I slept most of the way to the Wall, which made the journey just whiz by. As I was asleep, I didn't realise that due to the amount of traffic on the road, it took twice as long to get to the Wall as it should have done.

We had been taken to the Great Wall at Badaling, the nearest part to Beijing. It was also one of its most visited areas and the crowds today were huge. As the Wall is one of the landmarks in China and tourism brings in the almighty dollar, the government has

---

[41] Li is a traditional unit of measurement in China which equates to roughly 500 meters in length.

restored some of it. By restored, read made to look as it did during the Ming dynasty when much of it was rebuilt using stone instead of the earthworks of the original Wall. The car park area was full of tourist groups, souvenir sellers and restaurants. There was also a Great Wall museum (more on this later) and a Starbucks (more on this later too).

The students were a great help and good company. Neither of them had been to the Wall themselves, so they thought of it as an excellent way to spend the day. There were two routes that could be taken from the entrance and we took the one going south as the north route just looked far too busy. We could only hazard a guess at the total amount of people that were there on that day, but it wasn't very easy to move around. It didn't help that people would sit down in the middle of the walkway and eat their packed lunches, thus reducing the area in which everyone else could move. It was actually quite difficult to walk on the Wall as the surface was smooth and slippery so these blockages really didn't help.

The Wall may have been a very impressive thing to behold, but it was quite difficult to determine how far we had walked. The further we walked from the entrance, the more the crowds walking along seemed to thin out. Eventually, we came to the end of the bits visitors can walk on as the remainder had been blocked off. It was easy to see why because the un-restored Wall was in a terrible condition. It would seem that it's not only in modern China that constructions aren't built to last. It was a shame that the people who'd spent so much time restoring the Wall, had felt it necessary to obliterate a section of it to prevent visitors crossing from one part to another. There were signs up in multiple languages stating that the un-restored areas were out of bounds and at ground level, fences had been erected to also prevent access. Personally, these were the areas of most interest to me because the part we had walked along looked even more of a movie set than the Forbidden City.

We decided to take a breather, but random Chinese people kept asking to have their photographs taken with us, which made us feel like celebrities. We did draw the line at holding babies due to their split trousers. For a bit of a laugh, I told one group that it cost 10RMB to have their photo taken with me. As soon as I said that, their faces dropped and they walked away looking very disappointed. I grabbed them back saying it was just a joke, but all I could see whilst the photo was being taken was Sarah and Tana killing themselves laughing. Tana had another of her bright ideas and convinced the two students that they should try to gain access to the out of bounds areas, but Sarah and I thought it would be a bad idea, so we left them to it.

We decided to have a look at the Museum, which could have done with a bit of restoration work itself. It was an interesting place to go though as it was a history of the whole Wall and most of it had captions in English. There were loads of great artefacts but after we had finished, we decided to have a Starbucks. I did find it a bit weird and thought there should have been more of an effort to have a Chinese style tea shop in its place, but the Creamy Raspberry Frappichino was very nice thank you very much, especially as there was no one in there and we could make use of the comfy seats. We did keep hold of our receipt which clearly said on it in English 'Starbucks – Great Wall'. This was the only place were we ended up buying something touristy when we both purchased a Great Wall baseball cap.

Day 6 - We had planned to visit the Summer Palace with our guests, but we had a couple of medical issues that we really needed to deal with then and there. The girls said they would still go to the Palace as some of the others from the induction week were going to see them there. The girls all look exhausted and I suggested that they should go and get some more sleep. They agreed but said that they had arranged to meet the others and didn't want to let them down. It turned out that none of the others actually turned up. Anyway, back to the medical situation. Doug had knocked on the door to see if we could take him to hospital because the Chinese pizza we had had the night before had inflamed an on going condition he suffering from. Sarah called one of her students to come along and act as their translator.

I didn't join Sarah in helping Doug because the neck problem from the beginning of our stay had returned, no doubt brought on by sleeping in the beck of a bus that was not quite long enough for me to lain out straight in! Like Sarah, I also contacted one of my students and not the college, because I wanted the problem to be fixed straight away and didn't want to wait around until one of them was available. This would mean that I would have to pay for the treatment but it was so cheap, it would not make much of a dent into my money.

The Chinese Medicine Man remembered me, no doubt because he didn't get that many Westerners visiting him. Having the glass jars but on my back was as painful as last time, but I was happy to put up with it because I knew it was alleviating the problem. I was quite surprised when a woman walked in holding an intravenous drip which had one end embedded in her arm, and the bag containing the liquid above her head. She sat down, spoke a little bit to the Medicine Man and then walked out again, intravenous drip in tow. Weird! We were all glad that we didn't end up going anywhere that day because after lunch, the heavens opened. The rain was absolutely torrential, with thunder and lightning making the whole thing worth watching from our back balcony. This was the start of things to come. It was nice to have a relaxing day after so much travelling around earlier in the week when the weather had been excellent, if a little hot.

Day 7 - This was our guests last day in Beijing, so we decided to take them shopping. They spent an absolute fortune on DVD's, food from the Western Store and clothes from the market. Sarah managed to upset all the stall holders in the market by refusing to up her offer price to the level they were expecting. It started off as a bit of fun and became an obsession Sarah was determined to find a stall holder that would crack before she did, but it didn't happen. I was quite surprised when I found a stall that sold t-shirts in my size. As this was such a novel experience, I proceeded to wear it for the rest of the day with a big self-satisfied grin on my face. The DVD's were all bought from the shop where the bootlegs were missing from the shelves and I had been handed the piece of paper to view them in the back room. They had obviously not been raided this week because the piece of paper was conspicuous by its absence and they just showed all of us into the back room. It was sad to see our friends go as it had been nice to hear some British accents around the place, after weeks of just hearing American and Chinese ones. On the whole, May Week was great and it was just a shame that we had to go back to work on Monday.

The Sites, the Sounds and Smell of Beijing #4

The Summer Palace - With everything we had been and done in the proceeding seven days, the next few felt like one long Sunday. With a visit to the Summer Palace planned and our next load of guests arriving in the next couple of days, I thought that this would be a good time to make sure I had some lesson plans ready. I realised it had been a while since I had last picked up my teaching folder as two cockroaches fell out. After this we made a bee line to the shops to get a set of poisoned traps for the floor.

To finish the week off, we went to the Summer Palace but I didn't get that much from the visit as I was tired. I had played football with my students and I was fed up with being a tourist, so I really didn't get that much out of this visit. I saw enough to know that I didn't need to come back. Unlike the pandemonium earlier in the week, the bus to the Palace was relatively empty. We missed our stop and began to panic because the distance to the next one seemed to be vast. When we disembarked, we actually found that the bus has dropped us outside of the Palace's North Gate. This was a perfect day for sightseeing as it wasn't too hot, or too cold, and there weren't that many people milling around. The 'out of towners' had evidently gone back to their home provinces in preparation for the return to work.

The whole complex was massive, even though we didn't get to see much of the Palace itself. There is Kunming Lake, which was once used by the Chinese navy for training purposes, but it is now the home to tourist boats and on its banks, they have the odd wedding. It is a completely man made structure and one of the most famous feature of the lake is the infamous Marble Boat. We were told that the Marble boat was built using money that should have been earmarked for the modernisation of the Chinese navy in 1893. As with many other sites in and around Beijing, the Summer Palace complex was attacked by the allied Anglo-French armies during the Second Opium War and there were signs all over the complex telling us this, over and over again.

The rest of the complex is taken up by the usual series of temples and gift shops, but I was quite keen to see a Bronze Ox statue that I had read about before we arrived. Pictures in the map we had bought made it look very impressive but in reality, it was a good deal smaller than I had expected. Following this disappointment and the fact that I fell asleep whilst sitting down after lunch, I was really keen to get back to college. We hadn't really given ourselves enough time to see everything the Summer Palace had to offer.

The most memorable aspect of the day was the story Sarah told me about the ladies toilets, which she said were an experience all to themselves. They were western style, but under the toilet seat was a bag which went around the whole pan. When the user had finished their business, a button was pressed but instead of flushing the bag went into the basin to be replaced by another bag. Very hygienic.

More Guest Related Crazyness

With our return to work came our next set of visitors. I had worked with Dave and Mike, and I had gone to the same University as Lizzy and Richard. They turned up at Beihang in one piece, but their trip had begun with the all too predictable game of 'let's con the tourist!' Unfortunately for them, they had been caught unawares by someone who wasn't a registered taxi driver and they had paid roughly twice the price that an actual cab from the airport to the Uni should have cost! They learned their lesson pretty quickly as this was the one and only time they were conned during their whole trip. They were determined to beat jet lag by not spending any time napping so in an effort to keep them awake, I gave them a quick tour of the University and surrounding area.

By dinner time, they were all starting to flag so I decided it was time to give our guests an authentic taste of China. I therefore took them to our favourite Russian restaurant, Tractor! It was also my birthday and they would have plenty of time to have some proper Chinese food before they went home. Sarah took celebrating my birthday a bit too seriously by getting very drunk, and then blamed me for letting her get that way! This was the first of many alcohol-induced nights brought about by our latest guests. However, due to the fact that we were still working, we let them find their own way to the places they wanted to visit, which seemed to be mostly drinking establishments with a few historical sites thrown in just to make the journey worthwhile.

Shopping - On my one free afternoon, I decided to treat them to the Chinese shopping experience. We had some fun in the markets and DVD shops where Mike found a box set he fancied, but this wasn't like any of the other DVD establishments I had been to. It didn't keep the DVD's for box sets on the premises; therefore if you wanted to buy one, you had to pay a deposit and come back the next day to pick them up. Due to unforeseen circumstances, or a trip to the nearest bar (we couldn't be certain on this one), Mike had not been able to go in the next day so he had to go the day after and asked for his box set.

The shop staff said the DVD's were no longer on the premises and he would have to come back tomorrow. This was the last occasion Mike would be able to come to this shop and he said he would not be able to come back on another day. The shop staff said they would get them in that afternoon. Mike couldn't understand why they were not there in the first place and we decided they were trying to pull a fast one so we demanded his deposit back. They did seem reluctant to give him his money back, but after a few minutes of refusing to listen to their pleas of 'we will get them in' and a little bit of 'discussion'; we managed to get his money back.

Bowling - As a punishment for being a cheeky monkey in class, I had told Falcon Lee to help our guests buy their train tickets for the next stage of their journey.

As usual, his English was exemplary and he managed to get them the tickets they wanted. The guys asked him what I was like as a teacher and his response was a classic. He said that when I first turned up, I was more evil than the devil (by evil, he meant strict), but I had chilled out since then. Cue much laughter. I had to admire his style because when he left us he was pleading poverty, but proceeded to jump in a cab to take him to his girlfriend. Anybody else would have caught the bus.

Falcon Lee definitely had a confident air about him that made him a damn sight more mature than most of the other students. To begin with, I wondered why he was in my Class 9, but I was told by the other students that he was a bit lazy with his studies. No doubt he was spending a bit too much time with his girlfriend! If only his other work had been up to the standard of his English, he would have been in the highest group possible.

With their train tickets organised, I suggested we should go bowling. Back home, Dave had acquired a reputation for his unique bowling style that had led to him being given the moniker 'Dangerous'. Before they had arrived, I had given Dave a big build up and Doug was quite keen to see the man in action. Dave's reputation for mayhem on the lanes causing many to run for cover when he starts his run up may have preceded him, but he didn't disappoint. Dave managed to bowl the ball a damn sight faster than at home because he'd discovered that the finger holes on the lighter bowls were bigger than the ones he had used before. After watching a few of these, Doug would have been happier if he had been bowling on a different lane, in a different bowling alley in another country!

Beer Pong - After we had introduced him to Dave's particular brand of bowling, Doug thought he would teach us a drinking game called 'Beer Pong'. It is supposed to be played on a full sized Table tennis table but due to the lack of this piece of equipment, we had to improvise and use the small dining table in our flat. The idea is to throw a ping-pong ball into one of the opponent's six glasses. If it lands in the glass then the opponent has to drink it. This is not as easy as it sounds and it can get very messy! Tana had played this with

Doug a few weeks earlier and had been in a bit of trouble after drinking a little too much beer.

On this particular night, she had said that she was having an early night because she had an 8 o'clock lecture the next morning. It didn't take long for some badgering to make her change her mind. I got completely wrecked because whatever team I was on kept winning, so consequently I played more games than most. Eventually it got to the point where I really couldn't drink anymore and went to bed. The next day was not the best but at least hadn't had to get up for work. Tana was in an even worse condition than me but managed to get to her lecture only half an hour late, which isn't too bad, all things considered!

6-a-side (but in reality 8-a-side)

My Select (5) v The Flying College Staff (3) - William and Dean Tang knew that I played football so they asked me to organise a team for foreigners to play a team made up of the Flying College staff. I thought that it would be amusing if we were to play in Red Chinese shirts and William said that his team would play in white. William was also very insistent that Tana played. He most probably didn't know that Tana actually played in goal for her College team back in America, but I decided to keep this one under my hat.

A week before the match, some of my students rang me to see if I would like to play football with them. I was very interested and I asked Tana if she wanted to join me as I thought that this would be a perfect opportunity to see if she could cut it between the sticks. On the morning of the kick about, Tana was keen to play but only three of my students could be bothered to get out of bed and join us. The longer we played though, the more people joined in until we had a really good game going. Tana made a couple of good saves and was strong in her challenges, so I was pretty certain that she was up for the job. Aaron, one of my more able students really looked the part when we were playing. Both Tana and I agreed that he was by far the best player on the pitch.

In preparation for the game, I had told all three of my classes about it and the consensus was that they hoped that my team would win. Falcon Lee even requested that I put Dean Tang in hospital with a particularly fearsome challenge but he looked disappointed when I said that would be very unsporting of me to do so. I had requested that Mike, Dave and Richard bring their football stuff with them when they were packing for their holiday and had warned them they were expected to play.

I also suggested on the night before the game that instead of going out and getting smashed, we should stay in as this could be quite beneficial to our chances of winning. They agreed but Tana didn't need this type of request as she was still shattered from the beer pong, and had a very early night indeed! My request to play the match when my friends from home where in town had raised the suspicions of the Dean who had asked if any of them were pro's because he said would pick some of his own if they had been. Fortunately, none of my fine athletic friends ever quite made the grade!

Trying to lead by example, I only had a couple of beers and went to bed at a reasonable hour. They guys decided that they would all do their impression of George Best by proceeding to drink loads of beer and then washed it down with a series of vodka chasers. In fact, they had so many chasers that they managed to completely finish the bottle off. I wasn't best pleased when I found out the next morning, but there wasn't anything I could do about it and no point in getting upset. Whilst on our shopping trip a couple of days before, everyone had bought their bootleg red Chinese tops and Tana bought herself a white one as she was playing in goal. On the day, the only player who didn't have one was Drifter Christophe (who had agreed to come along to make up the numbers), but at least he turned up wearing the right colour.

To distract some of the more lecherous Flying College members of staff, I was tempted to pour a bucket of water over her so that a combination of her ample charms and the classic wet look would prove enough to distract the opposition. Then again, it would most probably have distracted most of my team as well.

Being in China I should have expected that things would not be as straight forward as they should be and by God I was right. The first thing to change was that the opposition decided the pitch was too big for only six players at one time and that it would be better if we had 8-a-side. Instead of allowing me to pick some of my students that I knew could play a bit, we were given two random Chinese guys who were just standing about on the sidelines. Their selection was not based on their ability but on the colour shirts they were wearing. Nice.

The Flying College also claimed to have booked a referee, but he had not turned up so after I producing a watch and whistle from my bag, Lizzie agreed to step in until he turned up. It was at this point I realised why I had not been able to pick any of my students. The Dean had picked one for himself as their goalkeeper and it would get worse as the game went on. Very sneaky! Fearing my reputation on the pitch (and God knows how they found out about it unless it was just my physical stature gave them a clue as to what might happen), I was reminded by every member of the college staff that this was meant to be a friendly game.

The whistle went and the Flying College players ran down the pitch and scored. The first my team touched the ball was when Tana picked it out of the net for the re-start. I got the impression that we were going to get stuffed and the loss of face would be too much to bear as about 50-75 of Tana's, Sarah's and my students had turned up to watch, specifically to see my team win. As it turned out, this was the kick up the backside we needed to get our game together and for the remainder of the half, we were the best team on the pitch. This didn't stop us from going 0-2 down though. In desperation after another attack, the Dean had punted a clearance forward and Tana rushed out to catch it. However, she miss judged the bounce, the trajectory, in fact everything that a goalkeeper should be able to do and the ball hit the ground at her feet, bounced over her head and went in.

We had plenty of shots but their goalkeeper was in inspired form and had kept everything out or had relied on the woodwork to save him. The nearest we came to scoring was when I hit the bar after a powerful bursting run through the opposition defence. It is in moments of hardship when big men step up to the plate and are counted. We had Dangerous Dave, a man not known for his subtlety on a football field or anywhere else for that matter. Running onto a delicious through ball from Richard, he scored from a very acute angle to make the 1-2.

I was by far the tallest player on the pitch and the Chinese reasoned that it would be a good idea to mark me tightly little realising that I was pretty useless when it came to heading. The marking got a little close for comfort sometimes. In one of the many photos taken of this game, the Dean was clearly seen to be holding me around the waist in an attempt to stop me from heading the ball from a corner. However, on one occasion I was able to slip my man and ran onto an inch perfect corner from Richard to even up the score at 2-2. It was at this point that there was a massive cheer from the sidelines from my students who had all been very keen for me to score. Having levelled, it was time for us to turn on the style. First, one of our Chinese guests (both of whom were actually quite useful, if not spectacular players) poked one in from range after a tidy team move and then Mike slotted in a forth to make the score at half time 4-2. It was during this period of sparkling attacking football that Richard found out the concept of what friendly means in China by receiving a black eye for his trouble from a flying Kung-Fu style kick from Louk. Louk apologised profusely afterwards, saying that he really didn't know how to play football.

The second half could not have been more different than the first.

1) The Chinese did what Sven Goran Erickson was prone to do with England National Football team and brought on nearly a completely new team, some of whom were a bit tidy. One of them was Aaron and I was told afterwards that he had played for China at Under 18 level. I knew he was good, but not that good. He was light years

better than everyone else on the pitch. The others tended not only to be better than the ones in the first half, but bigger in stature as well and they all had fresh legs. Damn Chinese.

2) We didn't have any substitutes and the age of the team coupled with the alcohol, lack of sleep from the night before and general low levels of stamina were beginning to tell.

We spent nearly the whole half under the cosh and there were many a last gasp tackle thrown in. One of which was so last gasp that we all thought Christophe had given away a penalty but fortunately the ref did not. This decision by Lizzie proved to be one of the best bits of refereeing ever seen on a football pitch because later that day, we discovered that Sarah had learned how to use the video option on her digital camera and had taken some footage of the game. On closer viewing, it clearly showed that Christophe had played the ball first before completely wiping the opposition player out. There also exists a photo of the same player laying pole-axed on the ground where the canaries flying around his head had to be digitally removed so we could work out who he was. After this French defending master class, this guy didn't stay on the pitch long which was a great help because he was a very good player.

The Chinese pulled one back as their ex-international was running our knackered team ragged and Mike could only say that he was blowing out of his arse at this point. I knew that if there was another mazy run, we would be in trouble. Low and behold, it happened again and we all thought he had actually equalised but Tana made up for her earlier blunder by producing a top drawer save, much to the amusement of his fellow students who proceeded to have a good laugh at their friends expense from the sidelines.

The scoring was not over and from another Richard corner, I floated in a cross that beat everyone, hit the post and bounced in. Another round of applause from the audience and Lizzie blew for full time which came as a great relief to us all. After a quick round of handshakes, we went home for a round of well-deserved showers, and more beer. Final score 5-3.

I later found out that a match report of the game was put onto the Flying College intranet and to give the score a better look, they gave it 4-3, but at least they admitted that we won the game. That could have been an Escape to Victory moment right there. I was asked at intermittent intervals by the Flying College if we could have a re-match. Not wanting to lose my moment of glory, the fact that most of my team was back in Blighty and the Flying College wouldn't let me pick the students, I always came up with the excuse that I would not be able to raise a team!

A Farewell to Friends

With our victory on the football pitch secured, we continued on with what turned out to be a day dominated by the beautiful game. All of the guests wanted to watch Beijing Gu'oan, the local Chinese Super League team play. As there were five of us, I was hoping that we would be able to find a taxi driver that would bend the rules a little bit and take all of us in the one car. It didn't take long to find one. The driver made me laugh because when I put my seatbelt on he turned to me and said in English that he was a good driver. He also complimented me on my pronunciation after I told him our destination in Chinese. The game was pretty poor in terms of quality and after we'd left the stadium, I tried in vain to find another cab that would take all of us to Club Football to watch the English FA Cup Final. In the end I gave up and chucked a couple of the guys in a cab and tried to find another one. Lizzie signalled to us from the cab and said that the driver had been surprised why we hadn't all got in, in the first place!

Sarah, Doug, Tana and Rob had all made their way independently of us to the bar and had secured the pool table, which we stayed on all evening. As I told them all about Club Football before they had come over, Richard had brought with him a Brentford scarf to add to the décor. As the place was already full of memorabilia, no one could see where it would go. The staff at the bar seemed pleased to receive a new piece of memorabilia though it didn't appear on the wall whilst I was in the country! The night itself was a great laugh. Tana bought all her team mates a drink to make up for her comedy goal keeping, but we did buy her a few back for the couple of saves she pulled out of the bag, and the FA Cup final was the best one any of us had seen in years!

Dave, Mike, Lizzie and Richard said their farewells the next morning as they were going to spend the second week of their visit in Shanghai and it was really sad to see them go. Their visit had made us a bit home sick, and not for the first time, we began to count down the days before we would be going home.

Watching Beijing Gu'oan

Even though my students had been anything but positive about the state of the nations football team, this didn't put me off and I was quite keen to catch a match or two whilst I was out in China. After a quick search of the internet, I found out that the National team and the local Beijing team both played at the Worker's Stadium which was based in the centre of town. I also hoped that there would be a club shop where I could not only buy one of the Beijing kits, but a Chinese National shirt as well. None of the shops that were in the stadium had anything I wanted to buy, even though I could have bought loads of European or South American team strips at inflated prices. They were the real deal though. After a quick visit to the local tourist information centre, it turned out that the Workers Stadium was being renovated for the Olympics and because of this the National team were playing their games in other cities.

I didn't think it would be too hard to watch the Beijing team, so I continued to ask around and look on the net to find out where they were playing. One of the Drifters told me that they played at a Stadium in the south of the city so after a quick look at our map of Beijing, I found what I thought was the right one. On a free afternoon, I made my way into town to see if it was the right stadium. It was not on the underground line and as I couldn't tell which bus to take, I decided to walk. It was a nice day which helped, but the walk seemed to go on forever and when I got to the stadium, there was nothing to show that this was the right place.

It turned out that I was in the wrong place. After walking into the stadium complex, I was accosted by a security guard. He didn't speak any English and with my minimal Chinese, we were never going to get anywhere fast. After conversing in two different languages for a couple of minutes, the guard beckoned me to follow him into a building, which I duly did. There I met with a lady who asked me if I had come to play table tennis. I mentioned that I was looking for Beijing Gu'oan but all she could say was that they didn't play here but she couldn't point me in the right direction. Back to square one.

I found the Bejing FC website, but the English section was at least two years out of date so it was no help whatsoever! I thought my students could assist me and even gave them the task of finding the right stadium for homework, but to no avail. Those that had bothered to look could only tell me that the team was based in the Workers Stadium. They did tell me about an English Language website that could be useful[42]. This helped enormously with club fixtures, but they still listed Beijing as playing at the Worker's Stadium. Even a quick email to the site wasn't helpful as they couldn't tell me where they had moved to either.

Lizzie before she came out for her visit actually found the name of the stadium they had moved to. Sarah and I went there during one of our May Week excursions and much to our relief, found that it was the right place. After looking at Sinosoc, Beijing were playing two home games over consecutive weekends, including the one when my friends were in town. I wanted to grab a game before they arrived though so I could work out how to get there easily. Sarah, Doug and Tana said they would be interested in coming along, if only to see what the fuss was about.

The journey down to the ground was more complicated than it actually needed to be. We had gone by public transport but once we got there, Doug said that he had been this way before and that it would only cost about 40RMB to get a taxi back to Beihang. There was a bit of a buzz around the ground and there were loads of people selling paraphernalia, so we bought team flags and head bands. There was a fair sized crowd to watch the game, but not enough to fill the stadium even though a third of one of the stands was full of military personnel. We joked that they had been either forced to come here to make the crowd size more acceptable, or that Chinese football had a massive hooligan element. As it was, it just seemed as though they were there to enjoy the game. The team ran out to the strains of their anthem, and what crowd there was, started to get excited and started to sing along.

The game itself was against Chongqing Qiche, the team I would no doubt have watched if we had been sent to our original teaching destination and the one Alison had been to see a couple of times. Chongqing were bottom of the league and it was easy to see why. They were terrible, but Beijing did not seem to be that much better. The game seemed to be played at a snails pace and everyone seemed to go to ground with only the slightest touch. A great disappointment and it was no wonder that neither Sarah, Doug nor Tana fancied going again. For the record, Beijing won 1-0.

Even though I didn't fancy it too much, I did play the dutiful host when Mike, Dave, Richard and Lizzie turned up. The game was against Liaoning FC and was of a similar standard, if not worse. Liaoning were reduced to ten men in the first half but Beijing, even though they controlled the game could not put the ball in the net. This game also finished 1-0 to Beijing. Needless to say, I was never tempted watch another game.

Class Things in Class #4

1) Tana and Sarah swapped classes to give each other's students oral tests, in the hope that they could reach some kind of consistency when grading. One of Sarah's students didn't endear himself to Tana by asking her why she was so fat! To put this into perspective Tana is about a UK size 12 – 14, far from fat in western eyes but

to the Chinese she is considered over weight. Tana was horrified and started to explain that in the US she is considered very slim. Interestingly they say that students often reflect the personality of their teachers. I was not surprised by this blunt, unsubtle, undiplomatically phrased outburst coming from one of Sarah's pupils!

2) Sarah had a puzzling moment in one of the tests with a student of Tana's. They were having a very good coherent discussion about the activities that the student had participated in during the May Week holiday until Sarah asked him what method of transport he used to get where he was going. The student very clearly explained that because there were eight of them they used a loaf of bread. Sarah asked the student to repeat what he said and he confirmed that because there was eight they needed a loaf of bread. Not sure whether to believe what she was actually hearing or not Sarah asked the student if he meant they travelled in small bus sometimes called a mini bus or people carrier. The student said yes but it was called a loaf of bread. Sarah asked the student why it was called a loaf of bread because she had never heard anybody call a mini bus a loaf of bread before. The student responded that Tana uses this word and that she knew what was meant by a loaf of bread. It turned out that a loaf of bread is the literal translation of the Chinese word 'Minibus' into English[43].

3) Determined to make her classes a bit more interesting, Sarah devised a game using a target and a gun. Having found a gun with suction darts in one of the campus shops, the class got over excited and proceeded to break the gun. Therefore various alternative bullets were devised by the class for shooting at the board until they settled on the time honoured method of the soggy tissue, which actually worked a

---

[43] The Chinese word is 'Mian Bao

treat and caused much amusement. Definitely one of the most fun lessons Sarah devised and miraculously the students actually enjoyed learning.

Part 7 - Summer Arrives-with a Vengeance!

<u>11-a-side</u>

Game 16 - Drifters (2) v Snickers FC (4) - After a couple of weeks off, the Drifters 11-a-side team was ready to spring back into action. I was a bit shattered from the game against the Flying College staff the day before, and was hoping for an easier less strenuous game. One in which we had loads of subs so I could chill out on the bench and come on for the odd moment of magic. Well that was the theory but it is amazing how things don't work out the way you would want them to.

The first I knew that we would be short of numbers was when Rupert rung up to ask me to pick up the kit as he was working. He had also heard from Christophe about the game the day before and wanted to know if my mates fancied making up the numbers as we were a bit short. It was really annoying that they had already left Beijing for their next destination. I rang a couple of my students to see if any of them fancied playing, but they were all either injured, busy or knackered from playing that morning. Things were not looking good.

When I eventually arrived at Club Football only Adam and Albert were there to meet me. We hung around for a while hoping that some other players would turn up, but when none actually materialised, we decided to make our way to the ground. Albert's Chinese was considerably better than either mine or Adam's so we let him sit at the front of the taxi. He was also the only person who knew that name of the ground as well, which actually turned out to be useful because the taxi driver didn't have a clue where he was going.

We were continually stopping along the way to ask random people and even other taxi drivers where the ground was. What would have helped, and would have been completely against the nature of the Chinese was for any of these people to admit that they didn't know where our destination was instead of sending here there and everywhere trying to find it. Some how, we arrived in time to find that we only had eight players. This was looking pretty poor until Arakawa got on the phone and

174

rustled up a couple of friends, one of whom had just got out of bed having been up all night drinking!

Lining up with ten players was a bit daunting because the opposition were a Chinese team that had turned up with a few subs, but I was given responsibility for being captain for the day. We played as well as we could under the circumstances and even had all of the early pressure before Amine scored a blinding goal from just outside the box. However, as the game wore on, our legs started to give way and we conceded two goals before half time.

The second half was more of the same and though I set Azat up for our second goal Snickers had already scored their goals and the game was out of our reach. It was very annoying because if we had had a full squad and a couple of subs, we could have had a better chance of winning this game because they weren't a very good. We did laugh afterwards though because Amine didn't realise that we only had ten players for the whole game and thought that he wasn't running around hard enough and needed to make more of an effort.

Put Some More Ice on the Fire Please

My students had warned me that Spring only lasted for a couple of weeks every year and by God they were right! The weather became exceedingly hot and it would remain that way for the remainder of our stay. The air conditioning (which we were glad to have access to, because our students didn't have it in their accommodation!) was always on when we were in the flat. Even when the temperature dropped, the heat was ever present because the winds that had once blown over the campus were now conspicuous by their absence which made sleeping a problem. To counteract the heat, some of the other teachers resorted to all sorts of measures! These included blankets and bacon foil over all of the windows in an attempt to block out the sun, buying fans or moving the bed into the lounge so they could sleep under the air conditioning unit.

All of the bedrooms faced either south or east so we were always hit by the sun at its hottest. What would have been sensible is if the building had been built at

180º so the bedrooms would have faced north. We bought ourselves a fan and put a blanket over the back window, but after a couple of weeks of the heat and the lack of sleep that went with it, we moved the bed into the living room. Having the air conditioning on all night meant that we paid a lot more electricity than before, but at least we got some sleep. Long gone were the days when we first got here of having two duvets on the bed and wearing pyjamas because it was so cold.

There was also an increase in the amount of storms that began to rage overhead. There tended to be on average at least one a week. They only seemed to occur at night and it was as though the government had organised it this way. Sunny during daylight hours, and wet at the end of the day, when everyone was going home to bed. Due to the poor nature of the building work, the balcony was more like a swimming pool after every storm and for a few weeks, it was never dry. The heavy rain also took it toll on other parts of the building. After a couple of the heavier storms, we would walk out into the corridor to find water and plaster from the walls everywhere!

The weather also made it into the pages of That's Beijing. My personal favourite was about the methods employed to produce rainfall for a city not far from a major desert. In the 'good ole' days', people would pray to the Gods for rain but the modern Chinese doesn't need to resort to these archaic methods anymore. When drought needs to be stopped, or in Bejiing's case, the city needs a clean, the government would shoot chemicals at the heavens with shells from anti-aircraft cannons. To compliment this, they would also burn cigarette like sticks containing silver iodine and low and behold, the heavens would open. These are great because we are able to sit in our balcony and watch the ensuing storm, but God knows what the health affects of this sort of thing was having on us (along with the almost permanent layer of smog!). The rain was most welcome though as it cleared the air for a while and lowered the temperature for a day at least.

The weather had an amazing effect on the Universities' park. Where once there was a dust bowl, flowers sprang to life with the lake full of lilies and the whole place bathed in colour. It was one of the few places that we saw in Beijing that was like this. What was annoying was that whenever you sat on the grass, random people would come up to you and give you grief. We can only assume that is what they were doing because they only spoke in Chinese, but we understood the tone.

Sarah and Tana used the sunny weather as an excuse to sit in the park sunbathing and studying. On one of these occasions, Tana suggested that they should buy an ice cream, so leaving the blanket and their books behind; they popped off to the shop. When they came back, they found that the gardeners had thrown all of their stuff into the bin. They were able to find and rescue it, but Tana realized that she had left her mobile on the blanket and that it was no longer with their stuff.

She asked a couple of the gardeners in Chinese if they had seen it, but they just shrugged their shoulders and claimed no knowledge of ever seeing it! Sarah, who had kept a hold of her mobile, decided to call Tana's and one of the gardeners pockets started to ring. Tana was absolutely furious but she decided against using some of the Chinese swear words her students had taught her as she was relieved just to have got her phone back. Doug, after hearing this tale told us that people are not supposed to sit on the grass as it is notoriously difficult to grow. This didn't seem to faze the girls who made a point of sitting on the grass once again just to be annoying.

Though they liked sitting in the park, Tana and Sarah complained that there wasn't anywhere they could go to have a proper sunbathe. They did bemoan the fact that the open air swimming pool opposite the Flying College was not in use (for reasons we were never able to fully find out. The rumours were that someone was killed during some shenanigans or that it was never refilled after the SARS scare). We pointed out that the Chinese men would just spend all of their time letching at them, which neither of them fancied.

With a change in the weather came a change in the things the mushroom speakers in the park started blurting out. No longer did they play happy birthday but loud bird calls came forth instead. As we started having the windows open all of the time, this was very annoying.

Consumer Rights

I have never seen Doug loose his cool, but he was very close to it when we tried to take the empty bottles we'd used for beer pong back to the shop below our building. The staff in the shop all spoke English to a degree, but when we brought all of the empties in, they started to converse with each other in Mandarin. After they stopped being rude and decided to talk to us in English once more, they said that they couldn't accept the empties without a receipt, which the shop hadn't issued us with in the first place.

We continued to press the point that we had bought these beers from this shop and the staff once again started to talk to each other in Mandarin. Doug's understanding of the language was good enough to translate what the shop staff were saying. He could tell that the shop staff thought he could understand everything they were saying, but no matter what we did, they wouldn't take the bottles. This was an absolute disgrace and Doug was left wondering what he was going to do with a case of empty beer bottles. We boycotted this shop from then on in protest.

The Quest for the China National Football Team Shirt

I didn't want much from our time in China and I thought that it would not be that difficult to complete. The wish list was:

1) Some teaching experience
2) A trip to the Great Wall
3) A trip to Xi'an for the Tomb of the First Emperor
4) A Chinese National Football Shirt

Number one was a given considering that was what I was coming out here to do. Numbers two and three would involve some planning and the ability to get up off of my backside to visit them. China, I knew, was mad keen on football so finding and completing number 4 should be easiest. However, this was as far from the reality of the situation as I could get and number four proved the most difficult one to achieve.

It all started in Shanghai. Discovering that the Chinese believe red to be a lucky colour and this is the colour of one of the team's strips, I thought that buying one before I started teaching to wear into my first class or two would go down well with the students. With only a week in Shanghai and not that much free time finding a shirt was never going to be easy. However, I managed to find an Adidas shirt for sale in the Shanghai Stadium shop for 480RMB. As the exchange rate at the time was 12RMB to £1, this was roughly £40 and the equivalent price for a not that much less for a football shirt back home.

An utter rip-off, or so I thought! The assistants on the orientation week said that a bootleg shirt could be bought from one of the markets, but when I found a stall selling football shirts, they did not have any Chinese ones. They only had the major league teams from England, Spain, Germany and Italy as well a selection of the better international sides like Brazil. I reasoned that it would be easier to buy it in Beijing, as that was where the national stadium was located and then I would also have more time to look around. As this was China though, what would be logical in the West is usually illogical or ignored.

Onto Beijing and the quest continued. Believing that the genuine article was just too expensive to buy on my Chinese salary (and only just acceptable on a Western one), I started to search the markets for a bootleg version. I made the mistake of mentioning to my students that I was after one, which they had trouble understanding due to the poor quality of their national team. They said that I should be able to pick one up for about 50RMB at any of the markets that were dotted around Beijing. For that price, I decided to buy a home and an away one. My first forays were not that successful due mostly to the fact that I could hardly speak any of the language.

When we visited the Silk Market with William during our first Flying College organised outing, I felt that this was the time to make my move. Finding the only stall that was selling football shirts, I tried my hardest to bring the price down from the ludicrous starting offer of 700RMB. It was here that we discovered two key things about bartering in the market:

1) The power of shopping as a couple
2) Not even the natives will get a good deal[44]

Sarah's obvious outrage at such an ridiculous price seemed to upset the stall holder who kept trying to shut Sarah out of the negotiations but where money is concerned this is not an easy thing to do. With Sarah dragging me away from the stall and pretending to look really cross, the price of the shirts started to fall rapidly until an agreement was reached.

I eventually bought a red and a white Chinese football shirt in the largest size available, 3XL. Having tried them on over a rather thick rugby top whilst in the market, I thought the slightly tight fit was because of it. Quite happy that I had finally bought the only thing in China I had come to buy, I tried them on again once I got back home. The shirts were both just too small. It turned out that a 3XL in China is the same as an L back home in Britain. The shirts would not go to waste however, as a couple of my friends back home were keen to have them.

The quest therefore was back on, but this time for a 4XL (or a XL in real terms) or even a 5XL to be on the safe side. Enlisting one of my more able students, I tried a string of markets in Beijing and nobody was selling anything larger than a 3XL. In the end I thought it would be best to ask the market nearest to the campus to order

---

[44] The best example of this that I can recall was when I went with one of the tourist markets with one of my students as he wanted to buy an England football top. As this was the tourist market, I thought I would do the negotiating, especially as I had been there on quite a few occasions and knew what sort of discount I could get for him. I had real trouble bartering on his behalf because the stall holders refused to believe that he was actually Chinese. After finally getting him what he wanted, he asked if he could help us. This didn't work out the way it was suppose to because the stall holders were really rude to him, asking why he was helping us and not letting them fleece us for as much money as they could get. It was on occasions like this that I wish I had a t-shirt printed in Chinese with the symbols "Just because I am Westerner doesn't mean I am made of money". I would still like to know where this impression of all Westerners being rich comes from. In fact, it is so bad that even though we can prove that we are teachers earning a Chinese wage, the majority of Chinese people trying to sell things still thought we were made of money!

one in because the shirts I had bought before clearly labelled a 4XL and a 5XL on the size tag. However, the seller claimed that the 3XL was the biggest shirt size he was able to buy and this was the case everywhere. No one seems to sell anything over a 3XL, which I did find a bit odd because I had students who were as tall, if not taller than me. When I asked them where they bought their clothes, they replied that they tended to buy them from their home provinces.

In the land of the fakes, I only had one choice and that was to buy the genuine article. Enlisting the help of another student, who said he knew all of the Adidas shops in Beijing (Adidas were the official kit suppliers of the Chinese team at the time); a whole afternoon was spent traipsing around loads of sports shops. Three shops had a China top and all with British sizes on them. All of them were the white shirt, which I was not so keen to own.

One was a Large (too small) and the other two were 2XL (too big). When I asked if he could order in a red shirt in the right size, all of the shops said they could not do this. Not believing what I was hearing, I decided to have a look on line to see if I could find a China shirt on Adidas's website. I couldn't, but I did find one on eBay back in the UK. I had to go home to buy a shirt for the country I was living in, where it had most probably been manufactured in the first.

A bit of rant this next bit, so you have been warned! The prices quoted for the genuine shirt and the bootlegs ones just go to show how much a rip off the genuine articles are, and who does Adidas think they will be able to sell these clothes to at these inflated prices! The lift girls earned approximately 600RMB a month, meaning that it would cost them a month's wages to buy a genuine Chinese football shirt. As the attitude of my student's showed, these shirts wouldn't be the biggest sellers anyway.

Any named brand (it is not just Adidas) costs a small fortune. Both Sarah and I were on a fairly good wage, but these shops were just too expensive for us to even think about going to. It is the same with DVD's. The government say they are cracking down on the fakes, but no one buys the real ones as they cost at least four times as much. Most of these items are made in China, but the companies charge the Chinese the same amount of money as they would a Westerner. It is ridiculous and just plain greedy.

Anyway, back to the shirt situation. I managed to win the eBay auction and sent it to my friend Lizzie to make sure that:

1) It turned up
2) It was the right size

For some reason that I cannot put my finger on, I knew that even after all this effort, the shirt would be the wrong size. Low and behold, I was right. I had to wait two weeks to discover this because Lizzie had come out to China to see me as it was being delivered and she didn't find out there was a problem until she got home. Luckily, the person who sold it on eBay turned out to be a company that specialises in sports equipment and they replaced it within the space of five days (good work fella!). I would not have been surprised if when I finally arrived back home there would be a small explosion in my head of either joy or sheer frustration as I took possession of this all too difficult to find item only to discover it is not quite right or that is was perfect. I was relieved to find that when I finally got home that it turned out to be the latter.

5-a-side

Christophe had informed me that football tended to stop during the months of June and July because the weather was just too hot to play in. However, Club Football decided to start a new season of 5-a-side matches that would keep us busy until the end of June. I expected to have a soaked shirt every game and always made sure that I turned up with plenty of water. Once again we were struggling for numbers and we only had five players.

The night was muggy and we knew that whoever we were playing, we were going to have our work cut out to get anything. I was back in goal as Rupert was on
182

another one of his business training sessions. There was even a change of venue, but no one had thought to tell Albert (or he hadn't actually read the email telling everyone where the game was) so he only just turned up on time preventing us from having to forfeit the game. As it was, the 3-0 defeat for doing so would not have made a blind bit of difference.

Game 1 - Drifters (1) v New Hope (4) - New Hope was a team of Chinese players, and by far the dirtiest team I have ever played against. When they decided to play some football, they were actually quite good but they seemed to spend most of their time trying to kick us into submission and then falling over and rolling around on the ground after one of us had administered the merest touches to them. We were a goal down pretty quickly. As I made my dive to try and prevent the goal, I felt a searing pain go all the way up my arm. My team mates knew I was in pain because they said they had never heard me scream out unless I was. I knew I couldn't continue in goal so everyone else took a turn through out the rest of the evening. It was only when I went out on pitch that I found out how dirty New Hope actually were.

I was continually kicked in the back of both ankles and after the first couple of hits I got a bit fed up with this. I started to put my weight about a bit so the New Hope players started falling down a lot. I started to treat their histrionics with the disrespect it deserved. One of them even complained that it was unfair that I could barge him off the ball (fairly I must point out) because I was bigger than him. It didn't stop him from kicking me a few times after we had spoken. We were all glad when this one was over and even Albert scoring a consolation goal didn't disguise the fact that we had been battered by a team with talent even if they chose not to use it.

Game 2 - Drifters (2) v British School Accies (4) - The British School had turned up with their A team, and we were nowhere near their level. We managed to keep up with them for long periods of the game, but in the end, the quality of Little Dave and their star midfielder (the one who can lose his shadow!) was too much, especially as we were bruised and battered from the game with New Hope. I surprised myself, as well as the whole Accies team by not only nutmegging Little Dave, but scoring from the space I had made! That was a special moment and as was expected, Dave congratulated me on my bit of skill. This was my only highlight of the evening.

This was a poor start to the second 5-a-side season and we all hoped that Rupert would get on the phone and rustle up some numbers for the following week!

Chairman Mao

Mao's legacy hangs over China like a bad smell and it can be argued that he is the best example of the old adage, absolute power corrupts absolutely. His cult may not be as great as once it was, but he is still held in high regard in China even though the country's current rulers follow next to nothing of what this bloated pie eater put in place. His images are still on public display somewhere in all of the parts of China we visited. The most famous of these must be the portrait in Tiananmen Square looking across the way to his mausoleum. The only portrait of him on campus (that I saw) was in Dining Hall 5 and it was almost enough to put me off my food.

I saw a lot of statues around the place and all of them made him look as though his coat buttons were fighting under the strain of his fat belly trying to break out of the corset he must have been wearing underneath. For a country where millions died due to starvation under Mao's rule, it is amazing that he never seemed to lose any weight himself even though in the 'official' literature, he was supposed to have suffered along with his subjects.

Authors in the West may have found fault with Mao, the 'official' line always tries to portray him in a positive way and as a dynamic leader. This is shown in the book 'Mao: Man not God', which, as Doug had said it was, an unconscious comedy classic. All it showed me about Mao was that if he didn't get his own way, he would throw all of his toys out of the pram and stamp his feet up and down. It must also the only book in history that goes into detail about a political leader going to the toilet.

The official party line on Mao is that during his leadership, he was 70% right and 30% wrong even though it is hard to find any evidence of any wrong doing. Beijing's Military Museum was an absolute classic when it came to Mao propaganda. Not only was there a massive white statue and portrait of him in the entrance, whenever he was mentioned in an information panel, it would never be critical of him. The Museum had quite a lot of information on the Civil War, but if there was a tactical mistake made during the conflict, the person or persons who made it would never be mentioned by name. The only name mentioned would be that of Mao, and it would be under his guidance that it was corrected. In my first lesson, one of my students asked me what I thought of Chairman Mao.

As I was new to all this and I not read that much around the subject, I said as such as a way of avoiding having to answer it. Later on in the same lesson, another of my students did say that Mao was a great man and from this point on, the students would mention on occasion that without Mao, there would not be a modern China. From all that I read about the man, I just couldn't agree with them. A lack of common sense may well be a Chinese trait, but this was a man who really had none! His ideas for the 'Great Leap Forward[45]' along with the 'Cultural Revolution' could be argued to have almost put China back into the Stone Age.

His policies kept his people in poverty and continued in the Chinese tradition of warmongering with his neighbours. Tibet became a part of China due to no

---

[45] The Great Leap Forward was a social and ecomic plan used from 1958 to 1960. Its aim was to utilise China's vast population transform the country from what was at that time, an agricultural based economy into an industrialized one. Mao predicted that this policy would enable China to surpass the steel production of the United Kingdom within fifteen years, but poor planning including diverting much of the labour force away from the fields caused the harvests not to be collected properly. Mao was also unlucky that the weather was poor in 1959 and 1960 which caused floods and droughts. The only outcome was famine and this policy was dropped in the hope of bringing normality back to the country. Some commentators on this period of Chinese history have labelled it 'The Great Leap Backwards'.

other reason than it was an easy target. He sent in the regular army to North Korea during the Korean War claiming they were volunteers, and then sat back in luxury as millions of them died on the battlefields. He even led his country to the verge of war with the Soviet Union because he didn't feel they were Communist enough. He was emperor in all but name.

Allegedly his poetry was not too bad, but this really doesn't make up for the fact that millions died under his rule. If there was a chart for the greatest mass murderers in history, he would be the clear winner. The only reason I could think that Mao was great, was because he undoubtedly had the best PR man in the business. This is definitely a case of the longer you tell somebody something, the more they will believe it.

The one thing I did learn from all this is that you should never let an assistant librarian rule a country!

The Postal Service

We tried not to use the snail mail because we had been warned during the induction week and by other teachers that post could be opened without reason so the Government could have a look at what was in it. When we did have to use the post, we experienced this invasion of our privacy. Due to the aforementioned problem with buying clothes, my parents were good enough to send me some. When the parcel arrived, it had clearly been opened and re-sealed.

The postal service will not allow you to send a letter or parcel through the post if you have sealed it before taking it to the post office. Everything had to be left open so that the cashier could have a look through it. Once they were satisfied that there was nothing in there that shouldn't be, they would seal it up in front of you. On the parcels, this would involve a load of packing tape and some plastic ribbon type substance. Whenever I sent home a parcel, I would always put a pen mark under this plastic ribbon stuff so I could see if these boxes had been tampered with once I had retrieved them. I had obviously been watching too many spy films of late.

Using The Internet

Without the Internet, living in China would have been a lot harder, especially in the early days. Email is the obvious one to mention because it kept us in touch with our family and friends in the outside world. We also used Skype which was a great service to have at our disposal. We were lucky that this service was available, even though we kept on hearing rumours that the government were going to block it because it was taking money away from the state run telephone service. Skype was never blocked, but it was a different story with some of the email services we used.

Hotmail was forever being blocked which was really annoying as this was my main email address. Whenever I asked the Universities IT Department why this kept happening, they would say that they were running security checks. To say that this was very annoying and even frustrating would be an understatement. As I was expecting some important emails via this service, there was at least one occasion when I would have to ring someone back in the UK so they could access Hotmail for me. There was never any warning that these blockages would occur and you would never be told that it was accessible again. The only thing to do was to keep trying in the hope that it would work once again.

One of the more useful sites I would have liked to have had access to during our stay was Wikipedia[46], which was always blocked. This was no doubt to stop the Chinese reading about events in Tiananmen Square in 1989, or the amount of people that died due to failings of Chairman Mao. In fact using any of the major search engines and putting in Tiananmen Square would bring up loads of pictures of happy tourists having a great time. Put the same words in outside of China and the iconic picture of the guy standing in front of the tanks would come up. I found another web site that used the

---

[46] Wikipedia is a Web based encyclopaedia that is written and edited by volunteers. As of the beginning of 2007, it has six million articles written in 250 languages and even though it has come under some criticism for displaying bias and is always in danger of content vandalism, it is in the top twenty most visited sites worldwide.

information from Wikipedia that could always be accessed, defeating the object of having a block on the source site in the first place.

All of these blockages can be put down to the near dominance the Chinese government has, no doubt fearing that if the people knew too much they would be ousted from power. Since 1998, they have been working on the Golden Shield Project, which is more commonly known to those outside of the country as the Great Firewall of China. They have sunk million upon millions of RMB into the project and is used to stop certain IP addresses being accessed within its national boundaries. A great example of this blockage is the news and sport sections of the BBC's website. What was strange though was that the rest of the website could be opened and viewed at any time. Other information that appear to be blocked relates to subjects such as Falun Gong[47], Taiwan, the Tibetan Independence Movement, and anything that puts the government in a bad light, especially when it comes to police brutality and the poor treatment of their own citizens.

The blockages could also be a bit random. A friend of mine had set up a blog about his new born son which I was unable to view for the whole time I was in China. Either the Chinese government can see into the future where he will be a threat to their national security, or having photos of a western baby would be detrimental to any Chinese person who just happens to see it.

All of the foreign teachers relied quite heavily on the internet for all sorts of things but the worst day we had with the Chinese Governments interference was when every web page outside of China was blocked. We considered complaining about this, but in the end none of us did because we all knew that it would achieve nothing

---

[47] Falun Gong is a method of 'mind and body cultivation' that was first introduced to China in 1992. Since 1999, the Chinese Governement has suppressed the movement for illegal activities. Some Western Governments have seen this suppression as a major violation of Human Rights suppression of Falun Gong practitioners has been regarded by most western governments and lawsuits have been filed outside of China charging the Chinese Government with torture and genocide as well as violating the United Nations Convention Against Torture.

and would not bring the internet back up any quicker. The IT department didn't seem to care that even though the service had been paid for, there wasn't anyway of having a refund on the time access wasn't available, no explanation why it was down was forthcoming, even an "it's called tough" would have been better than nothing. This lack of manners was something that would become very annoying!

Part 8 - Xi'an

As a follow up to the Great Wall at Badaling, Dean Tang told us he had organised a trip for us to go to Xi'an, and our trip there would be the first time we had left the capital since our arrival. The first we heard about it was when Sara knocked at our door. Even though we worked with Sara, we hadn't had that much to do with her as she had built up her own network of friends having been in China a lot longer than us. It was quite surprising when she came in and started chatting for about an hour. She did come up with some interesting it bits about the Flying College that we didn't know before.

1) First Years have to stand absolutely still for three hours and can't even move their eyes. God knows what this achieves.
2) The First Years seem to have it tough because they don't have that enough free time during the day to do everything they need to. It came down to deciding whether to clean themselves or their clothes. The clothes tended to lose out so after three months, the smell would become pretty bad even for Flying College students.
3) Allegedly, Mrs. Lu's husband has some influence in the University and it is the general consensus that she only has her position because of this. Sara did stand up for her by saying that Mrs. Lu had put her own hand into her pocket for wages when the University hadn't paid up. I do stress, that this was 'allegedly'.

The area around Xi'an is one of the most historically important areas of China, and some of the settlements around it had been ancient capitals of the country. It is also the home of one of the greatest archaeological finds of all time, the Terracotta Army of the first Emperor of China and we were very keen to go there. Sarah had even taken the unprecedented step of photocopying the page from the Lonely Planet about the warriors, highlighting the title and giving it to the college staff to really press home the one thing we were all keen to do. Tana was joining us, but Sara declined, having already been to Xi'an on her own. We left on Friday afternoon so we were missed we all of our lessons and were joined by Mrs. Lu, Mr. G, Emily and the Communist Party representative whom we had met at the beginning of May Week. Two cars were waiting to pick us up from outside the college and Tana commented that it looked like the Mafia had come to get us. Both cars were black with tinted windows. Sarah asked Mrs. Lu if we were going to see the Terracotta Warriors, to which she gave her standard reply of 'maybe'. Sarah was not best pleased about this as she was really fed up with receiving this answer to nearly any and every question she asked.

Day 1 - The college had arranged for us to be flown to Xi'an. Emily told me that compared to only a few years previously when the planes would have been virtually empty; the number of Chinese travelling by plane had increased dramatically. Our fellow passengers included a group of American tourists who most probably thought that they were blending in by wearing traditional Chinese style hats. A couple of the men had beards like those you see on Imperial era paintings. No doubt they felt they could pass for 'something' Chinese!

When we arrived in Xi'an, we were met by a lady who worked in the local Foreign Affairs department. She told us her English name was Lisa and that she would be looking after us for the weekend. Our first point of call was our hotel. We were absolutely astounded that they'd put us in such a nice one, especially as the College was footing the bill. It looked far too posh for us, but it was great to be living in a bit of luxury for a couple of days! Sarah and Tana were given a room to share whilst I had one to myself. Sarah didn't like this arrangement so moved into mine. All the hotel rooms we saw in China had the same twin bed arrangement in them as the one we had stayed in back in Shanghai.

We were not given that much time to relax. We were told that we had to meet in reception almost immediately as we were being taken out for a meal. Our first impression of Xi'an was that it was much cleaner and greener than Beijing. Apart from this, it had the same feel about it as the capital. The restaurant was really big and it served Muslim food. As we all enjoyed eating in the Muslim places outside of Beihang, we couldn't wait to eat. We were shown to a private room where we were joined by some ex-students of the Communist Party representative. We were told to wash our hands as we would be using them to eat.

The first thing we had to do was to break up a small loaf into very small pieces. This took forever as we kept being told that our bread pieces were not small enough. Once our bread pieces were at the required size, the waitresses took them away. We were then served loads of cold starters and they all tasted horrible. The same could be said for the main course. Sarah kept asking what meat we were eating, but Lisa kept asking her to guess. Sarah kept guessing pig, which was a bit of a strange choice considering we were in a Muslim restaurant. We were told afterwards that the dishes included cow's stomach, foot and tail as well as camels foot. After this revelation, I was quite glad that I was my usual experimental self and ate next to nothing. The girls looked a bit green around the gills and Sarah said she was glad that she didn't know what she was eating beforehand as she would not have picked up her chopsticks!

Throughout the meal, our host kept asking me if we should all get Baijiu, but I point blankly refused to do this and so they asked me what we should drink instead. Losing face might be a big deal to the Chinese, but I was getting to the stage where I didn't care what they thought of me. I said we should have red wine and we were treated to the only semi-decent Chinese wine I had in the whole trip[48]. For the remainder of the meal, there were loads of toasts and plenty of 'Ganbei[49]'. Emily was

---

[48] After studying the label, we thought its name was Nanxia and we spent a good deal of time trying to find it again once we returned to Beijing, but to no avail. We didn't really try that much wine during our stay. None of the other teachers had recommended it, especially the cheaper stuff! The ones that we did have tended to be passable, but they were always a little sharp and this included the reds. I must point out that we never had any of the more expensive stuff so we cannot tell you if the higher end wine was any good or not.

[49] This word is the Chinese equivalent of cheers, but with a slight difference. As it is mostly said whilst drinking Baijiu, the idea is to down your drink in

targeted the most and got very drunk very quickly to the point where her face went bright red!

At the end of the meal, the bread we had broken up earlier came back. It had been mixed with boiled lamb and beef along with noodles to make a sort of broth. This was actually very nice. After watching Mr. G and the ex-students argue over who was going to pay the bill, we left the restaurant and were taken to a massive square (the name of which escapes me), famous for the Big Goose Pagoda. The Pagoda itself was built in about 648AD and has been built up to its present level in the intervening years so that it towered over the square. I was so glad that we saw it at night because the whole place was illuminated and an impressive sight.

The night was hot, humid and the square was full of people milling about. It had a nice, relaxed atmosphere about it. Tana was her usual self and looked at all of the market stalls when everyone else wanted to move on. Back at the hotel, we all sat out and the Communist guy paid for all of the drinks and food we ordered. Both Emily and Mrs. Lu asked if Sarah and I we were a couple, claiming that they didn't know. This little get together was a very nice way to end the day.

Day 2 - We were taken to Hua Shan (Hua Mountain), one of the 'Five Sacred Mountains'. Even though I have not checked this out, it wouldn't surprise me if there turned out to be more than five. That's just the impression the country left on me. We wouldn't have chosen to include this on our agenda, but it turned out to be a nice day all the same. We were told that we would not have time for breakfast in the hotel but we would pick some up on the way. We all thought that we would be stopping at a restaurant but when we stopped, Mr. G got everyone a take out which he described as Chinese hamburgers. They consisted of loads of loose meat stuffed into a thick bread roll. They were very nice but very greasy!

After a two hour drive, which turned out to be the required length of travelling time for all of the sites we visited on this trip, we arrived at the mountain and all

one go.

of us were desperate for the loo. There was one in the car park which reminded me of a picture I had seen of a Roman toilet in Hadrian's Wall. The only thing missing was the sponge on a stick used for cleaning areas where most things just don't reach and, well the luxury. It was literally four walls with a trough. Without any plumbing, the trough didn't have a chance to empty so not only was it not that much fun to look at. The smell was something else, even compared with the general smell of China that we had experienced up to this point. I only saw the men's so I cannot imagine how bad the women's was in comparison. What was even more annoying was that about five minutes later, we found a brand spanking new toilet (with plumbing and actual porcelain) and had been built just up the road!

Before we set off onwards and upwards, we were given white gloves which made me feel as though I was auditioning for the Black and White Minstrel show. There were two options of getting to the top of North Peak. The first and much longer method was walking up. The Lonely Planet guide mentioned that this would take anything up to two hours. The second and much quicker route was to take the cable car, which would take about ten minutes. Unlike the Fragrant Hills Park, Tana showed a reluctance to do any more walking than was absolutely necessary so there weren't any arguments against taking the cable car. The fact that our Chinese hosts were paying for it also helped with our decision!

The Chinese concept of mountain climbing is to walk up thousands of man made stairs which had chains dotted along them. On many of these chains were padlocks but they were not actually used to lock anything up. We were told that it is traditional for lovers to buy a padlock and lock it on a chain such as this to symbolise that their love will last as long as the padlock. Others were for individuals who use them to hope for long life. As the walkways and steps had been carved into the mountain, some of these were almost vertical, so these chains proved to be very useful and the gloves prevented our hands from becoming dirty and covered in rust. It was staggering how many shops there were at the top, and there was even a hotel. The major selling point of

194

which was that the view from the North Mountain is meant to be stunning when the sun rises, but only if the weather is behaving itself. Whilst we were there, the cloud cover was quite low and so we could only imagine what the view would have looked like. I checked out the prices and the choices were quite wide. A single room was obviously the most expensive, but there were dorms where up to 12 or so people could camp down. These were a good deal cheaper than the single room, but still very pricey. It would be a real waste of money to stay here and then not see the alleged beautiful morning view.

Afterwards we were told that this mountain was historically important because it was traditionally the birthplace of Chinese martial arts and the location of several influential Taoist monasteries. After spending some time at the North peak, we tried making our way up the South peak, but we didn't get to climb it because there were so many people doing the same thing, it was jam packed and looked a bit dangerous. We took a more straightforward path around the side of the peak and chilled out along the way by enjoying the view.

The mountain was the only site we visited on this day, and I was a little concerned that we would not have enough time to visit the Terracotta Army as we were flying back to Beijing the next night.

The evening consisted of another terrible meal, but fortunately there was nothing as gross as the night before. Once again it was a Muslim style restaurant but when I asked for some of the dishes I had had back in Beijing, I was again told that they didn't have any of them. This might not have been the case, but it felt like our hosts had told the restaurant staff that we were not allowed to order anything for ourselves.

We met with the same people we had dined with the night before and once again, they did all of the ordering. It seemed to us that they didn't order food that they thought we might like, but would order the food they wanted us to try. This, combined with the fact that throughout the whole of dinner they were talking about us to each other in Chinese (very rude if you ask me) and going through another round of Ganbei, my patience was wearing a little thin. To get out of most of this, I pretended I wasn't feeling very well. I was left alone for most of the evening which was a good thing, especially when Tana was asked what she thought of China. Tana was able to give an excellent diplomatic answer, which I still think I would not have been able to give. The Chinese were also intent in telling Tana and Sarah that if they ate lots of the food in front of them, it would make them healthy and beautiful. All it did was make me feel sick.

We abandoned our hosts after the dinner to have a look around the city centre. I had seen a bookshop up the road from the restaurant and fancied paying it a visit, but by the time we got there, it was closed. The heavens then opened and the black cloud above my head was just getting bigger. Tana was quite happy to keep wandering around town window shopping, but Sarah and I had had enough and we went back to the hotel. I was so hungry that I went out for a KFC which was in the square we had visited the night before. When I walked in, I was the only person that needed to be served, but there were at least half a dozen people behind the counter all looking to for my business. As it was almost ten in the evening, I thought that the staffing levels were a bit on the high side. Picking the cutest looking, I ordered and it was the best tasting KFC I had ever eaten. It was such a great feeling to have some food that I could actually relate to.

Day 3 - Our last day in Xi'an and we were told today we would go to the Terracotta Warriors. For a nice change, we were taken to a restaurant that was selling an English style cooked breakfast. As I had done on the previous days, I lay down on the back seat of the coach little realising that we were not going to the Warriors, but were in fact being taken to Qian Ling Tomb. Normally this would have been of great interest to me as Qing Ling was China's only Empress who ruled in her own right. It is laid out in a shape of the Human body and although you need quite a lot of imagination to really see this effect, the scenery was some of the greenest I had seen in China.

This did nothing for my patience, which was becoming very strained as I really didn't want to be there and was expecting to be somewhere else. Not only did I throw all of my toys out of the pram, I had flames coming out of my ears. All we wanted from a trip to Xi'an was to visit the Terracotta Army and time was getting a bit tight to get there and make it back in time for our plane to Beijing. My actions, even though not the most grown up thing I have ever done, did do the trick and everyone was rushed along to our next destination; lunch.

The bus driver had been a bit on the sedate side with his driving before this, was obviously under strict instructions to get us to the restaurant as quickly as he could as he started to put his foot down much like the driver of the Good Old Boys bus in The Blues Brothers; just without the glue on the accelerator. At the restaurant, Lisa told the staff that we were in a hurry, that we needed a table now and that we needed our food yesterday. Now, this was more like it. We were even allowed to order some of the food we knew we liked. If only I had acted like this a bit earlier we might have been treated with a little more respect. This trip really cemented in my mind that we really have to stand up for ourselves or we would be taken advantage of.

After eating an enormous amount of food, we were finally taken to the Terracotta Army. The Army was worth the wait but we all felt that the English-speaking tour guide the Flying College staff hired for us would not score very highly on pronunciation if she were in one of our tests. Sometimes we had to go back and read the panels just to understand what she was going on about. I couldn't grumble too much though as her English was much better than my Chinese. She did make the mistake of asking me what I knew about the tomb and the first Emperor. After about five minutes of reeling off loads of information, the tour guide got a little bored by not being able to get a word in and went off to talk to somebody else.

The tour guide spent an inordinate amount of time telling us that the replica models in the on site shops were the only ones in the world made the same way and with the same materials as the originals. She also pointed out a miserable looking old chap who she claimed was the man who re-discovered the Warriors in the 1970's whilst digging a well. He was there to sign the official book on the site and Tana was hooked by the thought of spending her hard earned money on some tat. The Communist

Party guy kept telling the tour guide that we were running on a tight schedule and that we needed to go, and even I was getting annoyed by Tana's inability to hurry up. Having had to throw a moody to get this far, I was quite keen to actually see the warriors themselves!

The site was quite impressive and it is believed that there are over 8,000 warriors and horses buried there. They are housed in three buildings which looked as long and tall as an aircraft hanger. We were continually being hurried along which we all felt was a bit of a cheek, so we plodded along at our own pace feeling that it was not our fault that this situation had arisen. After taking all of this in, we felt that we <u>now</u> wanted to have a look at the gift shop! Emily tried to tell us that we didn't have the time but we were quite insistent, so they gave us 15 minutes grace. They made their way back to the minibus! The gift shop was a tourist trap of magnificent proportions. You could even buy a full scale replica of a warrior that they would post to anywhere in the world. Why anyone would want one that big was beyond me. Tana was trying to bargain with the stall holders whilst getting calls from Emily to hurry up. Tana couldn't be bothered with this and handed the phone to Sarah who promptly hung up! We'd humoured them all weekend doing things they wanted to do, treating us like children and generally allowing them to point and laugh at us like we were animals in a zoo. Enough was enough!

After Tana had bought a jade necklace (and for the price she'd paid for it, we could only hope that it was real!), we made our way to the car park. Emily was saying (down the phone) how angry she was about our lack of speed in leaving. Sarah couldn't be bothered dealing with this a promptly hung up again. When we finally returned to the minibus, Emily was very red in the face and upset that we had taken so long, even though we hadn't had that much time to look around. It turned out that the Communist Party guy had had a go at her for letting us walk around on our own without one of them to keep an eye on us. Our actions might have led to her losing face. Well this, and the fact that she was near to paralytic at the meal on the first night. Lisa was fine though and said we would get to the airport in plenty of time.

As with every other internal flight we had caught in this country, the plane was delayed so all of that hurrying up we had needed to do was for nothing anyway. We arrived back in Beijing very late on Sunday night and the first thing we noticed was the dust and dirt. Xi'an was a much cleaner place. The airport authorities also put the plane on the furthest part of the runway from the terminal even though it had been almost an hour late taking off from Xi'an.

It was quite a nice weekend, even with the frustrating bits, but we did seem to spend most of our time in the back of a coach. With the uneven roads, they were not the most comfortable that could be had but there were some moments when they hit a rather large bump, I ended up on the floor much to amusement of everyone else. This trip really wasn't about us, but was just an excuse for the Flying College staff to show off in front of their ex-student. After looking at the photos of our trip, we noticed that Mrs. Lu wore the same clothes all weekend, but she had the biggest travel bag out of the whole party with her. We did wonder what she had in it because it clearly wasn't any deodorant!

Part 9 - Counter Culture Shock!!!!

The Beginning of the End

After Xi'an, we spent most of our time relaxing but I was beginning to suffer from a touch of Counter Culture Shock. Doug explained this as the point in everyone's time in China when all the little things that would not even raise an eyebrow normally, start to grate. The thing that grated the most was the food, and by God, there is only so much rice and parts of animal you can realistically take especially when you are not sure which part of the animal it is! To try and get through this, we went out for a succession of Western meals that by the standards of home would be passable but out here tasted like it had been delivered from heaven!

We had both been feeling a little run down. Sarah had picked up her first illness, though we were not sure what it was! Running into Sara, I complemented her on her choice of not coming along to Xi'an. I also mentioned that we were a little put out by the Chinese all talking about us. She said that they don't do that around her as they know she has a pretty good understanding of the language. Doug also told me a useful expression I wish I had known before hand and it was one he has used to embarrass Chinese hosts when they had done the same thing to him. He would say (in Chinese) that he knew what they were saying and the response to this comment would always be the same. The Chinese would all turn red and look very sheepish.

After much harassment, we finally went to the SAFEA office to talk to them about the deposit they kept chasing us for. We cunningly went at the end of the month so we could play the poverty card once more. We explained to Lu Ying that we were not happy paying a deposit when the apartment showed a lot of damage and dirty marks from the previous tenants. As they had not conducted an inventory (which I explained was standard practise back home), we were concerned that we would be paying for the damage. Lu Ying said she would look into this so we left it and waited to see what would happen.

The end of our teaching assignment was close at hand and some of the students had started to take it all a bit more seriously. For some of them however, it was too little too late! It was nice to see the ones that have worked hard growing in confidence and speaking more English.

Cherry Picking
Having not learnt a thing from my experience in Xi'an just two weeks previously, I decided to take up the Flying College's invitation to go cherry picking. It was also a bit strange that I went because I don't actually like cherries that much, unless they happen to be on top of a Cherry Bakewell tart! It was same old same old, with lunch being bought for me but not knowing what the hell it was I was eating, as well as the Chinese talking about the foreigners in Mandarin and having a good laugh at our expense. I vowed never to be in this position again. I did make an impression with my students as I gave the first one I saw on my return to college the bag of cherries I had collected.

5-a-side
With my wrist still in a lot of pain from the week before and with Paul unable to leave Tainjin to play for us on Thursday nights, Rupert decided that some things in life are just too important to cancel for work and football was definitely one of them! This and the fact that he had won the 5-a-side league most important player award for the previous season gave him the necessary kick up the back side to relieve his gloves of the moth balls they had found themselves in of late. No one was quite sure why he had won this award, not even Rupert himself. If squabbling with one of your players to the point where he doesn't fancy playing for the team any more and then only playing six games in a fourteen game season is the pre-requisite for this prize, then we should all have got one!

I arrived at the underground stop where I would normally meet Christophe a little early, so I sat down to read my book. I was so engrossed in it that I didn't see Rupert and Christophe watching me. After they got my attention, Christophe said that I was the only person he knew who could stand in an underground station entrance and read. Rupert followed this up by stating that I was not a true Drifter because I could actually read and that I would be soon transferred out of the team!

Game 3 - Drifters (0) v Devils (3) - The last thing you need when you come into another series of games having been defeated twice the week before is to meet the team The Drifters had never beaten. This night was an opportunity to change the statistics, but it was not to be. Three defeats on the spin was not the way I thought that this season would start, but that is exactly what happened. The Devils were just too strong for us and we went down to them 3-0, even though things had started very differently. For the second week running we had only five players to draw on, but we started very strongly with me going close and Stuart hitting the post. With such a positive start we would have to do something drastic not to get anything out of this game, and in true Drifter fashion, this is exactly what happened.

The Devils were awarded a free kick and Stuart, in a moment of genius or lunacy, walked casually over to the ball and kicked it away. Result, a yellow card, ten minutes in the sin bin and the rest of the team having to play the next seven minutes with only four men. During this seven minutes we blocked everything they could throw at us and still didn't concede but there was only so long we could hold out and eventually the Devils took the lead. At half time, Christophe pointed out with a Napoleonic eye for strategy that we should have let them score straight away because the rule states that the sin bin lasts until either ten minutes is up or the opposition score. If only we had realized that at the time, we could have gone at them again with five men. Hindsight is a marvellous thing.

As we had given so much when we were down to four men, our legs were a little heavy and we went down 3-0. After this debacle, Rupert was seriously thinking of putting a new rule into place for all Drifter 5-a-side games from now on in which Stuart is a feature. He thought it would be a good idea to have two other Drifters hold him down whilst the others frisked him for

202

handbags as he had a habit of swinging them around at the most ill advised moments!

Game 4 - Drifters (4) v Athletico Red (4) – The second game was against Athletico Red, who in contrast to the Devils, we had yet to lose to. We were thoroughly knackered from the Devils game and Athletico came out all fired up and quickly scored a couple of goals. Now, normally this would give Rupert the excuse to start balling at the top of his voice about something or other but on this occasion something very different happened. With the Drifters under the cosh, Rupert remembered his MVP award and reading the game like a pro, he intercepted a dangerous through ball and then effortlessly glided past the first Athletico player he saw. With everyone in shock from this turn of events, the Athletico players stopped moving. Rupert saw an opening and ran up the pitch.

The Athletico players continued to let Rupert run towards their goal, either through fear and admiration of his reputation, or because they knew full well that he possessed as much threat to them with the ball at my feet as Professor Stephen Hawkins would in a similar position. With the goal beckoning, Rupert fired in a low shot that was just kept out by the opposing goalkeepers legs which would have been perfect for one of the other Drifters (who should have been in support of such a purposeful run) to knock in. However, not one Drifter was to be seen. As Rupert looked around to see, either a medic rushing on with an oxygen mask and stretcher to take him back to the goal or the team, he found that all the other Drifters had formed a wall across our goal face.

We were all concerned that Rupert would lose the ball and we didn't want to concede another goal due to our goalkeeper thinking he was the next Rene Higuita The first half was not a complete loss for the Drifters and for me especially as I scored two goals to try and keep us in it. The first was a run onto a through ball that I managed to slot beyond the despairing dive of the keeper. The second was something so special that I don't think I could ever repeat it. Just before the half time whistle, we were awarded a freekick just inside the Athletico half. As I was really fired up (and somewhat annoyed) by the evening as whole, I smacked the ball as hard as I could. Instead of flying over the fence and out into the park, I watched as the ball flew like an Exocet missile into the roof of the net. Due to this moment of unexpected brilliance, Christophe christened me the Drifters very own weapon of mass destruction.

These goals didn't inspire the team to great things and with only a few minutes left and leading 4-2, Athletico must have thought they would be able to break their run of losing results against us. Stuart however was a man with something to prove and after shouting something that sounded very rude and very Irish, he ran the length of the pitch going round every single player (including his own and at least twice just to re-enforce the point) before slamming the ball home. In celebration, there followed more words of Irish wisdom and we felt we could secure a draw. It is always at moments like this that a hero needs to step up and take the lead. We needed experience, a cool head under pressure, a suave accent but as Markus wasn't playing, we had to hope Christophe could do something. Now I had been informed by the man himself a Christophe goal is rarer than a smoothly run American military operation.

However, when we needed him most up he popped, forced his way through some despairing tackles and fired the ball home from an impossible angle. In fact it looked so impossible that Athletico protested that the ball was out before he scored but the Ref was having none of it and the goal stood. Four a piece and still there was time for more drama. With the Athletico players still fuming from Christophe's moment in the sun, they let their guard down and I was able to rush onto a Stuart through ball. I could hear the crowd cheering, my name in lights and hat-trick to my name. It was not to be as the goalie pulled off a great save. It would have been unjust for us to win because they had been the far better team, but we were happy enough with the draw but one point from a possible twelve was a poor start to the campaign. We all left the ground hoping that we wouldn't have a relegation dog fight on our hands.

* * * * *

Chinese Toilets

The toilets out in China were of the squatting variety and not the sitting down in comfort we had at home (except in our accommodation and in the hotels we stayed at, which we were both eternally grateful for). I may not have stepped into many of these squat toilets, but there were only a couple of occasions when I actually saw a clean one. One was in the first week in the Shanghai museum, and the only other one that springs to mind was in Tiananmen Square. This was a bit over the top with stone work and its own souvenir shop. Unfortunately they didn't have an 'I've been to the Toilet in Tiananmen Square' t-shirt which was a shame. I would have definitely bought one of those!

The majority of toilets were smelly, dirty and sometimes you had to pay for the privilege of using one. I managed to almost avoid using these, except on one occasion when the dreaded Beijing Belly got the better of me and I had no choice. It was the unfortunate Sarah that seemed to have to use them on a regular basis, especially when we started to travel around at the end of our stay. We always carried a roll of toilet paper with us just in case we were caught short and had to step into one of these potential health hazards.

Some of the horror stories she told me about the public loo's are as follows.

1) The women's toilets were very much like a men's toilets back home, in that it was open plan but dissimilar in that they were no urinals on the wall. The partitions between the stalls only came up to about chest height so when you are crouching down, you can still see the head of the person crouching next to you.
2) On occasion, there weren't any doors on any of the cubicles so you could really see everything people were doing. Not nice.
3) The flush hole was so small that if someone left a particularly large deposit, flushing would never clear the blockage.
4) A bin was provided in most of the toilets to put your used toilet paper in,

5) but if that was full, you had no option but to put it into the toilet which also caused a blockage.

Andrew told us about a blog site he had read where the author had ventured into a public toilet in the middle of nowhere to be confronted by a scene that a dung beetle would have taken exception to. The toilet had become full and excrement covered the floor. In the said excrement were body shaped patches where someone had obviously slipped on the floor and had become covered in other people's waste. Even if this is apocryphal, I would still say that it was entirely possible because of the disgusting state most of the toilets were in. Ray did say something very profound on this subject. 'It is not the toilets themselves that are dirty, but the people who use them'.

<u>11-a-side</u>
Game 17 - Drifters (5) v Tigers (0) - The Tigers were a Korean team that proved conclusively that Koreans, like Italians or any other any country that thinks long greasy hair is a fashion statement have trouble staying on their feet, falling over at the slightest hint of a breeze whilst kicking lumps off their opponents and not expecting anything of the same back is perfectly acceptable behaviour on a football pitch. They turned up looking a damn sight more professional than we did. They were all wearing the latest Arsenal kit, bootleg of course, with their names and numbers on the back! They even did the obligatory huddle and war chant to get them in the mood.

We played on the brand new fake grass 11-a-side pitch near the Lido Hotel that we had watched being laid whilst playing in my first 5-a-side league. It looked great, and as it turned out, played really well. We were short of a couple players for this one but Rupert had let me know in advance so I was able to rustle up a couple of my students to make up the numbers. Aaron, the ex-international player was one and the other was Carr, who had been bugging me for a game for ages. I had only ever seen him kick around with his friends before so I wasn't sure how good or bad he was going to be, but at least he turned up. Harry came along to give support, buy water from the local shop (good lad) and take pictures.

We only had eleven players so Rupert donned his kit and Paul, the regular goalie, went up front as he said he use to play there before injuries forced him between the sticks. It must have been weird for the Koreans looking at the Drifter front line, because neither of Paul nor me could muster a single hair on either of our heads. Paul proceeded to score four goals in the first half, the first of which led to very upset Koreans. The linesman flagged Paul off-side but the Ref said that he wasn't. Cue loads of Koreans pointing to the linesman and complaining, but to no avail. The football was a joy to watch, but that was all I could do because I didn't seem to have any energy what so ever. Even though I felt fine off the pitch, I must have been suffering from a bug but the rest of the team made up for my lack of running around by tearing the Koreans apart.

The best goal of the game was when Aaron played a smart one two with Amine, ran into the box and delivered an inch perfect pass onto Paul's foot that he side footed in. The half finished 4-0 but we could have easily had a fifth. Paul and I had beaten the off-side trap and were bearing down on their keeper. The keeper rushed out and I called for Paul to hit the ball early, but he obviously thought he had turned into Stan Bowles and tried to round the keeper. Now Stan Bowles Paul most certainly is not, and the keeper saved it. If only he had squared it, I might have added to the score line but once again it wasn't to be.

Half time was memorable for Paul using every Korean insult he had learned whilst working there to slag off any Tigers player that dared come close enough. Eventually I thought it would be beneficial for me to step in and to lead Paul away before he was killed. One of our other players had damaged his knee in a tackle and was unable to continue, it was going to be hard enough playing with ten men, let alone nine! Carr had had a great game at the back, which was to continue into the second half, totally surprising Rupert because he said that most of the Chinese players he had seen didn't think that defending was an honourable thing so would only ever want to play up front. We might have been down to ten players but that didn't stop us from running the game.

Amine scored one of his trademark blinding goals straight into the top corner and I hit the post. If only we had some subs, we could have reached double figures. We were just too good for them, even though I thought Aaron didn't seem to be doing that much. When I asked him about it at the end of the game, he said that if he had played to his best, the opposition would have just kicked him off the pitch. Fair enough as he shouldn't have been playing in the first place but the guy was so good that he didn't have to do that much to look like the class act. He made me laugh when he said that it was a great honour to have played football on the same team as me. I had to jump in to say what an honour it was to play with him. It wasn't everyday I got a game with someone who had represented his country, no matter what age level they were playing at! With this win we were guaranteed fourth in the league.

Staff Issues

By this stage of working at the Flying College, there were certain aspects of it that were really beginning to annoy me. One of these the tendency of the Chinese staff at the Flying College to change things or make new arrangements without actually telling us that they are doing them, and then expect us to know that they have done it. Mind reading is not a skill that either Sarah or I possess, but it does seem to be the minimal requirement when working here. Our first encounter, as you will have already read, was during the first week of classes when Sarah's timetable was changed without consultation.

Another one was the amount of students not turning up to my classes because Mr. G, or some other member of staff, would remove them for a punishment or some menial task, such as collecting laundry or the post. Dean Tang had said on numerous occasions that English was the most important lesson in the College. Matters came to a head when a 1st Year came in to my class and said that Mr. G wanted to see one of my students. I refused to let him go saying that Mr. G can see him in his time, not mine.

The 1st Year looked a little bemused by my comment (no doubt, teachers didn't refuse requests like this) and after he left, the students gave me a round of applause. With the words of the Dean in mind, I told all of my classes that if Mr. G (or any other member of the College staff) wanted to take them out of my lessons, he would have to ask my permission first. If my instructions were ignored, the student should tell me and Mr. G would have to answer to me. Needless to say, none of my students were missing from my class due to the actions of another member of staff.

The second and more annoying for me were the actions Lu Ding. The rumour was that Lu Ding had once been in the military and walked around the college like he owned the place. He was the person that had written the massive rule book that the students had to abide by, but his view was that he was above all of that. As has been noted before, none of the students were allowed to smoke (even though a fair number of them did) but he would always have a cigarette on him, no doubt trying to show his own self importance. He didn't have a lot to do with me or the other English teachers (which was nice), but when he did, I found him very rude.

He would walk into my class (without knocking which <u>even</u> the Dean did on the few occasions he would come in) and start talking to one or more of my students whilst I was teaching. Even though I would try to be civil and say hello to him (in Chinese of course, because the students told me that he couldn't speak any English), he would simply ignore me and continue on with what he was doing. Now, I had been led to believe that saying 'ni hao[50]' was bit like saying 'crackerjack'. Once it was said, everyone was meant to reply with the same word. Not Lu Ding though. I talked this over with Doug one night and he concluded that Lu Ding must have thought of himself to be so important that he didn't need to obey the social conventions like everybody else.

---

[50] Mandarin for 'hello'

Not long after the instruction I had given my classes regarding Mr. G, Lu Ding ventured into of my lessons. On this occasion, I made a beeline straight to him (and using the student he was talking to as a translator), demanded to know why he was in my classroom. Lu Ding looked a bit surprised by this, but as I was standing next to, and towering over him, he looked a bit threatened by this. Now, I can not be certain that my student was able to translate everything I was saying, but the tone in my voice didn't need translating. After telling him in no uncertain terms that when entering my lessons, he should knock first[51], wait for permission to come in and then ask me if he could talk to any of the students, he apologised whilst making his way sheepishly out of the room closing the door behind him. When I returned to the front of the class, the students' faces said it all. No one had ever spoken to Lu Ding in that way, but as I had told them many times before, 'my class, my rules'. Lu Ding never darkened my door again and whenever I saw him about the place, he would keep his distance. I was expecting to be pulled into the Deans' for not showing a member of his staff respect in front of the students, but it never happened. Being big, bald and a bit scary looking can sometimes work to ones advantage.

5-a-side

   Game 5 - Drifters (3) v Barbarians 2 (1) – The Dutch Women's National volleyball team were playing at Beihang on this particular evening, but I had already promised Rupert that I would turn up for the Drifters where I hoped we could claim maximum points, which would make up for missing a load of women running around in skimpy outfits. We started the game against the Barbarians at a slow pace as we needed time to adjust to playing styles of two guest players we had roped in for the night. They actually played for another team in the league but they had turned up on the wrong

---

[51] If I had been able to say it in Chinese, I would love to have repeated one of the rules from the rule book he had produced for the students where 'If you have to enter a classroom, knock on the door, say excuse me and then come in'. He was not a man to practice what he preached.

night for their matches. They fancied a game; we needed some players so they were in!

Even though we were camped in the opposition half for long periods, we were only 1-0 when the whistle went for the break. Our general play was pretty good, but it was our finishing that was letting us down. After the restart, our guests started to show some nice touches and set me up for our second goal before Mattieus went on one of his mazy runs to score our third and last goal. With the points in the bag, we took our foot off of the gas and gave Rupert something to (other than shouting a lot), which was picking the ball out of the net. Cue loads more shouting, tantrums and calls for a much needed smoke at the end of the game. We just claimed that with the job done, we were saving ourselves for the second, and potentially harder game of the evening.

Game 6 - Drifters (3) v Cosmos (2) – Christophe explained that meeting the Cosmos was always a special moment in a Drifter's life. The only winning strategy was to stick to them like glue and deprive them of oxygen because they were young, fit, good on, as well as off the ball. We were old-ish, not so skilled, and had definite problems with the ball, especially putting it in the net! Before kick off, Christophe made a special point of warning Stuart that he needed to stay calm as they were going to kick us, but he just stared back claiming that he was too tired to understand Christophe's English! After the game, we had a feeling that the real Stuart had not turned up, but had been replaced by his evil twin who stayed almost silent throughout game!

We were very sloppy at the start, and without Rupert between the sticks we would have been a bagful of goals down after the first couple of minutes. All these heroics caused Rupert's back to hurt quite badly, but the thought of one of the other players going in goal was enough of a spur to get us into action. We redoubled our efforts and the 'glue' strategy paid off; Cosmos mobility diminished and we scored three quick goals on the break, including one each from guest players. Of course, being The Drifters, sloppiness returned to our and near the final whistle, Cosmos scored twice.

Rupert lost his cool but managed to fix his back with staples to resist the last Cosmos attempt to equalize and we walked off with a maximum six points. A good night's work! Rupert asked our two guests if they wished to join us on a permanent basis and even though they said they were interested, they turned into a bit of a Jimmy (remember him?) and never darkened our doors again. I wondered it was down to our constant arguing that put them off

The Mafia Game

During the last month of teaching, I decided that the first two lessons of the week would be serious and involve some actual teaching. However, because I felt that my students were living under a very strict regime of work and no free time, I decided that the last lesson would be one where we could have a bit of fun whilst still using English. The most popular was the 'Mafia Game' which Doug had used with his own students. The rules were pretty straight forward and Doug had told me that his class had loved it. He also pointed out that his classes were about half the size of mine and he was not sure how it would work with nearly forty people in the room but I tailored the rules to my needs.

Apart from some willing players, the only other item needed is a full deck of cards, with both jokers and three of the aces removed. I did ask the students from one of their number to supply me a pack of cards, but as the Flying College had banned cards they seemed reluctant to bring them in even though I had had seen them playing card games on numerous occasions. To allay their fears, I told them that if they were to get into trouble that they should say I had requested the cards for a lesson and if that didn't work, to then tell me which member of staff they had got into trouble with and I would deal with them in my own inimitable fashion! Needless to say, this last point did the trick and there were more than enough sets of cards for us to play the game.

After shuffling the deck, all of the students were given one card each. Depending on which card they have received would be their role in the game. The different types of cards are as follows:

10, Jack, Queen or King in Black – Mafia
10, Jack, Queen or King in Red – The Police
Ace – The Doctor
Any other card – Citizens

The aim of the game is straight forward. To win, The Mafia must kill all of the Police or the Police must catch all of the Mafia. To begin, I would tell everyone to close their eyes and put their heads down on the desk. If I saw anyone looking up, unless I had told them to, I would take away his card and they would be out of the game. The people holding Mafia cards are told to open their eyes and then they can see who else is in the Mafia. I would then ask the Mafia which player they would like to kill. They would then point at their victim (Pointing was better because if they spoke, everyone would know who they were) and then I would tell them to put their heads back down. I would then ask the Police to raise their heads and ask them who they thought was Mafia.

Once they had decided on someone, I would give them a thumbs up to say that their selection was in the Mafia, or a thumbs down if they were not. The Police would then put their heads down and the Doctor would be asked to look up. There should only be one Doctor so three of the aces needed to be taken out of the pack before the game started, something that I would forget to do on occasion. He would be asked which person he would like to save from being killed by the Mafia and would pick someone randomly in the room. He would then put his head down and everyone would be asked to raise their heads.

I would then pick at random (by closing my own eyes and bringing my finger down on the class register) two people who would nominate two of their classmates who they thought were in the Mafia. Once nominated, these two would have to stand up and say why they were not in the Mafia. Once they had finished, the whole class would vote on who they thought was the Mafia person and once that was decided, that person would then have to show his card to show which category he was in.

It would then be revealed which person had been selected to be killed by the Mafia and then it would be revealed if the Doctor had saved him or not. The game would begin again with the only difference being that those people that had been either killed or voted out did not have to close their eyes and could therefore see what was going on.

Due to the large numbers of people in my class, I would normally wait until only about 15 people were left playing before brining it to a conclusion so that the people that had voted off early doors would not get bored. I would normally get through two games an hour. This game was a great success with all of my classes, and I looked forward to playing it. It did lead to some interesting moments:

1) Poor Jeffrey, the first student I had seen be straddled across the door because it was his birthday, seemed to be on the end of many of his classmates joke's. He would always get voted out very early for no other reason than he was Jeffrey!

2) Reasons for their classmates being in the Mafia would include such gems as "He looks like he is in the Mafia", "He has an evil smile", "He was in the Mafia last game so he will be in the Mafia this game" or my personal favourite "I don't know".

3) Defences by students that were up for elimination were equally as entertaining. The usual response was normally "I am a good man and could never be in the Mafia". In one of the early games, one of the students did not quite understand the rules so when he was up for elimination, he admitted he was in the Mafia and was duly voted off much to the amusement of everyone else. Another came at it from a different perspective and decided that he wanted to be voted off. However, his pleas did nothing for his cause and he proceeded to stay in the game for much longer than he had anticipated.

4)   Whenever I would ask the Class 8 Doctor who he would like to save, one of the students would always shout out "Me, save me". When he actually became the Doctor in one game, he just ended up saving himself every go. Even though this was not quite in the spirit of the rules, I had to hand it to him for his ingenuity.

5)   The look on one of the eliminated Policemen when he realised that all three of his classmates on his table where Mafia was priceless.

6)   In one game, I gave myself a Mafia card and when all of the other Mafia players had been eliminated, I proceeded to wipe out of the Policemen which raised a few laughs with those already out of the game and the fact that after this, all of the other classes nominated me for elimination even though I only did this once.

11-a-side

Aaron and Carr had, without any doubt what so ever, gone back to the other students and told them about the previous 11-a-side game in which they had played with me. For the whole week, two of their class mates (Victor, the Class 7 monitor and Daniel) had told me that if they were needed, they would love to play football with me. As it was, Rupert had rung me a couple of days before to say that we were really struggling for numbers to such a degree that unless I could find some players (because he had run out of options), we would have to forfeit the games. Aaron, Daniel, Victor and Carr said they were all available and willing to play. Harry said that he would come along again to take more photos and to see his friends play.

After the first nine games, Redberries had been languishing at the bottom of the league with nine straight defeats. That had all changed after the winter break as they seemed to find a team from somewhere and had only lost one of the next eight. They were definitely the form team going into this game especially as we couldn't even put one together. We were playing on the grass (and I use the term loosely!) pitches that we had played on for the first few 11-a-side games. As there was six of us, no taxi driver was going to take us in one cab so I wasn't sure how we were going to get there. The week before, Stuart had said that the ground was not far from one of the Line 13 stations. He suggested that we go there and then catch two taxis. He also said that he would meet us there.

We arrived at the station but Stuart was nowhere to be found and his mobile was off. Not knowing the name of the ground, I tried ringing Rupert but his phone was off as well (It turned out that his phone had been stolen the night before). I then tried Christophe who was on his way to the ground but said he would do his best to help. Fortunately for us, Christophe found Chinese Richard waiting and got him to ring us back so he could tell the cabbies where we needed to go. Rupert was very pleased to see me and my 'brood' as he called them because we only had ten players in total. Stuart didn't actually turn up for the game as he was working and had forgotten to tell me.

Game 18 - Drifters (1) v Redberries (3) – The game had the worst possible start (for us) because Carr had not warmed up properly and pulled his hamstring. He limped around for another ten minutes until Pablo turned up, but we still meant we only had ten. The pitch wasn't much help to us either as we were playing on the one which actually had grass on it. With all the rain and warm weather, the grass had grown some what since I had first seen it. It had actually grown very long indeed so that when the ball was kicked, it didn't get very far. This meant that the game was more long ball than normal. We were always going to struggle with a man less and this proved to be very much the case as we went into half time 3-0 down. It could have been a lot worse.

For the second half, we managed to field eleven players as Harry was persuaded to put his camera down, pull up his trousers and play. Even though he protested that he hadn't played for a while, he proved to be quite a useful player and we all wondered why he hadn't come on earlier, or played the week before against the Tigers. We managed to keep the Redberries out for the whole of the half, even though they did hit the bar three times. I missed an absolute sitter but with about ten minutes to
216

go, I was felled on the edge of the box. Aaron stood up and placed the free kick under the jumping wall to score our consolation.

A fourth place finish was pretty good considering that we played periods of two games and a whole one with only ten men. I was informed that this was a typical Drifter season. Not good enough to go up and but not bad enough to go down. After the game, I made a point of getting a picture of me and my students as a memento of the occasion even though I was quite glad the 11-a-side games were over because it meant the weekends were free to do some travelling around the place.

11-a-side Table
Position/Team

	P	W	D	L	F	A	Pts
01. Athletic Beijing	18	15	1	2	59	24	46
02. Beijing Celtics B	18	13	2	3	62	24	41
03. Beida Korea	18	13	2	3	53	27	41
04. DRIFTERS	18	9	1	8	41	44	28
05. Mafia FC	18	8	2	8	45	51	26
06. Snickers FC	18	7	2	9	41	43	23
07. Redberries FC	18	5	3	10	36	56	18
08. Tigers	18	5	1	12	37	53	16
09. BW Japan FC	18	4	2	12	25	47	14
10. Never Stop	18	3	0	15	23	55	9

The End of Teaching

With lessons coming to an end and the final exams imminent, this was traditionally the time when the students would give their teachers a present. Sarah had already received a number of gifts through the term which were:

1) A lollipop to celebrate children's day
2) A photograph of the student
3) Loads of sweets!
4) A mobile phone case in shape of Chinese tunic
5) Random sweet/fruit bar

At the end of term, she received a load more:

1) A set of two chopsticks in a presentation box
2) A pack of cards
3) A note giving Chinese name and wishing happiness
4) A mobile phone toy in shape of dummy that lit up when phone range
5) A Chinese recipe for Sarah's favourite dish (the student had to phone his mum first and then translate it into English for Sarah)

She also received a selection of more expensive items. These were all from students that knew that they were going to fail. With the final exams imminent and their future in the Flying College very much dependant on their results, they thought that a bribe might work in their favour.

1) Perfume
2) Beihang University pen in a presentation box. This wasn't a cheap biro either, but one that required proper ink
3) A gold looking bracelet

Sarah found it very difficult deciding whether to accept these gifts or not. Sarah is definitely not open to bribery but is partial to a free gift or two. She didn't want the students to think that by accepting the gifts they were going to pass when they were patently going to fail, so it was quite agonising trying to decide whether they were meant to be bribes or not. After the longest 2 seconds of her life, Sarah felt she should indeed accept the gifts, not least because these particular students had given her a hard time throughout the semester and she convinced herself that they owed her for wasting her time! She also felt that the students needed to learn an important lesson in life – don't expect foreigners to abide by your customs! One of her students even went so far as to write a note asking his teacher not to fail him. Sarah felt that this was the all the proof she needed that this student wasn't proficient enough to pass. She later found out that he had asked a friend to write the note for him, that he then copied out in his own handwriting!

My gifts............ None!

Well, this is not strictly true because, as has been mentioned before some of my students had taken me out for dinner. I had also been invited out for beers, played computer games as well as the occasional game of football. I felt that I'd missed out on the bribes; especially after seeing what Sarah came home with. Maybe it's because she's a woman that her students thought that she would be easily persuaded by gifts.

On reflection, I had a far better relationship with my students than Sarah had with hers!

Final Exams

We had reached the end of the teaching and we both had to conduct our final tests. The tests involved interviewing the students for about five minutes on anything I had a question for. I would also have to conduct a second set of interviews for my Class 7's as they were the first batch of my students to be sent to Australia. The first test was me on my own and it got very boring, especially as I had nearly 120 of them to complete. As there wasn't a dedicated examination room, I completed the tests in the classroom. The exam was a one-to-one so the students who were waiting their turn had to wait in the corridor. To make it fair, I picked the first name out of a hat and then that student would pick the next person out. As with anything like this, it is very unfortunate for the last person in and even though I said that the students that had finished could go back to their dorm to study, some stayed behind to give their friends some company. I wasn't worried that they would tell each other what questions to expect because I had a couple of hundred written down, and I even added ones off the top of my head depending on the answers I had been given.

It was during the test that the students revealed things about themselves that they may not have in front of their friends. The most interesting (for me anyway) was Aaron, the ex-international footballer when I asked him if he missed playing on a regular basis. He said that his parents had told him that he should get a proper job as there wasn't any money in football. He said he wanted to be a football star not a pilot, but he didn't want to upset his parents. Another one said that not only did there need to be more freedoms in the Flying College, but the government could also make things a lot freer. I was really surprised by this. Most of the time they followed the party line, because to become pilots they had to be members of the Communist Party. If they didn't, they would not have been allowed to enter the Flying College. A bit harsh you might think, but when I asked any of them if this was right, the reply was always "That's what I must do".

The second set of tests turned out not only to be my students, but some of Sara's as well. These students were tested not only in English, but to see if their flight knowledge was good enough to go to Australia. I wasn't the only examiner present as a Chinese woman who had worked at Boeing in the past and who could speak excellent English was with me. All of their questions were in English and some of them were so nervous that I could see their hands physically shaking. I did get a laugh out of my fellow examiner when I asked one of my students if the sunglasses he had bought to take with him to Australia made him look cool for which the answer was a hesitant yes. Just to really make him squirm, I followed this up by asking him if he thought girls found him cool because he had sunglasses. After replying with an even more embarrassed yes than before, I decided to get back to some more mundane questioning.

The technical questions were very repetitive (e.g. – how many types of engines are there, what are the six main components of an airplane, stuff like that) and I felt that after about seven hours of this, I could quite easily have answered all these questions myself. Once all of the tests had finished, we had a meeting with the Dean where we all discussed the marks we had allocated and why. I was by far the harshest marker, so guys that I had given low scores to had been passed by the others. It didn't seem to matter much what the marks were because the Dean was quite happy to have passed everyone. I asked if I could tell any of the students who I might see out and about that they had passed, he replied that it would be okay. Once we left the meeting, I made a beeline to my students' hostel where I took great pleasure in telling them the good news. They were all very relieved to hear such good news and were happy that I had made the effort to come over and tell them personally.

The end of the exams did raise an interesting question. As we had not been given any guidance about the levels of understanding and application the students were meant to achieve, we had no idea what the pass/failure level should be. Therefore, there was the potential for all sorts of inconsistencies. This could have meant that that a student whose work might have failed him with one teacher, may well have done enough to pass with another. It did make us feel that we should take the easy option and pass the lot of them, but neither of us could bring ourselves to do this as it would be punishing the students that had actually put the work in.

Class Things in Class #5

1) I set my students the task of coming up with a premise of a new movie or TV show. The one I liked the most was the guys who came up with the idea that one of the teachers was to go to 60 places around the world with a computer generated Chicken on his shoulder. Pure genius. The reason it was so funny was that the particular teacher they were on about's surname sounded like the Chinese word for chicken!

221

2) Sarah's students were asking her if she could tell the difference between Koreans. Japanese, Chinese, Thai etc, etc. Obviously if they were talking about food the answer would be yes but as they were talking about people she adopted the honest approach and confirmed her ignorance in her inability to tell them apart. She then asked her students if they could tell the difference about westerners to which came the immortal reply; "you can tell who the Americans are because they are fat". Interestingly (or not, depending on your point of view) the China Daily News English language paper ran an article on the growing problem of obesity in China. The words pot and kettle spring to mind.

3) In a lesson unconnected to mine, the students had been given a photocopied sheet with a diagram of a Western Style toilet on it where they were asked to fill in the blanks. Not many of them had ever used one of these toilets before but I thought making them a part of the lesson was a bit over the top. I instilled a bit of fear into them regarding these toilets for their trip to Australia by warning them of the red back spider and its habit of nesting under the rim of the toilet. Even though this story is no doubt apocryphal and most probably inspired by the song "Redback on the Toilet Seat" by Slim Newton, I still couldn't help myself.

4) I got a little fed up with walking into class, especially for the ones that stated at 8am to find some of my students were fast asleep. Remembering the whistle that Lizzie had used when she was refereeing the match against the Flying College, I thought that I would take it in to class. Without saying a word or trying to make much noise, I would walk to the front of the room and getting the attention of all of those who were awake, I motioned for them to put their fingers in their ears. As I had already put the whistle in my mouth, I think they had a good idea of what was going to happen next. Blowing

the whistle as hard as I could, those who had been dosing were instantly awakened. With a sarcastic 'Good Morning', I started the class. For those that had been awake, they spent the next couple of minutes laughing at those who had not been.

Part 10 – From Teachers to Tourists

<u>Dining Out, and About</u>

After Ashtray had closed, we were definitely scratching around for some other places to eat. We had made an effort to eat in nearly all of the restaurants outside of the West Gate, so we felt that we should really go somewhere new. This turned out to be one known as 'The Sizzling Pot Restaurant', which was opposite the North Gate. Apart from the dining halls, this was the closest restaurant to where we lived, but it took quite a while to walk to because it was on the other side of the Fourth Ring Road. That meant we had to walk quite a distance up the road to find a safe crossing before coming all the way back again.

The place really lived up to its name because whenever the food was delivered, the waiter would run from the kitchen to the table carrying a burning plate of food with only a handkerchief to protect his fingers from self combusting. We only visited here once which was a surprise because the food was very good, but Doug told us that none of the other teachers were willing to go there after Ray had found a cockroach in his rice. This and the walk was enough to make us think twice about a return visit.

For some weeks, Doug and Tana had been trying to organise a date when they would be able to have a Chuanr eating competition, as both felt that they would be the winner. Not wanting to miss out on anything that would be a good laugh, we went along and I said that I would act as judge. Rob and Ray heard about this also decided to come along as contestants. Doug had told us that the best place for the competition was the Beijing Culture and Language University (BCLU) which was based in Wudaokou.

This was chosen because it had the biggest and cheapest Chuanr in the local area. The campus at BCLU was very different from Beihang. It had more open spaces, felt less regimented and more multi-cultural due to all the foreign students milling around. The competition didn't really get going because the restaurant could not keep up with our Chuanr orders. The end result was a draw between Tana and Doug. They had given up, not because they had had enough to eat, but the standard of the meat had decreased considerably and the meat had started turning up in a semi raw state.

The English Speaking Contest

The next day, it was Sarah's turn to be a judge when she went to an English-speaking contest for primary and middle school children. Lu Ying at SAFEA had asked her to come along and she agreed as fancied doing something a bit different for the day. The offer of a huge wedge of cash for doing so also helped make up her mind. This was held at the Beijing Children's Palace, which looked like a smaller version of the Forbidden City. She told me that she had had a right laugh in the morning as the competitors were from urban areas in Beijing. The quality of English was extremely high and the performances were very entertaining. Most of the schools performed plays with an Olympics theme and one team even dressed up as the Olympic mascots which she said were incredibly cute.

Another team dressed up as the characters from "Journey to the West" which brought back childhood memories of Pigsy and Monkey. One team were so good that Sarah thought they had deliberately used some actual American school kids to see what score the judges gave them but it turns out they were genuinely Chinese. They just sounded incredibly American so Sarah gave extra points to anybody adopting an English accent.

The afternoon was for the schools in the Suburban areas. The performances were not up to the same standard as those that had preceded them in the morning. One of the other judges explained that urban area schools receive more funding so they attract the better teachers because they have the higher salaries and obviously the money to spend on costumes etc. She was also surprised to learn that that all of the children had been taught by Chinese teachers. She reasoned that in the next few years, there wouldn't be a need for foreigners to come over and teach English as the Chinese will be able to do it by themselves.

5-a-side

5:34 p.m. and I received a phone call from Rupert concerning the nights games. He had carefully studied the team sheet and no matter how he tried juggling the numbers, it would always come up with the same result. We only had four players. He had phoned everyone he could think of begging them to play, but even with the offer of a fully paid up weekend for one at the local brothels, no one was keen to don the infamous Red and White jersey. This might have been down to the fact that being shouted at in English and Gaelic was not everyone's cup of tea. I immediately got on the phone to Victor. Being the Class 7 monitor, I knew he would be my 'go to man' for rustling up a few players. Imagine my disgust when he replied that none of them could play as Lu Ding had said they must attend a meeting about their impending trip to Australia. Lu Ding, never my favourite member of the Flying College staff was definitely not be reinstated on my Christmas card list after this.

In desperation, I rushed over to the Flying College to see Dean Tang. The Dean had said that he would love to play another game of football with me, but he was unable to because his wife was flying back into the country and he needed to collect her from the airport. Daniel then rang me to say that if I spoke to Lu Ding I might be able to get them out of the meeting, but as Dean Tang knew that I was playing football, I was sure that we would get caught and the guys might well be thrown out of the Flying College. I was not prepared to risk their futures over a game of football. Victor on the other hand was about to pull off a masterstroke.

Victor told Lu Ding that he, Daniel and Aaron couldn't make the meeting as they all had been booked up previously to help me with some work regarding their final exam. Whoever said that the Chinese don't have any imagination was lying. As the three of them turned up at my door ready to play, I was informed of this ruse and asked to cover their backs if I was asked later where they were. Not a problem. For a moment of inspiration like that, I was more than happy to say whatever was needed

226

to make sure they didn't get into trouble. We had suddenly gone from four over the hill males to something resembling a team. In fact, we were going to look like a load of Dad's going out for a kick about with their sons!

Game 7 - Drifters (5) v Beijing XXXX (4) – The opposition really were called XXXX and this is not just me taming down Stuart's description of them. In fact, Stuart had turned up late and proceeded to spend ten minutes chatting on his mobile before deciding that he had actually come along to play some football. I couldn't help but say that after that sort of entrance, he'd better score a goal, which he duly did. He followed this memorable entrance with an equally memorably piece of screwing up. Making a mazy run down the left wing, he decided not to pass, go past the last man and then get dispossessed by the fence behind the goal. Rule 1 of football – always look up. With this fence clattering exercise out of the way, Stuart decided that his phone needed some attention so trooped off, whilst telling everyone else to run and tackle hard. We may well have been annoyed with him at the time, but you've got to admire his style.

Aaron and Victor combined well up front and showed some real class that tore XXXX apart. With about 5 minutes to go, we were 5-1 up and coasting. The passing was crisp, the shooting was deadly and most of the XXXX shots had been directed straight at Rupert. In fact, our domination was so complete that their goalie had waved a little white flag and scored an own goal, but our well thumbed self destruct button was about to be pressed. We conceded three goals in as many minutes to make the score look interesting but we managed to hold out to gain another three points. The XXXX left the pitch wondering what might have been if the game had gone on for another minute or so. Rupert was quite happy with their mumbling and said that they must be excellent judges of class though as he heard them saying 'Their fucking keeper saved them'. We only have Rupert's word for this.

Game 8 - Drifters (2) v Evil Spawn of the Devil Ninjas (or New Hope as they are listed on the league table) (2) – Normally a 2-2 draw against one of the top teams in the league would be seen as a good result, but

Rupert was the only player we had that was not nursing some sort of injury from this bruising encounter. Stuart used a few choice words to describe them after the game but I will not repeat them here for fear of upsetting someone of a nervous disposition. Anyway, against all odds and despite the opposition employing some of the most hideous tackling techniques since Torquemada, we managed to get a point.

New Hope thought that they had taken the lead when Rupert had dived at the feet of their striker and collected the ball. The New Hope player thought that this sort of thing was out of order and he decided that Rupert's head would be an equally worthwhile target and swung. His boot went whistling past Rupert's head, kicked the ball out of Rupert's hands and into the net. The Ref blew for a goal and it is at this point that Rupert decided it was time for a discussion about the finer points of footballing law. For those who had seen Rupert have discussions like this with players, Refs and linesmen before might have expected a story of headlocks and persuasive rabbit punches. However, on this occasion, they would be wrong.

He donned his white wig and robe and instantly became Queen's Counsel for the Defence. After a rousing final speech which would have been worthy of the O.J. Simpson trial, the Referee realised the error of his ways and reversed the decision. In all my years of playing football I have never seen anything like this happen before. After watching this surprising turn of events, the rest of the team were convinced that the way forward was for Rupert was to follow a career in law and also to query every single call ever made against The Drifters in any future games. Even though New Hope completely lost their rag, the Ref stood firm.

We took the lead when Daniel scored after a brilliant solo run from our own half and showing all the New Hope players a clean set of heels. New Hope raised their game and violence levels to score two goals of their own before I popped up in the right place at the right time to be on the end of a rebound off of the goalkeeper to toe poke in an equalizer. We spent the rest of the game doggedly defending our goal and this seemed to upset New Hope some what. We could tell this when one of their number decided to wrap both his legs around Victors neck. As Victor was standing up at the time, the Ref had no option but to send the New Hope ninja from the pitch. The rest of the New Hope team (including subs) decided to stand around the Ref abusing him much in the method of Manchester United (or Arsenal or Chelsea, or any supposedly top 'professional' team would). The Ref was not about to change his mind and as it was a straight red card, New Hope would be down to four men for the remainder of the game. We didn't get a chance to take advantage of this because the Ref blew for the end of the game not long afterwards.

As the final whilst blew, my students all walked up to Rupert to tell him what a good keeper he was. Rupert was only able to bask in the glory of this statement until Daniel asked him "Have you ever played for Germany?" We all had a good laugh at this and Rupert felt that his penchant for tantrums and lack of intellect (his words, not mine) would have marked him down as a true Brit. However as we left, Rupert said he needed to get back to his flat because there was a repeat of Knight Rider on the television, his Knockwurst was gently cooking in the oven and his Gewürztraminer was nicely chilling in the fridge.

Our Last Guests from Home

Clare and Rachel had been friends of Sarah's for many years and both were keen travellers, though neither of them had been to China before. They arrived early on a Friday morning. I was having one of my customary lie-ins, because I have never been the best at getting up early, and football the night before had been really tiring. After arriving at Beihang, neither Clare nor Rachel could get their British mobiles working so they stopped a random student (who luckily spoke English) and asked him if they could use his phone. Sarah had woken up early to give our guest accommodation a thorough clean so when they called, I was the only one available to answer the phone. The pleasure I had at seeing our guests arrive safely was negated by the fact that I would be grumpy for the rest of the day unless I got some more sleep. As my lectures didn't start until 2pm, I was able to power nap for the remainder of the morning.

For the most part, Clare and Rachel went about their visit without us because we had already visited most of the places they wanted to see. They were definitely our busiest guests covering the most ground and taking in the most sites. When we did go out together, Sarah acted as a tour guide taking her guests to the Summer Palace, the Pearl Market, Prince Gong's Mansion, Houhai Lake and the Night Market (even though this turned out to be the fake Night Market. Only in China!). Apart from the Summer Palace (which I didn't fancy traipsing around again) and the Night Market, I joined them in enjoying some of Beijing's tourist spots.

Houhai Lake - Houhai lake was a lot bigger than we had thought and it took us a few hours to walk around. In fact, it was so big that we didn't make it the whole way around it and that we stopped off for some food and a drink at one of the many bars on the lakes' side didn't help matters either. There were plenty of people fishing (even though we never saw them catch anything) as well as an artificial island that was used to by the local duck population, presumably so that the local restaurants will have a continuous supply to serve up. (`only joking, or I think I am anyway!)

Prince Gong's Mansion - This had been built quite close to the lake which included a very picturesque garden. Prince Gong was quite an important figure in the opening up of China to the West in the last days of Imperial rule, even though he was vilified for many a year after his death as he was said to have sold his country out to the 'foreign devils'. The first thing I noticed when we were walking in was the price list, which was a real throw back to a previous time. It stated that heroes of the revolution would be able enter the Mansion with a discount. Once we had paid, we were all handed a 3" DVD which turned out to be our entrance ticket. This wasn't the only tourist attraction where we received a ticket like this and it was a nice memento of the place, even if the actual content was a bit ropey with a Chinglish commentary as well a soundtrack of cheesey music.

230

There were numerous scenic spots, pavilions, a water feature as well as a curious rock structure. I have found it difficult to find the words to adequately describe this structure properly, but it was like a artificial cave but with more than one way in or out. It was whilst we were in the gardens that Clare and Rachel had first hand experience of the Chinese desire to take random pictures of us whenever they could. Just outside the Mansion was a very curious sign. It was quite big and on it were loads of pictures of different types of dogs. We hazarded a guess that this was the list of the types of dogs permitted near the lake[52], but Clare decided to take a picture of it to show here work colleagues, saying that she would tell them that it was a restaurant menu!

The Night Market - Sarah used her one night off during the week to spend some quality time with her friends. This involved a trip to the Night Market which Sarah had been keen to visit ever since we'd arrived. The main reason for this was to see if the stories she had heard about it selling all sorts of exotic food were true and she wasn't disappointed. What was available had been skewered onto a stick and was cooked by being put into a vat of boiling oil. It was what went into the oil that stopped me from joining them. The thought of watching people eating deep fried scorpions made my stomach turn. They didn't only sell scorpions but seahorses, snakes, beetles and grasshoppers!

Tractor (Yet Again!) - For the most part, Clare and Rachel would return in the evening from a long day sightseeing. As Sarah was mostly teaching at those times, I did my best to entertain them and this included the obligatory Russian meal. During the consumption of our sumptuous repast, Clare noticed on the bar a massive jar full of snake vodka on the bar. Being a little braver

[52] One of the more curious laws we came across was the one that stated that no large dogs were allowed inside the limits of the Forth Ring Road. This seemed to be one of the few laws that were actually obeyed because the only time we ever saw a dog of more than a foot in height was when we travelled away from Beijing. The Forth Ring Road was a massive structure, comparable to a motorway back home, but with more lanes and running in a circle around a city. There were five of these roads, but for some reason, there wasn't one called the 'First Ring Road' The first one was actually the second on, if you see what I mean. Truly bizarre!

than everyone else, Clare decided that she wanted to try this and the verdict was that it didn't taste too bad. However, Ray also had a good taste of it because Clare spilt the majority of it on his meal. Ray was not the biggest drinker at the best of times and he especially didn't like spirits, but he put on a brave face and continued to eat.

As with all of our guests, we were sad to see them go as they reminded us of home and how much we were looking forward to getting back there. The girls were really helpful in taking some of our belongings back with them, saving us from posting or putting them in our suitcases. Seeing as they were both seasoned travellers, they had arrived in China with the minimum needed so there was plenty of free space in their bags for us to fill.

Going Bye-Bye #1

With their studies over, contact with our students became almost non-existent, but we were invited to join some of them at a restaurant outside of the East Gate. All of the students in attendance all came from the same province, as well as the owner of the restaurant. He had told the students that they only needed to pay for the food they were going to eat. All of the beer was free. Needless to say, we didn't have much to eat. This was an enjoyable night out as it made a change to see our students relaxing, even though I was under strict instructions not to tell the Dean. Even though they stank of fags and booze, the students made an effort to get back to their dorms before the curfew.

It was weird to think that I may never see any of my students again and they had been such an important part of my life for the last four months. Some of them asked me to keep in touch which was nice. Over the coming week, they would all be sent back to their provinces before they were shipping out to Australia and it was quite sad when I saw them catching taxi's to the airport. With the students gone, my ready supply of able footballers to help out the Drifters in times of need had dried up. I could only hope that Rupert would be able to persuade the squad that they really needed to make themselves available for match days.

Before they all left, a couple of the students made a special effort to come and see me to say their goodbyes. We were given a CD that one of the students had put together for the whole of his year group so they could remember their first two years at the Flying College. It was made up of video footage and pictures, including one from their first day, it was amazing how young they all looked! We were also shown a news report from Australian TV about the Flying school the students were about to fly to. It was unintentionally hilarious because the two Chinese students they interviewed already had Australian accents and they even used rising inflections with every sentence.

Accommodation Issues

Even though we had never told them, the Flying College knew that we were a couple, but whenever they have asked if we shared the same room, we were always vague with our answer because even though we did, the spare room had been very useful. One day, William asked Sarah if she would see him in his office. Sarah was a little worried by this as we had still not paid our deposit and it reminded her of summonses to headmasters' office at school.

When she walked in, William seemed really embarrassed and apologised for what he was about to ask which really freaked Sarah out. However he then proceeded to ask if it might be possible for her to share a room with me because they had another foreign teacher coming here and they would like to borrow her apartment. They obviously didn't have anywhere for him to stay and didn't want to pay for a hotel. Sarah trying to hide her relief at this harmless request and simultaneously trying not to laugh out loud at the apologetic way in which it was made, said that she would check with me about this. It all went a bit quiet for a week.

The Flying College then rang me about this same issue but I said that they must talk to Sarah about this as it is her room they were trying to use. When Sarah met with the Flying College to discuss this further, she had such a long list of things she wanted in place before she could agree to it, so that she frightened them off the idea. They decided it was better to pay for a hotel for their visitor instead of trying to deal with such outrageous demands as ensuring that the amenities were paid for by the Flying College and the most outrageous demand of all, making sure the university would cover any damage the visitor made to the room whilst he was here – Some people are just so demanding!

5-a-side

The Drifters had always been known as a cosmopolitan team but this night was a first in that we managed to field a team of six blokes from six different countries.

Game 9 - Drifters (2) v Beijing XXXX (1) – After the previous weeks lucky escape against XXXX, we were all looking forward to a game of good passing, team work and accurate shooting. Any of these would have been good but in the end, we settled for brute force and the long ball instead. It did have its moments though. In a team comprising me, Amine, Stuart and Rupert, there was always going to be a good chance of a heated 'discussion'. Those Chinese spectators who came to see Westerners explode for little or no reason were not going to go home disappointed:

Explosion 1- Amine. Set a new Drifter record as it took him exactly 27 seconds and one tackle before he went up in flames.

Explosion 2 - Stuart. Displayed excellent levels of focus, he failed to notice two balls on the pitch and as Rupert threw one of them to the Referee, Stuart decided our keeper was trying to give the game away. Friendly words were exchanged between them and stalemate was reached when we ran out of ways to insult each others families.

Explosion 3 - Me. Well, I had to get in on the act somewhere along the line. I was less than impressed with Rupert's use of so called encouraging words and guidance to the team that I took time out to remind him of the inherent dangers of pointing out the weaknesses of guys bigger than himself. Rupert was actually quite welcoming of this advice and looked around the crowd for a Gnome to pick on.

Explosion 4 - Rupert. With only ten seconds to go and a clean sheet a distinct possibility, we did what we do best and fell asleep. The resulting goal was more than Rupert's fragile mentality could handle. Fireworks went off in his head and he spent the next ten minutes (which include the first 2 minutes of the following game), explaining to the team why he knew more about football than anyone else on the planet. Or at least we think that is what he was on about.

This game was also quite a bruising encounter, especially for me. Even though I had paid penance for the knee to the Never Stop goalie's face in the return match, it seemed that the Korean football Gods had not forgiven me and had plotted some extra retribution. I went in for 50/50 header, but whatever happened next left me sprawled out on the floor with a massive pain in my knee. Amine, the only fully qualified Doctor in the vicinity of the playing field rushed to his bag but instead of coming back to administer some much needed first aid, he pulled out his phone and proceeded to chat to his wife! Needless to say, I made sure that my fingers and toes were working before I hobbled off of the pitch and wondered if my night's excursions were over. Some of the opposition came up to see if I was alright which was a nice touch, and they couldn't understand why I had gone down in such a heap either as they said what had happened had looked pretty innocuous.

At half time, Amine actually remembered what he did for a living and had a look at my leg. He then proclaimed that it was too big (and by big, I am hoping he meant muscular) to know what was going on in my knee. Thanks Doc. My knee felt up for a little more action towards the end of the game and I wandered back on, but this might not have been the best move as all I could see were stars in my eyes, and not the good ones either. It might have been my lack of vision that meant XXXX were able to score a late goal, but a wins a win so it didn't matter.

I was informed after the game that we had managed to score a couple of goals but I must have missed them whilst lying on my back, looking at the sky wondering if I was every going to walk again.

Game 10 - Drifters (9) v Barbarians 2 (0) – Rupert was too busy continuing his rant from the end of the first game to be concentrating on his own game. In the first minute he proceeded to twice pass the ball to the opposition which could have been seized upon by other Drifters to gain revenge for his earlier tantrum but instead we hoped that it wouldn't happen again and got on with the game. Realising that he was now treading on thin ice, Rupert proceeded to remain quiet for the duration of this match. The Drifter outfield players decided to grab the game by the scruff of the neck and absolutely destroyed the Barbarians, who actually gave up any pretence of playing after the fifth goal went in. I managed to continue my good scoring run by netting one and keeping things tight at the back for what would turn out to be our only clean sheet of the season.

We did have some trouble during this game, but for once it wasn't the football. As the name Paschalis is not one many of us had encountered in the past, we managed to call him 'Number 10', 'Pasquale', 'Pushkin', 'Pinocchio' and 'Peschisolido'. At least he understood what we meant and didn't get upset. Markus also had a problem realising that the only people who understand German are people from a German speaking country. This did not stop him demanding that Stuart "Spielberg balloon" (or something like that). Miraculously Stuart seemed to understand him and passed the ball. The miracle here not being the understanding, but rather that Stuart passed!

All in all a good evening and another six points in the bag. As the World Cup was on, the park authority had decided to put up a massive screen and open a bar not far from where the pitches were sited. To celebrate our nights work, we all went for a drink to celebrate and watch England bore the football world for 45 minutes. They should have put the Drifters on instead. We were far more entertaining and sometimes for the actual playing of the game! At half time in the England game, there was a downing of a pint of beer competition and Amine said he would compete on behalf of the team. We don't think

236

that he quite understood what was going on because he had only just sipped his beer before the bloke next to him had already finished his and was waving his t-shirt around his head in celebration. After our poor start, we had been unbeaten in seven games and had zoomed up the league. Talk of promotion and championships had entered into the conversation, and rightly so.

<u>BBQ Time</u>

With the Universities continued restoration work on the building (what this actually meant was they were plastering over the cracks!) the door to the roof had been left unlocked, so we decided to have a BBQ up there. Doug bought some steaks and a grill and everyone else contributed to the night with other food and beers. It was great being able to stand up there because the 360-degree view was spectacular, especially as the sky was clear. We were able to see a beautiful blood red sunset to the west and the moon came up in the east. As we were not meant to be up there, we were eventually thrown off (not literally of course!) by the Universities security team, but at least they waited until we had finished eating before doing so. It was great timing as the beers were running low at that point.

<u>5-a-side</u>

Rupert sent out the call to face the unbeaten Athletico and the unpredictable Accies and it was answered with aplomb. Rupert was quite pleased with the team that had made themselves available and sent out a break down of each player (that has been reprinted here in full).

- "Stuart - Midfield dynamo who has been lucky enough to get out of the asylum on day release.
- Ross - A commanding presence on the pitch, much in the same way as an iceberg in a pond might catch your eye.
- Markus - By far the fittest 53 year old in Beijing. Is sure to play a starring role as long as he doesn't get lost on the way to the ground (which is what happened the week before).

- Matthias - Flair, creativity and a hairstyle from this decade. May think of himself as German but the aforementioned qualities suggest otherwise.
- Amine - Haaaayyeeeeee Guuuuyyeeeez...... He is in, he is hungry, he, is bound to lose his temper.
- Paschalis - The looks and skill of David Beckham, so sure to have a good first five minutes but then spend the rest of the match playing with his hair.
- Me - Ah well, every chain has a weak link. However, as no-one else is willing to pour themselves into the yellow shirt, you are stuck with me."

Don't let this fool you. Rupert was quite a good keeper and had kept us in a couple of games during our impressive run that we would have lost otherwise.

As I had been forewarned of who was going to play, I thought that this would be a good opportunity to take a team photo. Stuart seemed to be less impressed with this idea claiming that any team photo had been the kiss of death in the past and that the Drifters had lost every game that had happened. Well, it had actually happened during the 11-a-side game against Athletico but surely lightning couldn't strike twice could it.

Game 11 - Drifters (1) v Athletico Red (2) – Well, this result really grated. Athletico remained unbeaten for the season and recorded their first ever win over us in a 5-a-side match, but it was a close run thing as the winner was scored with the last kick of the game. This may have been karma as we got a last minute equaliser against them last time out, but it didn't make it any less annoying. We were woefully let down by our shooting. We absolutely pummelled their goal but we just couldn't get the second that we all felt would have broken their resolve. Had it not been for the fact that their keeper had an outstanding game, things could have been different. Never mind, spilt milk and all that.

It must have been a great game to watch though, as it was a blinder to play in. We were a bit guilty of too many long balls early on and they had a player we

238

hadn't seen before who looked a bit on the tidy side. I thought that this would be a good time to introduce my team mates to my as yet unheard of man marking role which enabled us to dominate the game. It also meant that their star striker saw more of the floor than the ball. He was a lot shorter and weighed a good deal less than me, but he seemed to want to take me on in a physical game that he was never, ever going to win! I did feel after a while, that he was going to ground a little too easily for my liking and was caught on more than one occasion screaming, "Get up you Fucking Woman" as he writhed about in pretend agony. The Ref saw through the histrionics and gave him absolutely nothing for his play acting and a good job too. After a while, he got a bit fed up with his play acting not getting him anywhere so he substituted himself off. Job done I thought.

      With the clock ticking down and the scores level at one a piece, a draw looked on the cards until one of the players managed to burst into our half. Amine and Stuart tried to nick the ball off of him but somehow he wriggled through. The player I had been man marking had brought himself back on at this stage and was running into our half. I had to weigh up whether their forward player was going to shoot or pass. I went with he was going to shoot but he passed it and from the resultant shot they scored. I was absolutely gutted. Their star player hadn't had a sniff of the ball all game, but he'd managed to score the winner. Our fantastic unbeaten run was at an end and we trudge off the pitch disheartened to have taken them so close and got nothing in return.

      Game 12 - Drifters (7) v British School Accies (1) – After yet another one of Rupert's 'positive' team talk's, we discovered our shooting boots and absolutely annihilated the Accies. This was all the more sweet as they had brought Little Dave along as well as their defender who reminded me of me. To say we destroyed them would be a fair description of play and everyone had a cracking game. Even with the mercurial talent of Little Dave, we were rarely troubled and at the end of the game, he said we were the best team they had faced so far. I managed to keep up my scoring run by putting in an absolute blaster and I also had a tussle with their version of me. Well, it wasn't much of a tussle, but more of a hardness contest. He was taking a corner that I blocked and knocked out for another corner. This continued for quite a while and all the time he took them, the kicks became harder and harder. In the end, Rupert called for the pair of us to get a room, so the rest of the team could get on with the game!

The game was not only notable for the score line, but from some top quality quotes, both of which came out the mouth of the ref.

1) "Stop fucking moaning and get on with it". We couldn't be sure which Drifter this was directed to, but Rupert was going to request that this guy referee both of the following week's games as he liked his style.
2) "Goal kick (when it should have been a corner). " Sorry lads, but to be honest I wasn't watching". This just strengthened Rupert's resolve to get this bloke refereeing all of our subsequent matches.
3)

This wasn't the 'six-pointer' that we hoped for, but the other results from the evening worked out in our favour. Our two closest rivals for the second promotion spot were both on the end of some big defeats. New Hope were trounced 6-0 by the Accies (told you they were unpredictable) and most of the Devils team had gone to pastures new and their scratch team was quite rapidly sliding down the league. By the end of the night, we found ourselves occupying second spot. If we were still there the following week, then we would be promoted. A Drifter first!

As an aside, whilst we were annihilating the Accies, New Hope and Athletico were engaged in a mass brawl. Athletico left the pitch, forfeited the game and New Hope gained three points. New Hope had managed to get themselves a bit of a reputation for dirty play and fighting with the opposition, which would come back to haunt them.

* * * * *

Shanhaiguan

We had finished teaching a couple of weeks before, were a bit fed up with looking at the same four walls everyday and wanted to experience something other than the Beijing. As this was our first trip outside the capital, we didn't want to go too far away in the hope that it would be easy to get return tickets for the train. As this was going to be our first solo outing, we thought we'd be brave and buy our own tickets instead of using our students or Doug. Sarah reviewed the chapter in her Chinese phrasebook on travel, and then as prepared as we could be, we headed off. Fortunately, the ticket agent spoke a little English so between Sarah's Chinese and his English we successfully purchased our train tickets to Shanhaiguan. As usual, I kept my use of Chinese to a minimum as there were no cold beers to be ordered.

Shanhaiguan is located between the Yan Mountain and the Bohai Sea. The literal translation of its name is 'The Pass of Mountain and Sea' and as it is only 300km from Beijing and it has been called 'The Key to the Capitals'. It is famous (or infamous!) because the cities gates were opened without a fight by it defenders during the last days of the Ming Dynasty to let the invading Manchurian army in. This act helped contribute to the fall of the Ming and establishment of the Qing Dynasty, the last of the Imperial houses.

The train was packed and people were standing or sitting on the floor in front of us so there was no chance of stretching my legs out. I was so glad to get to Shanhaiguan and the chance of getting some blood back into my legs. It could have been a lot worse though. We could have made the trip without a seat. There was even the occasional member of staff that brought along a buffet cart, which not only didn't hit anyone, but seemed to be chock full of Pot Noodle type containers that everyone bought with relish. The hot water for these noodle pots was contained in the areas between the carriages and I was quite worried that someone was going to spill one over me as I was sitting on the end of the seats. Thankfully, this didn't happen. The journey was quite uneventful and the hard seat area didn't smell as badly, as I had been led to believe it would.

The station at Shanhaiguan looked brand new, but the area surrounding it looked like a bomb had hit it as there were craters in the ground and bits of rubble lying everywhere. It didn't look as though there was any other works planned for the area which made the station look a bit out of place. Our first job once we were off of the train was to book our return tickets. We only wanted to spend one night away, because according to the Lonely Planet there wasn't that much to do to stretch a visit over more time than that. The only return tickets that were available were for the hard sleeper as all of the seats were fully booked, even the soft ones so we had little choice but to buy them.

When we walked out of the ticket office, we ran into a couple of Westerners who were being pestered by a taxi driver to let him take them to a local hotel. No doubt he had been paid by this hotel to pick up travellers from the station because he only mentioned one in particular all of the time, even though we asked him for other options. Our new found friends were Marie and Eva, a pair of sisters from Sweden who had spent the last six months travelling around South East Asia. Their English was excellent as they had spent the early years of their lives in Canada. They asked if they could tag along with us and we were glad for the company.

We didn't spend long trying to negotiate with the taxi driver. We reasoned that if the hotel wasn't up to scratch, we would just go somewhere else. The city walls were still pretty much in tact (a marked contrast to Beijing!) and the hotel we were taken to was inside of them! It backed onto one of the old city gates and I was quite happy about this, because one of the things we had come to see was close at hand. Sarah really came into her own as she was able to negotiate a lower price than we had initially been quoted by the hotels' receptionist. As there was four of us, I'm sure this gave us a position of strength than if we had turned up in groups of two. The receptionist started by quoting us a price of 280RMB per room per night, but Sarah managed to knock it down to 150RMB. All of those Chinese lessons were beginning to pay off and the rest of us were suitably impressed. We all agreed to meet up in an hour to go out for some food
242

and drinks as all of the tourist sites would have already closed for the day.

We were all hungry, so we went to the local Western Fast food place called 'Mike Hamn Fast Food', a chain none of us had ever heard of. It wasn't the best (and far from the worst), but it hit the spot and was more memorable for the cheesey pop hits, not sung by the original artists, playing in the background. The restaurant was just outside of the old city walls and it was a real shock going from the old style into the new in such a short distance. We noticed that the days of the old city might be numbered as there were piles of rubble where once there had been homes.

After wandering around being hassled by taxi drivers, we found a small pavement bar that was selling ice cold beers. To get them really cold, they were serving them from a cabinet that would normally have been reserved for ice creams and lollypops! A round of four beers cost only 7RMB, which was considerably cheaper than it would have been in Beijing. Whilst we were chatting with our new friends, they told us that they had travelled around a good deal of South East Asia and China was by far and away the most expensive country they had been to. They also had a similar complaint about the Chinese markets, but from a slightly different angle. The exchange rate for the Swedish Krona and the RMB was nearly one to one, so they were really annoyed when the Chinese market stall holders would use the same argument they had with us, that they knew we had money just because we are Western. For them, everything in China was the same price as it would be back in Sweden.

It was a great night though, made even better by the woman who was selling us our beers who kept coming over to us to have a chat. Her English was as basic as our Chinese, but with some tactical use of some phrase books, we were able to understand each other. Marie and Eva even gave her their phrase book as they weren't going to be in China for that much longer and didn't have any more use for it.

The Next Day - Our first port of call was the Old Cities East Gate known in Chinese as the 'First Pass Under

Heaven'. The Chinese symbols were above the gate in massive letters to emphasise this[53]. The entrance to the site was next door to our hotel so we didn't have to walk very far. We arrived as it opened and the first hurdle was the ticket office. The cashier didn't speak any English and we couldn't work out what we would get for the different tickets that were on sale. After a short discussion between ourselves, we decided to buy the most expensive ticket available which would allow us to enter three different historical sites, even though we had trouble working out what they all were. We knew one was the Wall and another was a museum, but even after consulting the site map, we were still a bit in the dark about the identity of the last one.

We started by climbing up the city wall, but as we had arrived at such an early hour, we had the place to ourselves. As had been the case at Badaling and the Beijing city wall, we could only access a small part of the structure. Unlike the other sites, more of the wall had been restored than we could access. These inaccessible parts were dotted with wax works of soldiers with ancient weapons. They had been placed in such a way to make them look as though they were preparing for an attack. Being allowed to walk next to them would have added to the whole experience because standing next to them would have made for some memorable photo opportunities.

Talking of photos, it was in Shanhaiguan that my yet as unknown celebrity status was confirmed. Before this visit, I had been asked by random Chinese people to be in photos with them, but here it went into overdrive. I still cannot put my finger on why this was, but at the time I thought it was down to the fact that I was wearing a

[53] Much like Ancient Greece, the view of Imperial China was that they were the only civilization in the world, and that everyone outside of their borders were barbarians. This manifested it self in the 'Mandate of Heaven' that I have mentioned before in which the Chinese Emperors believed they had the divine right to rule over all others. The fact that the gate had the legend 'First Pass Under Heaven' written on it was designed to emphasise this point. It is with an irony that at least one invading barbarian armies from the north (the Manchurians) conquered China using this gate. Judging by the way in which the Chinese think, they would say that the Manchurians were actually Chinese, much in the same way Genghis Khan was!

football shirt because, initially the only people asking to pose with me were guys also wearing them. As fun as it was for the first couple of occasions, it did get a bit tedious after a while and I was looking to the time when I could get back to being anonymous. What I should have asked some of the people that wanted to pose with me why they didn't want any of the women I was with to join in the picture. Oh well. Sarah joked that the Chinese couldn't get enough of me and it would only be a matter of time before there were calendars, notebooks and posters with my face on them!

The area of Wall that was open to visitors had not been restored to the same level as Badaling, and it made the whole thing seem a bit more real to me and not like a movie set. A lot of the wall was accessible and as we walking at quite a leisurely pace, it took us a while to reach the end. Once there, we could see the Great Wall snaking off into the distance through farmland until it reached a mountain. We could see the bottom of the mountain but we not how high up the Wall went because its top was being obscured due to low lying pollution. Shanhaiguan might be tiny in comparison to Beijing (or any of the other cities we had been to) and on the coast, but pollution was still a problem.

As usual, there were the purveyors of tat, but there were also fun and games to be had. One guy had set up an archery target that I just had to have a go on. I might not have hit the paper target with all of my shots, but my aim wasn't too bad because all of my arrows ending up hitting the cardboard backing the target had been stuck to. When I stood next to the target to have a photo taken of my handy work, I realised that if I had missed, there would have been the possibility that the arrow could have flown over the side of the Wall and into the field below. Even though this would have been fun to have had another go just to do this, it might not have gone down too well, especially if I had hit somebody, or something, as there was a particularly sorry looking donkey staring back up at me.

We proceeded to our next port of call, the Great Wall Museum. This was on a par with the one at Badaling, just newer. We found out that the third part of the ticket would have given us entry to a traditional style Chinese mansion. Fearing that we would run out of time, we knocked this on the head and caught a taxi to the 'Dragon's Head'. This is where the Great Wall meets the sea. We weren't sure what to expect from this. We had seen pictures of this at the Badaling Great Wall Museum, and all it had shown was a pile of rocks. This picture had been taken in the mid-80's so we were sure that there would have been a bit of restoration work since then.

Catching a taxi down to the coast, we thought we should get a bite to eat. Outside of the entrance was a whole series of restaurants. After looking at all of the Chinese written menu's to see if there was any symbols we could recognise, we eventually found one selling Muslim food. The restaurant was empty and the owner was very keen for us to come in and have some of their fresh fish. She even took us out into the kitchen to show us how 'fresh' it actually was. With the asking price of 100RMB and the sea just over the horizon, we thought this was a bit of a rip off. I couldn't help but think of the health and safety issues that we would have raised if we had entered a kitchen back home. We ordered what we knew, and our Swedish companions were happy to go along with our suggestions.

Over lunch, Eva had told us that she was a student back in Sweden and we proceeded to tell her how she might be able to get a discounted price from the cashier. Sarah and I thought we would try our luck pretending our teaching cards were students ones, but the cashier was having none of it. Not even Eva could get a discount (you win some, you lose some). Once inside, the site turned out to be a lot larger than any of us expected. Apart from the wall, the buildings that once housed the garrison had been restored. In fact, the buildings had been restored to such a degree that the only thing missing were the soldiers. The Wall itself had been completely rebuilt and the only thing missing was the 'Dragon's Head' itself.

It was a really interesting place to have visited, especially as we were standing at the Walls' end (or beginning of the Wall depending on your view), looking down into the sea. It was really nice to have spent some

246

time away from Beijing, sitting on the beach, enjoying the breeze. The weather helped as it was pleasant for the entire time we were there. As with plenty of the other sites we had visited around China, we saw plenty of signs telling us how the Western Powers attacked this bit of the wall at the turn of the last century. What did make me laugh was they claimed to have a French cannon on display, but what they didn't take into account that it looked as though there was a British Crown embossed on it!

When we had finished walking around, I was accosted by a parent who was very keen for her child to have his photo taken with me. Even though I was fed up to the back teeth with all this photography, I agreed in the hope that they would move along once it was over. The child on the other hand was not so keen and had to be forced to stand with me so the photo could be taken. His mother seemed happy with the result though. When we left the Wall, we went straight to the train station. Marie and Eva were going to stay another night as they were planning to do some sun bathing. Sarah and I hoped that the weather would be a bit clearer than it had been when we were with them. We swapped email addresses and agreed to meet up when we were all back in Beijing.

When we were waiting for our train to arrive, a Chinese child accosted us asked us if we could sign her shirt. I explained that I wasn't anybody famous where as Sarah (being the more sensible one) asked if her parents knew about this not realising that they were standing directly behind the child nodding their heads frantically. It turned out that she had come first in her English class and wanted some Westerners to write a congratulatory note on her shirt. She seemed happy even if we were a little bemused by this, but they seemed pleased so who were we to argue. As we had had to buy tickets for the 'hard sleeper carriage journey' home, we were able to stretch out and relax in a way that would have been impossible in the seats. As we were travelling back during the day, the carriage was almost empty and because this was our first experience of travelling by sleeper, I thought that this would be a good opportunity to see if I could get in the top bunk. I just about managed to fit, even if my feet stuck over the edge a little.

5-a-side

On a rather sad note this was the last Drifters game of the season and I thought it would be my last one as well. Stuart was also going back home so there were two of us making our bows on this particular evening. I had also asked Rupert if I could keep my shirt as a memento of my days playing for the Drifters. He was good enough to say yes, which I put down to the number of heroic performances I had given whilst wearing it. It could also have been the fact that I actually made the effort to play in nearly every game. The reality was that the club were changing the strip for the next season and Rupert was glad to have one less shirt lying around his apartment. I had picked up another bout of the Beijing Belly, but it didn't seem as bad as previous times and I was hoping that this wouldn't affect my performance in the biggest games in Drifter history. Rupert had been sending out emails all week claming in a 'Bill Shankley' way that these games were more important than life and death. Everyone who could should come along to play, bringing with them as many family and friends to cheer us on in what could be the clubs finest hour. As it was, there was a very good response, especially from players who didn't normally play. The call had most definitely been heeded!

The day had been very hot and sunny but it might have been to my benefit to pay more attention to the aged man, with long grey beard and long cloak I'd seen about the place, as he led his procession of paired animals into a big wooden boat! This was a man who knew his weather! Just as I was about to leave Beihang to meet up with Christophe, the heavens opened, lightning flashed and thunder hammered its way across the sky. It was in fact like any ordinary summers day in England! Not even that well practiced Beijing art of raising a newspaper up over ones head was enough to prevent an instant drenching!

I rang Rupert to see if the games were still on and he said that however unlikely it was at this stage, I should turn up just in case. I had planned to walk to the underground, but it was raining so hard that I decided to get a cab from outside the North Gate. I first had to negotiate the massive puddles outside Dining Hall 8, which I failed to do as I proceeded to lose my right leg up to my knee in water. This wasn't really a puddle, but more like a lake. Only an hour earlier, there had not been any water on the ground, which goes to show how hard it was raining. I arrived to the entrance of the underground station to find it full of people that had been as unprepared for this deluge as I had. Needless to say, the umbrella sellers' were out in force!

Meeting up with Christophe, we searched, and found, that Rupert was holed up in The 'Den' waiting for confirmation as to whether our games would go ahead! He had got that far on his scooter, before his clothes had become so waterlogged that he decided that going indoors might be a good idea; that and the fact that he could have been struck by lightning at any stage also played a part in the decision! The weather was not exactly conducive to a good night's football or any football for that matter, but even as we were sure that the whole thing would be called off, in the back of all of our minds, we were hoping that the game would go ahead; because we wanted to get this over and done with, and Christophe had even brought his video camera to record what could be a moment of history!

Those who arrived at the ground to play at 8pm, discovered that their games had been cancelled. Those of us cowering in The Den were surprised to say the least when we discovered that water logged pitch, lightning bolts and the metal rimmed fence surrounding the pitch, had not deemed reason enough to cancel ours? So it was that Rupert got on the phone to send out word to our Drifter cohorts that the matches were on and that their services were needed.

The mission for the evening was simple. We needed six points and plenty of goals to stand any chance of promotion. Our opposition were the Swiss (whom we had never beaten) and Beijing Cosmos (who had gone the last 3 weeks undefeated). When we arrived, the pitches resembled a swimming pool that had been half drained. The rains continued to come down and in the pre-match warm up, a number of well struck shots from 3 metres out were held up 2 metres short by the lake that had taken up residence in the penalty box. It was disconcerting that we displaced water every time we put our feet on the ground.

To show how much this had meant to us all, Mathias had rushed from a business dinner. Kelvin finished work early (which actually cost him money, and it was a shame he didn't get more time on the pitch) and everybody else who endangered their lives to play. Just because the rain had stopped didn't mean that the lightning hadn't. I remember looking up at one point in the second match to see a massive fork of lighting crash across the sky and I wondered what the hell I was doing here.

Game 13 - Drifters (4) v Devils (1) – At last! It only took the Drifters four seasons of trying but we finally beat the Swiss Devils. Breaking the habit of losing by one goal every time, we put four past them and it could have been more. Raising a team had become such an issue for the Devils that their normally solid keeper was playing out on pitch. This didn't stop him from thwarting me by making a goal line clearance from one of my shots. I could spend hours describing this, oh so sweet victory, but everything paled into insignificance when it came to Stuart on his final competitive night of Drifter football.

For those who were paying attention earlier may remember that in the last game against the Devils, we were left with only four men after Stuart chose to whip out his handbag and swing it around a few times. That kind of behaviour was never going to be repeated. Who needs a handbag when you can grab an opposition player around the neck and threaten to do something to him that may mean he would never be able to have children. No one actually knows why Stuart and his Swiss counterpart decided to throttle each other but it made for a great spectator sport. They swung each other round in a butch version of a barn dance. Rupert admitted later that he was rather disappointed when I stepped in and told the Swiss player in no uncertain terms to let go of a by then blue faced Stuart. I might need lessons in the art of impartiality, but all my team mates were clearly impressed by my dealing with the situation, especially, and I quote that "Ross could loosen people's teeth purely with the sonic boom effect of his voice". This might not be strictly true, but it did the trick. Stuart and his dancing partner let go of each other and were sent from the field. We weren't sure if they had been sent off because we were able to bring on replacements for them both, but they were not allowed to play for the remainder of this game. Regardless of this little tête a tête the game had been won and 50% of the night's objective was achieved. It was a great team effort, but now we were preparing ourselves for the final hurdle.

Game 14 - Drifters (3) v Beijing Cosmos (1) – The Cosmos came into the game having just held Athletico to a 1- 1 draw, which was a good result for any team. They played their usual fast paced passing game but our defending was about as solid as it had ever been. They might have dominated possession but by half-time we were 1 - 0 up. The goal was a real touch of class with Stuart and Paschalis combining well to slot home. We were under continued pressure for much of the match, which wasn't helped on a couple of occasions by:

1) Stuart, who had taken over control of the video camera and asked Christophe how it worked. Christophe was at that time jockeying for position with a Cosmos player and this might not have been the most opportune moment to ask such a question.
2) When the referee decided that he would do whatever he could to help Cosmos. It must be pointed out at this stage that the ref and the Cosmos team were all Chinese.
3) Cosmos decided that they would play with six men on the field. The ref deciding that this was ok as one of the six players was injured. If by injured he meant that he limped a bit before he dribbled the ball down the wing to shoot at goal, then he was right.

As the ref was now a Cosmos player in all but

name, the second half of this all or nothing game became a farce. Any Cosmos guy falling down within a kilometre of a Drifter was immediately awarded a free-kick. In fact, an elderly man tripping over a loose tile on the floor of his bathroom on the other side of town was almost given a penalty. Mathieus 'nut-megged' his man time and time again only to be barged out of the way without any attempt to play the ball. Not only did he never receive a free kick for his troubles but on a number of occasions he was actually penalised. To add insult to injury, a Cosmos defender stuck his hand out and blocked a shot in the penalty area. That was quickly waived away as accidental. These decisions only worsened as we scored a second and then a third, which came courtesy of my right foot.

I robbed a Cosmos player just inside our half and ran toward their goal. It was then that strange thing happened. Stuart made a run to my left and was the only Drifter player in their half. The two covering defenders and their goalkeeper decided that Stuart was such a threat and they all moved to mark him. Even though I was just over the half way line, they had decided that I posed no threat whatsoever. How wrong they were. I whacked the ball as hard as I could. The goalie realising his mistake, was too late getting back into position for the ball to sail in the net. I was greatly relived that my celebrations were not caught on camera. I can only remember turning to the Drifter subs, clenching both fists and waiting for a vein to pop in my head as I scream 'Come on' at the top of my voice. The whole sideline had massive smiles on their faces, so it mattered not.

With the clock running down and since Stuart had already lost the plot in game one, it would have been asking a lot from him to repeat his tantrums. With this in mind, Rupert stepped up and taking on the captain's role, explained to the referee in simple, concise English that he was not having a particularly good game. For this, read he actually started a massive swear word induced diatribe in the direction of the ref. Thirty seconds later, he was watching the game from the sidelines and I stepped into the breach to cover the goalkeeping duties. Cosmos were able to sneak a late goal and they didn't even score it.

Mathieus stuck out a leg and deflected a pretty harmless cross into the net, but this was literally the last action of the night. The Cosmos had never looked liked beating us in the final three minutes as we had just shut up shop and frustrated the hell out of them.

The fun didn't stop with the final whistle though. Rupert decided that he wanted to clarify a few points with the ref. All the ref could say was, and I quote, "I am Chinese so I want to see Chinese men win". Rupert so lost the plot that I had to block him off from the official to prevent anything that might result in our victories being nullified by the league. The New Hope Ninjas, whose games had been cancelled earlier but had decided to say around and watch then put their oar in claiming that one of our players shouldn't have been playing in this game because he had been sent off against the Devils. I dealt with this by telling them, in no uncertain terms, that this was ridiculous and they should worry about their own behaviour. Well, it might not have been as well phrased as this but the intention was the same.

The English ref from the other game decided to join us to find out what the fracas was all about. After a few bouts of swearing from Rupert, I explained about the bias refereeing and that we had it on video. Things calmed down quickly enough when Christophe mentioned that the battery on his camera was failing and he wanted to capture the moment of triumph for the official DVD. It was decided that a 'Klinsman' style dive across the pitch led by Mathieus was the way to go. All I remember when standing up from said dive was hearing Christophe telling me I wasn't getting in his car after that. The job done, all we could wish was that New Hope (our only challengers to the second spot) would not be able to catch us. They needed to get a maximum six points from their remaining two games and score eight goals more than they conceded to catch us.

Drifters Epilogue #1 - The games that were cancelled due to the weather were played a week later. Rupert went along to watch as well as cheer on both Barbarians and Beijing XXXX (who were both propping up the league). They were playing New Hope and if they could either take points off them or at least limit the goals then we would be promoted. Knowing that we would need some luck, Rupert went to the games armed with a four leaf clover, a rabbit's foot and a voodoo doll in the image of a Chinese psychopath. The first game saw New Hope play Barbarians. The Barbarians didn't live up to their name and were annihilated. Rupert actually lost score but he suspected that it was somewhere in the region of 7 or 8 - 1 to New Hope. This pretty much signalled the end of The Drifters hopes of gaining second place in the league. However, New Hope were about to let their reputation hamper their progress.

In the second game, New Hope played Beijing XXXX. For the first five minutes it was end to end stuff. New Hope were up 2 - 1 but XXXX refused to fold. The tackles came in thick and fast until after one head high tackle by a New Hope player, everything exploded. Disappointed at not decapitating the XXXX player with his tackle, the New Hope guy decided to finish the job with a flailing right hook. His team mates, concerned that fighting one against one went against the spirit of not getting involved unless you outnumber the opposition by at least 300, all piled in too. Random Chinese spectators, sensing a chance to slap a couple of Westerners at little risk to themselves, also joined in. The long and short of it is that XXXX conceded the game rather than concede their lives. Rupert felt that this was a bit out of order, especially as New Hope had pulled the same trick against Athletico and been awarded the points. The next day, he had a chat with the league organisers about this sort of behaviour just not being cricket. The net result was that XXXX were awarded the game and New Hope failed to get the six points they needed. We were promoted. Not bad for a team that had only one point and a goal difference of -8 after the first 4 matches!

5-A-Side Table (2nd Season)
Position/Team

	P	W	D	L	F	A	Pts
01. Athletico Red	14	8	3	3	48	33	27
02. DRIFTERS	14	8	2	4	47	27	26
03. New Hope	14	7	2	5	47	31	23
04. Devils	14	7	2	5	46	38	23

05. British School Accies	14	7	1	6	43	54	22
06. Beijing Cosmos	14	5	2	7	38	36	17
07. Beijing XXXX	14	5	1	6	41	46	16
08. Barbarians 2	14	2	0	12	23	63	6

Clothes

Buying clothes turned out to be a real problem for both of us. We had taken mostly winter clothes due to advice that we should buy summer ones when we needed them. However, people of mine and Sarah's shapes and size were not catered for, especially in the bootleg markets. Trousers were the biggest problem as I never found a shop or market that had any that fitted except in the brand shops. It turned out to be cheaper to get my parents in the UK to buy clothes from the supermarket that had originally been made in China, and then ship them out to Beijing. Madness! Not quite a food parcel but just as essential. The funniest thing was finding a fat man stall in one of the markets. The jeans were massive and I'm sure it would have taken two of me to get into a pair. China might be suffering from an increasingly obese population but we never saw anyone who would have fitted into these particular garments.

The Quest for the D Cup Bra - This search concerned neither Sarah, nor myself, but Tana. Being a little on the busty side (she is a D cup, hence the title), she had found bra shops in the markets a frustrating experience as most of the women in China were struggling to make an A cup. All of the bras designed for the Chinese market that Sarah and Tana had seen were all padded, which is something that Tana didn't really need. After a couple of months of fruitless searching, she heard a rumour on the teacher grapevine that there was a branch of the lingerie shop Victoria's Secret in down town Beijing. Dragging Sarah along for company, they went in search of this elusive shop.

Finding themselves at the China World Trade Shopping Mall, they felt they had entered another planet because it was full of shops such as Gucci, Prada, Armani and the like. As expected, these shops were stocked full of the real deal and not the fake clothing found in the markets. As they walked around, they said they could literally smell the money that was floating about and they couldn't believe that anyone could afford the prices they were seeing. It did make us all wonder how long the country can remain officially communist with these prime examples of the capitalist shopping experience establishing themselves there. They felt that the Mall would only be frequented by foreigners, but the only place they saw a foreign face was in Starbucks as they felt this was the only place any of them could afford to buy something. Sarah felt that they were the scruffiest people in the Mall and was sure that they would be asked to leave at any time.

Going into one of the designer stores, they were amazed by the amount of sales assistants the shop had, especially as there was a real dearth of customers. All of the assistants were wearing black suits and looked like a cross between the FBI and bodyguards. The girls were constantly asked by one or more of these assistants if they needed any help as though they were receiving instructions through an earpiece. Sarah said that all this constant attention made them feel like criminals as they never seemed to have a moment to themselves just to look around. After examining quite a few pieces, they both came to the conclusion that the more expensive the piece of clothing was, the uglier it looked. It is for this reason that I haven't mentioned the store by name just in case they want to sue me.

If the Mall ever had a Victoria's Secret in it, it had long since gone. After stopping off at the nearby China World Hotel to seek help from the English speaking concierge, they were directed to a department store with a large lingerie section. When they arrived, the assistant didn't seem to understand that Tana needed a D cup. She kept offering Tana an A, B or C cups. It seemed that the assistant had only learned the first three letters of the alphabet, or no one had actually asked for this size before. Tana felt that the way the assistant was talking that she had invented a brand new letter. After much searching on their own, Tana found a couple of suitable bras and proceeded to spend over 1000RMB on them. Needs must I suppose, but surely it must have been cheaper to buy them in the US and ship them over.

Fashion Faux Pas - Not content with centuries of foot binding (a practice now thankfully outlawed), 21st century Chinese women have felt the need to continue with the tradition of foot torture. I could not be sure if it was vanity, idiocy or just a lack of appropriate footwear but more often than not you will see women walking in the most inappropriate areas in high heels or smart office/dress shoes. Examples of where this had seemed most ludicrous include climbing the Great Wall and hiking up the Fragrant Hills mountains. Kinky boots and stilettos were just not designed for these types of activities but try telling the Chinese that!

The Chinese sense of fashion amongst the young was reminiscent of a bad 80's film. Big hair (which no doubt used as much hairspray as it takes to put a permanent hole in the ozone layer), t-shirt (with a slogan on it of some description) very short white skirts and white shoes. There even seemed to be a uniform for anyone who was in a relationship and wanted to shout about it. They would wear matching T-shirts or a set where one would say 'Our love will' and the other 'Last forever'. We would never see couples out wearing them the wrong way round!

How Not to Handle a Situation – Chinese Style

By the end of June, everyone had finished teaching so the University had a short ceremony for all of the foreign teachers. All of the teachers received a small present to say thanks for all of their work over the previous semester. The guys received a Beihang tie, where as the women received a hideous Beihang scarf. Lu Ying knew that it wasn't the nicest present and told Sarah that she would be able to swap it for a tie if she wanted to. There was even an award for excellence in teaching which was a monetary bonus of a few thousand RMB. It would have been nice to have received one myself, but the rules stated that you had to have been teaching for two semesters before a teacher was eligible to receive it. Ray won one of the prizes, so we were all happy for him, as long as he took us out for drinks afterwards. The head of the University gave a short speech and it turned out that she was actually one of Doug's students. They took a group photo and read out all of the teachers names to thank you once again, but they forgot Tana which did give us something to laugh about. The frivolity soon stopped though.

After the ceremony, we were asked along with all the other teachers who were living in our building to stay behind as the SAFEA wanted to tell us that they were going to refurbish the apartments on our floor. This meant that we would all have to move out. This got a mixed reaction because they revealed that they didn't have enough apartments to put people in individually, so there would be some who would have to share. Not a problem for Sarah and I, and when I mentioned this, the Head of the University replied that 'I know of your situation' as though she was looking down her nose at us. I felt a little peeved by her snobbish tone as I thought I was being helpful. That'll teach me.

The timing of this announcement was poor because it was at this time that most people want to travel around, or even go home until the next semester started. Ginger Tom was particularly annoyed because his apartment had only been refurbished six months previously he was not in the best of moods anyway, as he had only turned up to the ceremony because his boss had promised him that he was receiving one of the prizes. He later told us that he had cancelled two private tutorials to attend this ceremony and he had lost 400RMB. As he didn't received one of the prizes, it was no wonder that he was pissed. Needless to say, no one was particularly happy with this arrangement and nobody wanted to move. We didn't see the point as we would be going home only a couple of weeks after the proposed date for us to leave Building 114.

This situation was a perfect example of how the Chinese system of democracy works. They said we had the choice to stay in our rooms whilst the decorations went on around us, but Ginger Tom pointed out they would no doubt kick us out whatever we said. It gave us the illusion that we had a say in matters but in the end, we didn't. The debate did become a bit heated in places and Ginger Tom's background as a lawyer began to show. The Head of the Uni said she knew that it was not in our culture to share rooms, but it would only be for a short time. Tom quoted all sorts of things from the contract that said we were entitled to our accommodation.

After Tom had paused for breath, Sarah asked about the internet. As we had paid in advance, she was concerned that we would lose it. The Head of the Uni replied that it would be up to us to sort this out which got everyone's back up even more. We were asked to give her an answer in a couple of days, but none of us were happy with the arrangement and walked out muttering to ourselves under our breath.

With the deadline up, Ginger Tom had told the SAFEA that he wasn't moving and they had said this was fine. He told us that he had had visions of returning from his trip back to America to find that all of his stuff was missing and he would never see it again. Doug went to SAFEA and they had said he would get a room on his own, but that we would be put up in the campus hotel and that the Flying College would have to pay for it, which we thought was a disgrace. SAFEA had caused these problems but were trying to get other people to sort out their lack of vision. We asked to have a look at the hotel room they wanted to put us in and it looked exactly the same as all of the other hotel rooms we had seen in China.

We turned it down because it didn't have access to the Internet and even though the Flying College said we could use theirs whenever we wanted to, we said we needed it at unsociable hours because we spent a lot of time using it to talk to our families back home. The room also didn't have a fridge in it, so we couldn't have milk for our breakfast cereal. After dismissing all of their previous suggestions, we left it with the SAFEA to sort us out with an apartment on a par with the one we already had.

The Sites, Sounds and Smell of Beijing #5

With a lot more time on our hands and wanting to avoid the 'moving apartment' arguments that were going on, we decided to do a bit more sightseeing. After a cursory glance at our Lonely Planet Guide to Beijing, we saw that there were plenty of places we fancied paying a visit to, and now was definitely the time to go out and see them.

Beijing City Wall and Ancient Observatory - There isn't a lot of this left and only in the southeast corner of the old city, near Beijing Railway Station, does any significant part of the wall remain. As with a lot of other Chinese landmarks, the remains of the wall have recently been restored back to the state they were when it was first built, no doubt in attempt to attract the tourist pound. The city wall was built around 1435, and it had nine gates, three of which are still standing. This wall stood for nearly 530 years and even survived WW2 almost intact, but in 1965 it was mostly demolished as part of Mao's Cultural Revolution when the 'We'll destroy the old world to build a new one' policy was in place.

On the south side of the wall, a park had been laid out enabling those visiting the wall to be able to walk along its path. This park was built as part of the restoration of the city wall but under the ground, there was some interesting archaeology to be found. It was in the later years of the 18th Century that the British and the Russians built some of the first railways in the country and the lines were laid where the park is now. In fact, the British built railway station is still visible at the southern end of Tiananmen Square, even though it had now been converted into a series of shops.

Some of the old railway tracks have been excavated as part of the restoration project and the original British built signal house from the early 1900's is still standing. It is now used as a place for the caretakers of the park to hang out and deposit their equipment. The modern railway was just to the North of the wall and runs parallel to the old one.

The wall ended with a fully restored gate which is listed in the Lonely Planet as the Southeast Corner Watchtower. As with all the other restoration work we'd seen throughout the country, the wall looked as thought it had been built yesterday. Looking to the West and down to the un-restored bits really enforced this and like the Great Wall, these were inaccessible to the tourist. The watchtower had a museum inside of it as well as, for some bizarre reason a gallery of modern art. If you like modern art, this is for you. As both of us have a real dislike for this sort of thing, we walked past this as quickly as we could.

The museum had some English panels in it, telling the story of the wall. This included the attacks on it by the army of the Eight Nation Alliance[54] during the last years of the Qing Dynasty. A point was made in the exhibition about the damage done by this army, especially the graffiti that the some of the soldiers etched into the brickwork. This graffiti is still visible on the towers' wall and whoever P Foot of the USA was, he has left his mark on history!

Not that far up the road, and mounted on a watchtower on the eastern end of what was the city wall, is Beijing's Ancient Observatory. According to the Lonely Planet, the original observatory was built in the days of Kublai Khan[55] as he used astronomy to plan his military campaigns. The tower was built between 1437 & 1446 and the astrological instruments were built by Jesuit scholars throughout the 1600's. They are allegedly a curious mix of Chinese and Western styles, but unless you are an expert in these things, I don't know how you could tell.

Not all of the equipment was located at the top of the tower. At ground level, there is another building containing more astrological instruments, including ones used for navigation. The building was also dedicated to more of China's attempt to say they did everything before everyone else. This was something that did appear in a good deal of the historical sites we visited. For any invention, there tended to be a plaque saying that some Chinese bloke did it first including football, musical notation and bureaucracy (if the last one is true, the

---

[54] The Eight Nation Alliance included armies from Austria-Hungary Empire, France, Germany, Italy, Japan, Russia, the United Kingdom and the United States. The alliance was formed in the wake of the attacks on foreign nationals and businesses by the Boxer Rebellion 1900. With the conclusion of the Alliance in 1901, the Imperial Government was forced to sign the unequal Boxer Protocol of 1901.
[55] Kublai Khan was the Grandson of Genghis Khan and the first Mongal to be Emperor of China.

world <u>really</u> thanks China for that!). For a country with a 5000-year history, they have a real inferiority complex.

Dead Mao and the Military Museum - Our visit didn't get off to the best of starts. It all started when we decided to go to the Mao Mausoleum or "Dead Mao" as we affectionately referred to it. We had risen early and along with Ray, we went to Tiananmen Square where Dead Mao resides. Unfortunately, when we arrived we discovered that he didn't like having visitors on Mondays. What made this more annoying was back in February during our first visit to the square, I had taken a picture of the opening hours sign so this sort of thing wouldn't happen. With time to kill, Ray and I decided to go to the Military Museum which was so important it has its own underground station. Sarah decided this was not for her and went shopping.

We had an absolutely fantastic time because their handling collection allowed us to sit in tanks, anti-aircraft guns and jet fighters. Mucking about on the tank was a great laugh, especially as I had taken along a lairy pair of shades that Ray and I wore as we took multiple photos of each other mucking about with the gun. I wanted to ask if this tank had been used in Tiananmen Square back in 1989[56], but I didn't think I would push my luck and the Museum staff would most probably not have entered into this anyway (well, they wouldn't would they!). We paid 5RMB for the privilege of sitting in/on the military hardware, but it was money well spent. The Imperial War Museum back in London never lets you do things like this, which is a shame really.

As could be expected from a Chinese museum, it was all part of the Communist propaganda machine (e.g. Mao never made a wrong decision during the civil war, it was unnamed others that did that, the Communists are seen as being heroic during World War 2 where as in reality, they did next to nothing but hide etc[57].) but in my

---

[56] Doug had been in the country during the 15th anniversary of the 1989 protests and he said that anyone seen wearing a black armband or taking photos in the Square on that date (5th June history fans) were harassed by the police. When I looked up the date, I fancied going down to the Square on the day but in the end, thought that staying in and chilling out was a much better option as it was a little on the warm side.

opinion; it was one of the better museums out here. Apart from its faults, it was very interesting and actually had a lot of information written in English. The objects had been treated with respect and it looked as though there had been a great deal of care taken to make sure it looked as good as it did.

There was so much weaponry on display, it was scary. There were fire arms from throughout history, machinery dating from before the Second World War until the modern day and a couple of galleries dealing with warfare during China's Imperial age. As usual, there was the obligatory anti-foreign propaganda blaming them for all of China's ills during the last days of Imperial rule instead of looking inwards. The most revealing bit of the museum was the section dedicated to the Korean War, or The War Against American Aggression as it was called above the entrance.

Unlike the rest of the Museum, we were not allowed to take photos and none of the captions were in English. It was though they were trying to hide something. It could be that they were criticising the same Western powers that are currently pumping millions into the country to maintain the morally bankrupt government. Mao would no doubt be spinning in his grave (if he had one) at the way the Government has prostituted itself to stay in power.

There was even a gallery showing all of the 'great' (and I use this term loosely) Communist leaders. I had come to expect images of Mao to show him as well fed, but all the other leaders were also shown with rounded stomachs as though the great periods of starvation that China has suffered whilst the Communist have been in power had not effected them. Funny that.

Natural History Museum Take 1 and around Tiananmen Square (Again) - The Natural History museum had an interesting write up in the Lonely Planet guide and sounded like fun. Again we got up early and headed to

---

[57] Well, this is not strictly true. The Chinese Communists tried to avoided large-scale combat against the Japanese, but instead fought a guerrilla campaign against them. With the official government weakening themselves by fighting a convential war, the Communists hoped that they would emerge from the war and be in a strong position to fight the Nationalists.

Tiananmen Square. This time we walked south from the square for quite a distance in the heat till we finally reached the museum. We asked the security guards where we bought the tickets from and they replied "closed". It turned out it that like Dead Mao, it was also closed on Monday's. Great! After this, we headed back to Tiananmen Square because there are still a lot of sights in and around it that we had yet to visit. The first one of these was the Imperial City museum. This was actually very interesting seeing how the city has changed down the years. They had a massive model based on the cities layout from about 300 years ago. We then decided to go to the Imperial Archives but when we got there, there were several builders hanging around and yes you've guessed it, it was closed because they were refurbishing it. Doh!

We then headed back to the Square, which is actually more of a rectangle but tell anyone around here that and they will get upset. As has been said before, walking around Tiananmen can be a real pain because as this is arguably the most visited place by tourists in the whole of China, the amount of people trying to sell things increases ten fold. For a change, we were accosted by random people trying to get us to visit their art exhibition housed in a building just off of the Square. As we had been warned we would be on the end of some hard selling techniques if we agreed to go for the viewing, we just kept on walking.

Anyway, back to the tourism. We went from the Imperial Archives to the Tiananmen Gate via a small park which was not listed in any of our guide books. This was a shame as it was beautiful. Security was very tight when we went to the gate as we were not allowed to take any bags with us. Maybe they feared we would throw propaganda from the gate into the Square, but as usual, no reason for this decision was forthcoming. On the gate, we ran into a young soldier who had brought his father and grandfather for a visit. The older men were both wearing green Communist style clothes with all sorts of medals attached. They were taking loads of pictures of each other so I motioned to them that I would be more than happy to take a picture of all of them. I think they

264

were all quite surprised that I had made this offer, but they all thanked me afterwards. The young guy even insisted in taking a picture of Sarah and I with our own camera to return the favour. After they had gone, I pulled out a piece of paper and stood in the spot Mao made his proclamation, declaring the formation of the People's Republic of Ross. As this is China, I hadn't filled in the necessary paperwork to get the microphone delivered on time.

Confirmation is being sort by the United Nations for statehood, but I am not holding our collective breath.

The Lama Temple – The Temple was originally used to house court eunuchs, but was converted to be the court of Prince Yong who would in turn become Emperor. After Yong's ascension to the throne, the Temple was given over to Buddhist monks. The Temple was very reminiscent of the Temple of Heaven park; an area of calm in a sea of chaos. Apart from at the most northern reaches, the constant noise from cars and their horns couldn't be heard. As this was still a functioning temple, people were continually lighting scented joss sticks that after a while become a bit too much for the senses to handle, though it didn't block out the almost ever present smell of pollution that we associated with Beijing. The Lama Temple was one of the few places we have seen that is critical of the Cultural Revolution and it was lucky to survive that time in China's history when so many other things were lost. Its survival can be attributed to Zhou Enlai, who was the Chinese Prime Minister at that time, so well done him.

Deshengmen - Deshengmen is what is left of one of the Northern gates of the old City Wall. Once we arrived at its base, we had some trouble working out how to get in. We arrived at the south side of the structure, which was where we thought the entrance should be. Even though we found a gate, it didn't look like it led anywhere in particular, so we walked around the whole tower before coming back to where we originally started without finding another doorway. Concluding that this was indeed it, we walked in. The gate itself housed a Monetary Museum that we also had trouble finding. Believing it would be in the tower itself, we climbed up

265

only to find an art gallery (what is it with the old city gates and art galleries), which wasn't that exciting. As we had climbed to the top of the tower, we thought we would have a look at the view but as usual, the pollution in the air meant we couldn't see very far. What we did see at the edge of the viewing platform were two portable toilets, which is always nice to see!

The Monetary Museum was back the way we had come, and would have been a bit more interesting to us, if some of the captions had been written in English. We really couldn't complain too much on this subject though because we can't think of any museums back home that have anything but English in them. The museum had coins and notes dating back hundreds of years and was interesting to see how beautiful their money used to be before they stuck Mao's ugly mug on it.

The Old Summer Palace – Having been to the Summer Palace, we thought that we should also go to the original version; which turned out to be not that far away from Beihang. Work started on its construction in the 18th Century and it was famous for its architecture, gardens, and works of art. It was known as the 'Garden of Gardens' and it even contained a few buildings that were of a European design, appealing to the Emperor Qianlong (1711-1799) who had a taste for the exotic. It is only the shells of these European style buildings that have survived, because the site was looted and burned in 1860 by an allied army from France and Britain. The Chinese buildings were more easily destroyed as they were made solely from wood where as the European buildings were made mostly from stone. This destruction is still seen today as symbol of China's humiliation during the last years of Imperial Rule, or that it how the Government uses it anyway.

Even though there has been some restoration work, it is unlike the Great Wall for instance, because it has not been returned to its original state. It actually looked more real because of the state it was in. It is old, it was destroyed and it still looks that way. It was very difficult to grasp the grandeur of it all from the models and pictures dotted around the site. The biggest downside for me was that the panels were very difficult to read as

266

the words were in gold and were put on an off white reflective surface. There were a good many references to the destruction, but by now I had come to expect this. It would have been nice to have some parity, by detailing the destruction Mao, and the Cultural Revolution had done to the ancient sites of China, but we can't have that. That would be showing Mao in a negative way. However, I digress. It was a beautiful site and very peaceful, even though there was always the dull drone of traffic in the background. The site was absolutely massive and we spent a good few hours there without covering any distance whatsoever.

The Saddest Thing I Saw in China #2

There were many things in China that raised my eyebrows. The persecution of Falon Gong practitioners (even though I didn't see any this first hand), the wanton destruction of the historic city to pay for the morally bankrupt government and the amount of people going through bins looking for items they could recycle, just to earn some money to buy food with, to name but a few.

However, this was nothing compared to the sight I saw one day in Tiananmen Square. It was a man sitting crossed legged up against the underground stations wall begging for money. Nothing out of the ordinary here because there were always loads of people begging in the areas the tourists would be going to but this one was slightly different. In front of him he had photos of himself as a younger man in good health and dressed smartly. This was a real comparison to the way he looked that day.

He was stripped to the waist and his torso was covered in scars, especially where his arms should have been. We had all heard the horror stories of working conditions in China and even though this is conjecture on my part, I could only guess that he had been in an industrial accident which had resulted in the loss of his arms. If the reports were too be believed, there is hardly any help given to people in his situation who must therefore find ways of supporting themselves. With all of the supposed prosperity around him, this really did ram home the human cost of China's economic growth.

Part 11 – Who Knows Where the Time Goes

<u>Chinese Trains</u>

Travelling through China by train was one of the things I wanted to experience during our stay. Due to the size of the country, this is the best way of getting around, especially when living on a budget and not in a hurry to get to the next destination. Those with money to burn or time not on their side, should really stick to flying. Travelling by train can also be a great way of practising your Chinese (which is what Ray would do) or having them practise their English on you (this is what tended to happen to me). Smoking was allegedly prohibited on the trains, but that did not stop people from having a crafty burn either at the end of the carriage, or in plain view of the passengers and train staff, who never did anything about it.

Before even considering getting on to the trains, you have to run the gauntlet of buying a ticket. There are two ways of doing this. The first, is to go to the railway station itself and join the ever present queue (which was always massive), and then there was no guarantee that the ticket you wanted, on the date you wanted it for, would be available. The second was to get a travel agent to get them for you, for a small finder's fee of course. The main reason for this is that you can only buy a ticket one way. This was a real pain in the backside and whenever we went anywhere by train (except Dandong), the first thing we would do was to queue up to get tickets for our next destination or the return to Beijing!

There were four classes of ticket available:

1) *The Hard Seat* - Not only was this the cheapest ticket, but definitely the most uncomfortable by a long way. We travelled this way to Shanhaiguan which is a relatively short journey by Chinese standards. The seats had a little bit of padding on them but after two hours, they became unbelievably uncomfortable but due to the overcrowded carriage, there was no room to move in. It took me about half an hour to get

the regain any feeling in my backside after this trip.

2) *The Soft Seat* - This was the one journey by train that we were not able to experience, even though we tried to buy them on the occasions when other tickets were not available. According to Ray (who managed to travel on the Soft Seat), the seats were massive and very comfortable with no one sitting or standing in the aisle.

3) *The Hard Sleeper* - This was the usual train journey because most of the majority of them took about twelve hours to complete. We would always try and catch the overnight train because sleeping through most of it made the whole journey seem a lot shorter than it actually was. Each of the hard sleeper carriages were made up of loads of door-less compartments that had six bunks divided into three tiers. Each bunk came with its own sheets, blankets and pillows which always seemed clean enough, but they did smell on occasion. The price of the bunks would be different depending on which one you were in. The bottom bunk was the most expensive with the top being the cheapest. We were advised that the middle bunk was the most preferable because all the other passengers in the berth and even some from outside of it would sit on the bottom one eating, drinking and making a mess. The top bunk meant that you had to negotiate the low ceiling but this was the one I found to be the best option for me as my feet could stick out of the end on the bunk and I would not have to worry so much about being knocked by people walking to the toilet. Some of the newer trains had air conditioning which was a bonus because they tended to be a bit of sweat box without it, making sleeping very difficult. Some of the non-conditioned trains would have a very small fan in the ceiling which could be of benefit to the person on the top bunk but of absolutely no benefit to those in the lower

ones, if it was in fact working. The cabin lights would be turned off by the guards because when travelling in cattle class, people can't be trusted to turn them off by themselves.

4) *The Soft Sleeper* – Now this was bit more like it. There were only four bunks and it was a room, with a door and privacy. The beds were bigger, seemed cleaner, and we were in control of the light switch. The one time we travelled on the soft sleeper, we had a TV at the end of the bed but other travellers told us this was not available on every train. One of the other benefits of travelling this way was the soft sleeper lounge. At the entrance to the lounge, there would be inspectors who wouldn't let you in if you couldn't produce the right ticket. The riff-raff needs to be kept at arms length you know. Once inside the lounge, there were loads of comfortable chairs, a private bar and on the occasion we visited one, it was very quiet. The waiting area for the 'hard' options was always crowded, smelly and very noisy. Getting a seat here was a rare occurrence so most people sat on the floor, which didn't look that clean.

I was really surprised by the number of different tickets you could buy, especially as I thought that this was meant to be a Communist country where everyone was supposedly equal. You learn something everyday.

The trains themselves had massive diesel locomotive which pulled about twenty coaches. A couple of the carriages we went on were double-deckers big enough for me to stand up without the need to slouch. I was told that there was a buffet car on all of the trains we went on, but I never bothered to walk along the train to check them out. I didn't really need to bother as there was always a member of the train staff coming along with a trolley full of food. This would include biscuits, fresh fruit or the obligatory massive pot noodle. Hot water was provided on every train in either a massive thermos flask style container or a tap in the wall, or even both. People would also bring along their own food and looking at the amounts some brought on board, it looked as though they were planning to feed the five thousand!

The toilets in the 'hard' carriages were just a hole in the floor and there were instructions stating that it should not be used whilst the train was stationary by the platform. You could easily tell when someone was using the loo at a station, and a most disturbing sight it was to boot! Washing the toilet involved pouring a bucket of water over the floor, but as it tended to be wet even before this occurred and as was the norm with Chinese loos, the smell of stale urine was ever present. This all added to the experience and nothing quite lived up to the view of railway sleepers passing beneath you at high speed as you take a pee. Thankfully I never had the need to perform the gymnastic display needed to stay upright whilst having a number two.

Ray had commented that he had had to do this on a train and it had been a little tricky. I must console myself that all over the Chinese countryside, there are little bits of my DNA degenerating at this very moment. The 'soft' option was a bit more civilised in that it had a western style toilet and a lockable door. We would always try and sneak up to those carriages if we really couldn't hold on any longer hoping that none of the guards would ask to see our ticket and thinking that because we were Western, we could afford to be there. Sometimes that view did have its advantages.

Inner Mongolia

Back in the days when we actually did something to justify the money the college was paying us[58] some of my students had said that a visit to Inner Mongolia would be a memorable experience. When Ray mentioned that he was organising a trip up there, we both said we would be interested in tagging along. We were joined by Eddie (a friend of Ray's mate California, who was over on a visit), a Chinese friend of Ray's who's English name was Sammy, Tana and Rob. Ray had been the main driving

[58] Even though we had finished teaching in early June, our contract lasted until 31st July. We were essentially on gardening leave for the remainder of our contract; but being paid to sit around is not as interesting as it sounds.

force behind the trip and he (with the help of Sammy because a native Chinese speaker is always helpful) booked this excursion through a travel agent near to the University. Due to the inherent racism or xenophobia (I am not sure which word serves the most precise purpose here) in China, all of us had to pay 100RMB more than the Chinese would have done, simply because we are not Chinese. If someone tried to do this at home, or nearly anywhere in the Western World, they would be sued to high heaven. There was no use complaining though because if we hadn't paid up, we wouldn't have gone.

Day 1 - Well, just the evening really. Our destination was Hohhot ('Blue City' in the Mongul tongue) which was an overnight train journey north of Beijing. It didn't look that far on the map but the train had to cross some mountains and would therefore take a rather tedious 12 hours to complete. Hard sleepers were the order of the day. We had all arranged to meet at 17:45 to go for a KFC, as it was quick and most importantly, not Chinese in any way shape or form. The day before we set off I had begun to suffer from another bout of Beijing Belly. It had been a bit touch and go if I would actually make it at all but Doug came up trumps producing some super strength diarrhoea type tablets that I hoped would keep everything nice and tight, if you know what I mean!

As always with a group of this size and especially one with Tana involved, we were running late so couldn't go for food. We rushed our way down to Beijing West Railway Station, which annoyingly is not on the underground system. Luckily for us, there was a KFC just outside the station so we purchased a load of take-outs. Ray then pulled out the tickets and told us that we would not be all together. As there was seven of us, we always knew that one person would be sleeping outside of the group and Ray did the honourable thing (feeling it would add to the experience if he were to sleep amongst the locals) and took the odd bunk. To pass the time before lights out, we played some card games and had a bit of a laugh. The lights in the carriage were turned off at 11pm sharp by the train crew so we took that as our cue to get some shut eye.

Day 2 - We woke up just as the train pulled into Hohhot. We met the local representative of the travel company outside the station and she seemed to be in a hurry to get us to the camp site saying we were going to be late, even though the train had arrived on time[59]. It was here that I asked where the nearest toilet was because my stomach was beginning to feel a little dodgy. Doug's super pills had worked wonders on the journey up, which was a relief as I didn't fancy trying to use the hole in the floor that passed for a toilet on the train.

There was a set of toilets near the station entrance but before I had a chance to step inside, the smell that was emanating from it was enough for me to realise that this was not the cleanest of establishments. In fact, the smell was so bad that I thought I was going to be sick. God knows what would have happened if I had actually gone in. What made things worse was that anyone using these loos was expected to pay for the privilege. I wish I knew what this money went towards, because it was definitely not on cleaning products.

I went back to the bus to ask the rep if there were any other toilets around and she looked less than happy with this because it meant a further delay for whatever it was that we were going to be late for. She then said that there would be some in the station in the hope that they would be a little cleaner. The toilets may have been but the Chinese people using them most definitely were not. When I eventually made it into a booth, the guy that had used it before had emptied his bowls but had forgotten to flush the damn thing.

I had never been comfortable using the squat toilets and I was beginning to get a little agitated by it all. After once again trudging back to the bus, I claimed that only a western toilet would do for my condition. Even though the tour rep was getting a little stroppy herself, she took us to rather the rather nice Regency Hotel,

---

[59] There was a definite trend for this to happen whenever we went anywhere with a Chinese host or tour guide. The trips to the Temple of Heaven, Forbidden City and Xi'an had all been the same. We had been rushed when our contracts had arrived when we were still back in Britain. Due to this rushing around, we would always end up arriving early to whatever destination we were expected to arrive at.

which was just up the road from the train station. I was allowed to us one of the western toilers in a guest room, but it turned out that I only had wind. With the emergency over (and thankfully the only one of the whole trip), we all got into the minibus for the trip to the grasslands. Ray (who had come into the hotel with me) and I had both agreed that it looked very nice. We made a note that if we were going to stay in a hotel after our return from the grasslands, we should consider this one. Arriving back at the bus, we had been joined by two Korean girls who were also planning to spend some time riding around on horses.

The journey took over two hours but half way through (where there was no chance of escape) the tour rep revealed it would cost an extra 200RMB each if we wanted to go horse riding. Understandably, we were not too happy about this. Ray started to examine the contract the travel agent had given us as he and Sammy had been led to believe that horse riding was included in our fee. They spent the remainder of the journey trying to negotiate a better deal but all that happened was the price was lowered to 100RMB and the time on the horses halved. Therefore, we didn't get any sort of a deal what so ever. Unsurprisingly, it also transpired that we were not in fact late for anything. It might have been that she wanted us there early so we would spend more money taking a trip on the horses. Well, this wasn't going to happen after what had happened in the bus now would it.

On disembarking from the bus we were greeted by the camp site owners who were dressed in traditional looking costume. They sang to us and passed out cups of Beijiu. None of us had any liking for the stuff, though out of politeness we drank some, but things were definitely not looking up! After the journey, a few of us needed the toilet (not me this time) and only a stones throw away, we could see a small brick structure with WC emblazoned on it in big red letters. It was literally a big ditch in the ground without a roof and a bit of concrete on the floor. At least there were separate areas for the different sexes but there wasn't room to be coy as the walls weren't tall enough to obscure the heads of the other people using it.

As it was outdoors in a baking hot day there were hundreds of insects and huge buzzy things flying around making the whole experience for those who actually dared go in there, less than pleasant. The almost unbearable smell didn't help either. Drains, sewers or even a cesspit; this toilet had none of those things. However when needs must, you just have to use whatever facilities are available[60].

The heat was repressive, but not as humid as Beijing and we all decided to take time that afternoon chilling out. I spent all of my time in the tent lying down and wishing there was some air conditioning. I felt that going out and doing anything in that heat would not have been beneficial to my health, but Tana and Rob (in their infinite wisdom) decided that they would go for a walk to a mound of rocks they could see on the horizon. Needless to say that when they returned, Tana looked a little on the red side and Rob had also broken his belt. It was on its last legs when we got here, so was not much of a surprise, but it didn't stop any of us making all sorts of hilarious japes about what had they really been up to when they disappeared over the horizon!

After the earlier revelation about the extra cost of the horse riding, Ray was given a few more things to get wound up about. The tour rep told him that for an extra fee, our dinner would be a special one. As they were not clear what this meant, and feeling that this should have been part of the all-inclusive price, he declined. None of us disagreed with his decision either. The second thing was that all seven of us were put into one tent, but were only given bedding for six. The two Koreans had been placed in a tent by themselves, which was exactly the same size as ours and with the same amount of bedding. Ray's blood was beginning to boil.

When it was time to venture out on the horses, it was significantly cooler but it did not stop the amazing amount of insects that populated the grasslands from

[60] A little later on, as we were waiting for lunch Sarah noticed that there were some buildings behind the dining tent with the words WC on them. She went to investigate and found proper toilets (Chinese style of course) with sinks and running water. You live and learn I suppose and no doubt that locals would have a good laugh at anyone who used the outdoor toilet.

landing on the horses or us. The horses didn't look the biggest any of us had seen and I was very especially worried that mine might collapse at any moment considering that I was by far the biggest and heaviest of the riding party. Whilst the guides showed us how to control the horses, this turned out to be a complete waste of time. They don't pay any attention to what we instructed them to do as they are conditioned to listen only to the guides. The guide controlled the pack by a series of grunts, clicks and shushing noises so even if we didn't want our horse to do something, I would to the instruction of the guide. This became very annoying, very quickly.

Tana's horse was a little feisty and had kicked out randomly throughout the early parts of the trip. Unfortunately for Sarah, as her horse was approaching Tana's from behind, it kicked out and connected with Sarah's ankle. Not being the most comfortable of riders, Sarah decided enough was enough, refused to go any further and wanted to go back to the camp. Sarah had learned that in China, the best way to get something done is to throw a bit of a strop. Her ankle turned out to be fine, but her nerves and confidence had been shot to bits. Having had two bad experiences on horses from her childhood, Sarah decided that her only contact with them from now on would be from afar.

One of our guides rode ahead and brought back some guy on a motorbike that proceeded to take Sarah back to camp. Sarah said that this was excellent and much better than the horse riding. Sarah left us just before the halfway point so she missed sitting in a Mongolian style tent and eating some local food. Being my usual adventurous self I didn't touch any of it, which Eddie said afterwards was a very good idea. It was here that we all noticed how sore our legs were from the saddles.

For the journey back, Tana was given Sarah's horse and one of the locals rode the fiery one back. Well, I say ride. I mean that he beat it with a strap which he continued to do for the remainder of the trip back. Animal lovers be warned, China is not the sort of place you want to come if cruelty to the animal kingdom is something you frown upon. We rode back the same way we had come and stopped at the site we had been promised. This turned out to be a random set of rocks. No one could or would tell us what was so special about this site either. A good place to take pictures; but not much else I am afraid.

Dinner was almost the same as lunch and none of the other tour groups seemed to be having anything different from us. We concluded that the idea of a special meal that they were keen to sell us earlier in the day was another ruse by the tour rep to get more money out of us and we were glad we hadn't fallen for it. A show was put on in the evening, which involved the people who ran the place dressing up once more in their 'traditional' Mongolian costumes to perform song and dance numbers. It had its moments but they were so badly out of tune, we all felt that we would have seen better performances at the local karaoke bar.

They also set off some fireworks, but being China, there was a total disregard for health and safety, as they seemed to make a concerted effort to hit the living areas with them. Remember, the accommodation was made of canvas and no doubt would have burned easily. One headed straight for Rob as he made his way out of the toilet, and I never saw our Australian friend move so fast again!

Ray and Sammy had not given up trying to improve our sleeping arrangements but after failing to obtain another sleeping area (allegedly they were all full even though we could clearly see that they were not), some of our number went and shared with the Koreans who were more than happy to help us out. As there was an absence of clouds that night, this was the first time we had seen the stars since we left Britain. The night was so dark that we could see the lights of the nearest town miles off in the distance.

Day Three - We were woken at some ungodly hour for breakfast and Sarah decided that filling up with a hearty breakfast would be a good idea whereas I decided that having as much sleep as possible would be beneficial. Before we left (and once again, we were told we needed to hurry as we would be late!), the locals put on a very short horse race and then showed us some native wrestling. I decided to stay in the mini bus to guard everyone's belongings, which saved me from being dragged up to wrestle myself, something I cannot say was true of Rob. After a few throws to the ground, he decided that wrestling wasn't for him. As we made our way back to Hohhot our two Koreans friends left us, as they were going on a trip to the desert. Good luck, we all thought!

The tour rep took us to a local temple (which looked very similar to the Lama Temple back in Beijing), and the Inner Mongolia museum. This was the same as nearly every other museum we had seen in China: propaganda for the Communist party with a few other bits of interest thrown in for good measure. It was amazing that anyone could actually believe what they were reading, because the smell of bullshit emanating from them is almost overpowering. The other bits of interest included some skeletons from a few prehistoric creatures as well as some bits on Genghis Khan who seemed to be a bit of a celebrity in these parts.

After we had finished, we were taken back to the Regency Hotel as we fancied a bit of luxury after our night in the grasslands. As she was leaving, the tour rep said she would drop our return train tickets at some point later in the day. After everything that had happened, Ray was keen to go to another hotel because he thought that the tour rep would get a cut from our stay, but we convinced him that as we were already here, we didn't know the town and the railway station was only a stones throw away that we might as well stay where we were.

Everyone looked really tired, so we all took some time out. Sarah and Eddie spent a good deal of this time looking out of our rooms' window at the building opposite the hotel where some Chinese guys were painting it from the roof downwards. They were both amazed that the Chinese considered the procedure for this safe as all that seemed to be between the painters and certain death was a piece of wood and rope. Once again, Health & Safety back home would have had a heart attack looking at this.

For dinner we went to a Mongolian style restaurant. It wasn't a restaurant in the traditional sense because the tables were in individual tents and they looked similar to the ones we had slept in the night. Unlike the previous day's accommodation, this one could have easily slept seven people and had air conditioning. The food was tasty, but we were quite surprised when they mentioned that they didn't serve rice. When we thought about it, we could see why it wasn't included in the Mongolia diet because the grasslands aren't conducive to its growing. When the bill came, the receipt came with a scratch off panel. Sammy explained to us that this was a receipt lottery and that if we were lucky, we could win some money. We didn't, but the panel did have 'Thanks' written in it. This was a great idea that could (and maybe should) be implemented in Britain. We arrived back at the hotel just as the heavens opened. Even as the rain fell, Ray had plans for a massive night out, but the exertions of the last two days had taken it out of us, and we all had an early night.

Day Four - Our train tickets for our return trip had still not arrived so Sammy spent most of the morning on the phone trying to find out where they were. We didn't have any plans for the day, but Sarah remembered that she had the phone number of a Chinese student (whose English name was Dot) whom she had ended up talking to in the Beihang Park one day. Dot was from Hohhot and said that if Sarah were to visit, she should get in touch. After making contact, Dot arranged for her father to bring her to our hotel. For the first part of our Dot guided tour of Hohhot, we were in the local milk factory, which was one of the biggest and most famous in China. It was surprising how vocal the support for this was (except for Tana who came from cow country back in the States) so we all went (including Tana who didn't want to get left behind). Dot's Dad drove some of us in his rather posh car, whilst the others went in a taxi that had been paid for by Dot's Dad to follow.

The milk factory was a right laugh. Dot organised a tour guide who first took us to see the cows being milked. This was as expected, except for the self milking machine. It was explained to us that when the cow wants to be milked, it steps into this machine and a computer milks it. No humans needed here. These particular cows were fed the best types of grass and this milk is only available for government officials. As you can see, Communism is alive and well in China. Anyway, we were actually given a batch of this to take home for ourselves in a presentation box. Most of the milk produced was long life (or UHT), but with slightly different process so it actually tasted better than the crap we get back home. We were given a presentation box of this milk (which the tour guide had allegedly paid for with her own money) and when we tried it on our return home, it just tasted like full fat milk. None of us could really see what the fuss was about.

In certain parts of the factory, we had to cover our shoes in plastic wraps so we wouldn't contaminate the place. My feet were too big for the standard foot covering, so they had to give me the ones that they normally handed out to put on your head. When they have finished packing the milk, it all went into a massive warehouse and all of the machines were computer operated. No humans needed here either. The tour guide told us that the loading systems were once used by the government to store missiles, but were now being used for more peaceful endeavours. One of our number said that it looked like something out of The Matrix, but I was more concerned as to how many missiles were stored in a warehouse as big as this. A frightening thought.

The tour guide didn't speak any English so Dot spent the whole time translating for us. Not only did this give Sammy a break, but it meant that Dot could show her Father that all the money he had spent on her education had not gone to waste. Dot's father had joined us on the tour and he had a big cheesy grin on his face for the entire time we were with him.

After lunch, Dot mentioned that she had taken classes in foot massage, so we all agreed to continue pampering ourselves with one of these. This was fantastic. Firstly, our feet were bathed and then washed. After this, they were massaged for about forty minutes. Paradise. On the walls were a series of diagrams drawn by the man who owned the place showing how the nerves in the feet were connected to the rest of the body. Dot told us that the masseur can tell what is wrong with a
280

person from massaging the feet by 'bubbles' (her words, not mine) under the skin. All very interesting!

After it was over, each of our masseurs told us what was wrong with us. Sarah had bad neck, a bad stomach (news to us) and a lack of sleep. For me, they said I had had a bad stomach and a bad back. I was actually surprised that that was all they said was wrong with me. Rob was the only other one I can remember and they told him he also had a bad stomach which he knew nothing about. This was about to change because by the end of the trip, he was beginning to suffer from the Beijing Belly. When they finished the foot massage they gave us a neck, back and bum massage too!

The train tickets had still not been delivered and Ray was getting concerned (as well as a good deal angrier about the whole thing). Sammy then received a phone call from the tour company. She told us that there were no tickets available for the 20:15 train that we had expected to be travelling on and that we would have to go on the 23:00. Ray was very annoyed about this as he had to be back in Beijing for 14:00 the next day to pick up another friend from the airport. To let off steam and have a look around Hohhot, we went for a walk.

We ended up in a street market where Rob was able to buy a new belt so he no longer had to keep pulling his trousers up. As we left the market, we came across a park that we decided to walk around in to kill some time. There was a selection of fairground rides here, but none of them looked particularly well maintained so we decided not to go on any of them. In fact we're pretty sure that the place would be condemned as unsafe by western standards.

Dot recommended a restaurant for us and we went there for dinner. However, she said that she wouldn't be joining us, which was a shame because we wanted to buy her something to say thank you for all of her help during the day. On the way there, we were called by the tour rep to say that our train tickets were ready and it turned out that the train was not at 23:00, but 23:57. Ray was almost ready to explode and vowed to get some sort of revenge when we returned to Beijing. With more time to kill, we made our way back to the

Regency and managed to book a room for a couple of hours just to chill out. Some of our number used this as an opportunity to use a shower and a western style toilet before the 12 hours train journey back.

Overall, it was this a brilliant experience and an excellent laugh, but it was a shame that our dealings with the tour guide/company were the only real low points. Ray was not at all pleased with the service and was most annoyed by the fact the tour rep had been so smug about the way she had conned us and made life difficult. This left us in no doubt that China is all about ripping the traveller off, especially if you are Western.

There were some other things that stuck in the mind from this trip:

1) The amount of staring we had aimed in our direction. I was convinced that all of the Chinese people were looking at the girls, but everyone else in the group said that they were actually looking at me. The sight of a tall bald Westerner isn't an everyday occurrence, especially in the Wild West that is Inner Mongolia. I am actually thankful that I am not famous because I did not find the experience to my liking.

2) Apart from the odd tourist trap enclosure, there was a whole lot of nothing for miles on end. The plains were just a massive expanse of empty space apart from grass and the odd tree. Contrast this to Beijing where personal space is almost non-existent. This was the darkest night I think I have ever seen because once the site lights were turned off, it really was pitch black.

3) Genghis Khan is the Mongolian equivalent of Chairman Mao. His face was on everything you could possibly imagine and the similarities don't stop there. Both were mass murders and warmongers, but what was bizarre was the complete lack of Mao related bits and pieces.

* * * * *

Random Jet Fighters on Public Display

Having grown up in a country where there are plenty of statues and public monuments on public display, I thought I had seen everything. This view changed once we started travelling around where we would see the rusting hulks of fighter jets randomly dotted about. In Shanhaiguan we saw one on the beach and in Hohhot there was one in the middle of a housing estate. There were some more but for the life of me; I cannot remember the names of the places I saw them in. After pointing this out to our social group, they all started to notice them. As far as I could tell, they were all MiG-15's (or J-2's as the Chinese called them when they built them themselves).The engines had been removed and all the planes showed signs that they had been used as a trampoline in their retirement. No one seemed to know why they had been put on display like this and to me; it was just another really bizarre thing to do.

Moving Home

When we returned from Inner Mongolia, we found that an earthquake had hit Beijing. One of our fellow teachers said that it was strong enough to shake him out of his bed. Our feelings that Building 114 wasn't the safest of buildings weren't helped by this news, especially as it already had loads of cracks in it from just standing still. We were glad that we were in a train many miles outside of the capital when the earthquake hit. The weather continued to be on the warm side topped off with some violent storms, one of which seemed to be raging directly over our heads as it woke both of us up. One of these deluges of rain caused a part of the road to collapse near the North Gate. Chinese workmanship at its finest!

We had tried to delay moving out of Building 114, especially as we would be going home in less than a month, but SAFEA were adamant that we had to go, so after much mumbling under ones breath and pouting a bit, we did. When we went to have a look at it, we were surprised to find out how big and spacious it was compared to the one we were in. It had two bedrooms, a dining area, a kitchen but a very small toilet/shower room. In fact it was so small that it would be possible to use every facility in the room from the one spot. Another downside to this otherwise positive relocation was the doorways had been measured to accommodate the average Chinese height. Our neighbours must have wondered what the regular thudding noises were, but needless to say, I spent a good deal of my time nursing a headache. Nearly all of the light switches had been put on the walls upside down so instead of saying 'On', they said 'No'.

Other positives were:

1) The double bed which the first one we had seen in China. This made a pleasant change after the one and half size bed we had had before.
2) We even had our own key to the wash room which meant we could wash our clothes whenever we wanted to.
3)

These turned out to be the accommodation for married couples. If only Sarah and I had been married when we had come to China, we would no doubt have been put in one of these. That would have been a shame though as we wouldn't have had the spare apartment for our friends, and would not have spent as much time with the other teachers.

I was a little bit sad to be moving out of our apartment that had been our home for the past four months. I thought that the day we moved out would be the day we came home. As we were only going to be in the married quarters for just under a month, we never really unpacked and spent our time living out of our suitcase. The move didn't do down well with everyone and Ginger Tom decided that he had really had enough of all the bullshit that comes with living as a foreign teacher in China and went back home to the States. Even though Doug was losing an acquaintance of a couple of years standing, the blow was cushioned by the amount of Western food and other luxuries Tom gave him.

Dinner on Dean Tang

Eating good food was very much on the agenda. A week before, Dean Tang had asked me (even though Tana and Sarah had been in the room at the same time)

284

where I would like to go for dinner as a way of saying thanks for all our hard work. Doug had said that the Dean would take his teachers to a German restaurant in the city and as we hadn't been (or actually knew where it was), I suggested we should go there. We all thought it would be nice to go out to dinner with the Chinese and not have food ordered for us that no one in their right mind would want to eat. It turned out that this was Dean Tang's favourite restaurant in the whole of Beijing and he was very pleased that I had requested it. He promised a night of good food and plenty of beer. A perfect night out if you ask me!

The restaurant was in the Lufthansa Building, which I had seen on many an occasion as I drove past on my way to another Drifter game. Walking in it for the first and only time, I was struck with the way in which the place seemed to ooze wealth. This was shoppers paradise, but only if you had the money. Along with Dean Tang, we were joined by Mr. G, Mrs. Lu and Emily. We let Dean Tang order, and he instantly asked for two massive plates of mash, salad, sausages, sauerkraut, bread and pate. The food was amazing and the beer was to die for (and at 70RMB for half a litre, it should have been). Everything the restaurant sold had been imported from Germany and it was a refreshing change to drink something other than the Chinese beer.

The Dean had heard us talking about eating fish and chips at home and decided that he should order some of this as well. We really should have learned our lesson from the previous occasion we had dined with the Dean because by the time it arrived, we were beginning to feel a little full around the edges. The German beer was affecting us more than we thought. Mrs. Lu and Emily really struggled to finish their beers (which I thought was a bit of waste considering how much it cost). Mr. G had decided that he would try and keep up with Tana, but he failed dismally. She only had three beers and I had to help Mr. G out by finishing his. He had a big drunken grin on his face for the rest of the evening whilst the two ladies were falling asleep.

After the meal, Dean Tang had a moment of genius and said that he was taking us all to Häagen-Dazs.

Häagen-Dazs was as expensive as the restaurant and we estimated the whole night cost about 3000RMB for the eight of us. That was almost the same as our monthly wage. After stuffing ourselves full of ice cream, we made our way back to Beihang. This was where the only down side to the evening occurred (because being us, there had to be one). Our taxi driver decided to start the journey before I had put my right leg in the car. The back wheel of the cab ran over my foot. This was very painful but luckily, nothing was broken.

We might have been paid less than the majority of the other Western teachers at Beihang who were earning 6000RMB, but the perks of working at the Flying College were better. This and trips to Xi'an saved us a load of money and gave us moments to remember, if not always for the right reasons.

Tianjin to Dalian

After a few days of inactivity, Sarah was getting itchy feet and decided that we needed to get away from Beihang. Unbeknownst to me, Sarah had armed herself with a list of destinations and possible train times and marched down to the ticket office early one morning with plan A,B.C,D and E for the 'Escape from Beijing'! Eventually after exhausting all options for A, B and C, the ticket clerk finally had tickets available for plan D which was Tianjin[61], a city about an hour away by train.

Sarah proudly arrived back at the apartment with the news that I would be joining her on a little journey. What really woke me out of my slumber was the fact that we needed to leave Beihang at 6:00am to get the train. Springing into action, I rang my fellow Drifter, Paul who lived in Tianjin. We told him the time we were turning up and asked if we could stay the night in his flat.

---

[61] Due to the Treaties of Tianjin signed in 1858, the port was opened up to foreign trade. Concessions were created with the British and French being the first to establish self-contained areas of control. These areas would contain barracks and it was the presence that would cause later hostilities and resentment. Concessions were later formed for Japan, Germany, Russia, Austria-Hungary, Italy and Belgium. Its importance as a centre of trading was helped when a railway line was built connecting Tianjin to Beijing.

He was more than happy to put us up and also said that he would be available to spend some time hanging out.

    Day 1 – Tianjin - I was told by Sarah that the train journey was very pleasant, because I fell asleep as soon as I sat in my chair. Sarah spent the time reading the Lonely Planet to see what we could expect in Tianjin but the next stop on our travels. When we walked out of Tianjin East Railway Station, the first thing that caught our eye was a rather extraordinary looking clock. It was a free standing monstrosity located over the road from the entrance. The clock face was actually a reasonable size, but the rest of it was a horrible metal structure that had two arms coming out of the side with one facing down and the other upwards. The second thing to catch the eye was the amount of taxi drivers who came up to us offering us their services. Even when we walked away from them, a couple followed us. Only after about five minutes of ignoring them were we finally left in peace. Sarah told me that she had read about the ferry which goes from Tianjin up to Dalian and that would be an interesting experience, especially after all the train journeys we had completed recently.

    I rang Paul who said he would be able to meet us in about an hour. With time to kill, we thought we would check out some of the local area. It didn't take us long to stroll into what used to be the Italian concession. It was a bit strange seeing architecture that looked so out of place. One minute, we were walking through your typical communist designed high-rises and the next; we might as well have been in Europe. We would love to have examined this area in more detail, but most of it was boarded up for renovation work so we made our way back to the station.

    Meeting up with Paul, we told him that we wanted to book some ferry tickets. He said he knew of a travel agent so we jumped in a taxi. Our journey wasn't helped by the driver, who didn't know which stretch of the road the travel agent was down. To be fair to the man, it was a very long road. When we eventually arrived, we were the centre of attention because there were seven assistants ready to help us out. After much debate, contradiction and reduction of the numbers of staff trying to help down to one, we were told that the only ferry tickets available would cost 380RMB plus their fee of 100RMB. We decided that this was far too much especially as they wanted us to pay up front and we would have to go to the ferry port ourselves to pick up the tickets. Essentially, they were telling us that we were paying them 100RMB to make a phone call. We made our excuses and left.

After this, we decided to stay overnight with Paul and then make our way to the ferry port and buy the tickets ourselves. We also decided that if we couldn't get them, we would just make our way back to Beijing. The exterior to the building Paul's flat was in was your typical Chinese block of flats (a grey, concrete monstrosity) but the interior was very modern and western looking. It was nice to see fixtures and fittings we hadn't seen since we left Britain and made us feel homesick once again. We parted company with Paul who had to do some work in the afternoon and made our way to Binjiang Dao, one of the major shopping streets. This was no different from Beijing (loads of Western shops selling goods at Western prices) so we decided to check out the Antiques Market.

This was a real highlight of the trip. It was in a hutong area and this added to the feel of the place. The shops were filled with all sorts of goodies including an old gramophone with a selection of pre-war Chinese opera 78's, loads of artworks and sculptures as well the obligatory Cultural Revolution posters. The only difference between these posters and ones I had seen previously was the layer of dust and the rips in corners as though they had been ripped from the walls. These looked like the real deal instead of being a reproduction.

The shop that took my fancy the most was full of all sorts of electronic and military goods. There were sniper sights (no rifles though), jet fighter pilot helmets and early mobile phones; that were the size of a brick and only weight lifters could carry! This shop also had what looked like a genuine Red Guard bag from the Cultural Revolution that I just had to have. We only thought it was genuine because it smelt old, and it didn't have a pocket for a mobile phone like the ones I had seen in the tourist markets.

After finishing there, we had a look at our location in the Lonely Planet and saw that there was nearby Hyatt Hotel, so we thought we would chance our arm and see if we could book the ferry tickets there. We walked into the reception looking as scruffy as possible and no one batted an eyelid, nor were we asked to leave for lowering the tone as it was all a bit posh. It must have been because we are Western and they thought we must have some money somewhere. The receptionist directed us to the Business Centre where we were shown into an office where a lady asked us in perfect English how she could help us. The lady was unbelievably helpful, especially as we were not guests at the hotel, but luckily for us, we were never asked this question.

She phoned the ferry ticket office, booked the tickets for the time we wanted and wrote down instructions for a taxi driver to take us to the ticket office to collect them. The tickets were almost 100RMB cheaper than the ones we had tried to book at the travel agent, and there wasn't a charge for booking them either. We both mentioned that we were quite concerned by the weather as it had been bit stormy earlier and Sarah particularly so as she had read that the Dalain ferry had been prone to sinking. Sarah asked if the ferry still sailed in bad weather which caused the lady and her colleague to start laughing, but it didn't stop her from ringing the ferry office once more to ask them the question. What service! The woman told us that if it was "Eight degree wet, the shit doesn't sail". We thought we knew what she meant, but we did have to bite our tongues stop us from laughing.

Walking back out of the Hotel, we asked the concierge to hail us a taxi. Being the Hyatt, these were a little bit more expensive than the normal ones, but they were still comparable in price to Beijing taxis. The ticket office was quite straight forward and it turned out that they actually offered a coach service to the ferry port for only 10RMB. We booked our tickets for this there and then. Feeling relieved that this was all out of the way we thought that we would check out some of the other concession areas.

We didn't have too far to walk. Like the Italian concession we had been in earlier, this was a real contrast the rest of the city. Some of the buildings reminded us of home and Richmond upon Thames in particular. There was a metal horse and carriage that Sarah took great pleasure sitting in, but we couldn't find any rhyme or reason why it had been put there. The local tourist board had also done a great deal of research because any property in this area that had famous residents during the concession era had a plaque put on the wall.

The only one that caught my eye was that of Eric Liddle, the Scottish Rugby Union international and one of the main characters in the film 'Chariots of Fire'. I had known that he had died in China but didn't realise that he had actually been born in Tianjin. It was a great pleasure to stand outside that house, but a little saddening that it was unoccupied and in need of some restoration. We finished the tour at the Earthquake monument. We only knew that it was such a monument because that was how it was listed on our map. We couldn't see a single sign that would have shown us what it actually was.

Stopping off at a supermarket to pick up supplies for our ferry journey, we were called by Paul who suggested that we go out to a bar he liked. The bar didn't actually look like it was anything other than a closed building. There wasn't a sign outside, no lights on and all the windows were boarded over. How they ever did any business was anyone's guess but when we walked inside, it was obvious that this place was the haunt of the foreign community because the only Chinese faces in the place were behind the bar. We didn't stay long because we were all knackered. It had been a long day and the constant muggy heat had really taken it out of us.

Day 2 – Tianjin - It turned out to have been rather fortunate that we had managed to see everything that we wanted to see in Tianjin the day before, because this was a complete wash out. We both struggled to think of times when it had rained this hard during the day before. Granted, we had seen plenty of massive rain storms in our time in China but they only seemed to happen at night. It meant that we were able to sit back

290

and chill out for the afternoon. We thought we had left Paul's to catch the coach in plenty of time but due to the amount of rain, the roads had become grid locked and we were quite concerned that we would not make it to the bus before it left. The cab driver guaranteed us that we would be there on time and he was as good as his word as we arrived with about two minutes to spare.

When we stepped on the coach there didn't seem to be any spare seats until we noticed that they had fold down seats in the aisle which we duly sat on. No one quite packs them in as well as the Chinese. The coach journey was a real tester on the backside as the seats were quite hard, the roads were very bumpy and the suspension wasn't up to the job but it did drop us off at the ferry terminals entrance. We didn't have to wait long for the ferry to leave and we knew it was time to board when we saw a massive plume of smoke coming out of the ships stacks.

The cabin was as basic as you could get. It had eights bunks and nothing else. Sarah was also quite worried because our cabin was on the lowest deck and the water line almost covered our port hole. If the ship were to sink, there would be no chance of us surviving. The stairs to the higher levels would not have been able to cope with the amount of people trying to use them and would have been a re-run of the Titanic, but without the subsequent movies. I was particularly happy to discover that I was sharing a room with six women for most of the evening, until some random bloke took up the spare bed later on. I was a little upset because I had my eye on that bedding and was going to pinch it. My annoyance was compounded by not being able to get to sleep for a couple of hours and matters were not helped by the fact that the girl in the bed next to me kept farting. Tianjin was a very nice place but the abiding image of the place for me was the numerous condom vending machines that were dotted around in public places. We never saw anything like this anywhere else.

Day 3 – Dalian - We arrived in Dalian at 08:30 and a bus took us from the ferry to the main terminal. In a complete contrast to rain in Tianjin, it was a lovely sunny day with the odd cloud in the sky. Once outside the

291

terminal, we tried in vain to get one of the numerous taxi's that were lined up to take us to the train station. At first, none of them believed that we wanted to go there because they kept pointing at other areas on our map that they thought we should go to first. Eventually, we found one that would take us to where we actually wanted to go (I thought that's what taxi's were for in the first place), but he insisted that we pay 20RMB and refused to use the meter. Knowing from experience that we were going to get ripped off, we walked away from the terminal and quickly found a taxi that would take where we wanted to go using the meter and it cost significantly less.

As usual, the station was heaving and the queues were massive. Once more, Sarah had prepared a list of train times and plans A,B,C and D for onward destinations and more exciting adventures. Unfortunately, the only train tickets we were able to get to any of our proposed next destinations was back to Beijing that night. I managed to continue my now semi-official tour of China's KFC's by having a quick Chicken burger for breakfast. I did feel that after eating at so many KFC's that I should try and make a Morgan Spurlock style documentary on how KFC is taking over China because they really were everywhere. They seemed to be so popular that every other fast food chain served them. Going back on this day meant that we would be able to say goodbye to Ray, who was planning to fly back to the US.

Over breakfast, we had a quick look at the Lonely Planet to work out which sights we would like to visit, and Sarah got very excited when she saw there was an Aquarium with a whale and dolphin show. The impressively titled "Polar Aquarium and Tiger Beach Park" was a real treat. In fact, the only things that looked poor were the Polar Bears, who were a bit on the sad side, lying around in their rather small enclosure. The diagram inside the Aquarium showed three cross sections of floor detailing where each exhibit/fish were. We found floors 1 and 2 no problem, but we couldn't find any stairs, lifts, or elevators taking us to the third floor.

We walked around the aquarium several times each time hoping to find the hidden passage that would take us to the next level. After getting really dizzy wandering around, we looked long and hard again at the diagram and realised that there weren't three floors after all but that there were two cross sections of the second floor. We saw the whale and dolphin show, but the thing that really stuck in the brain, was the sign behind us showing a child pissing on the ground and a red line going through it. Obviously they had had a problem with children using the wall we were standing next to as a toilet.

The Tiger Park surrounded the aquarium so it was quite difficult to miss. However, it wasn't the most interesting of places especially when the temperatures reached westerners meltdown levels. One thing that did catch the eye was a zip line over the bay that you could abseil down. After watching a few Chinese guys do this, it still looked appealing but the one major factor that stopped either of us doing this was all of these guys ended up going into the water. As I weighed considerably more than the average Chinese person, I knew that I would be drenched through by the time I reached the other end so we knocked this on the head. With lunch time approaching, we made our way back into town for a bite to eat. We also wanted to work out what to do next.

After consulting the ever useful guide book, we made our way to the Labour Park. On entering the park, we saw a massive football. One of the two things we knew about Dalian before we went there was that their football team (Dalian Shide) were considered to be the Manchester United of Chinese football. Not the most popular club but definitely the most successful since the creation of the super league. The other thing we knew was that in an attempt to stamp out the practise of spitting, the local Dalian government would fine anyone caught doing it 50RMB. In the remainder of China (except when I was playing football), I had refrained from spitting but in the middle of the Labour Park, a fly flew into my mouth so as a reaction, I spat it out. Realising my error, I waited for the spitting police to turn up to fine me but they never materialised. Not wanting to stay in one place too long just in case, so we moved on.

At one end of the Labour Park was a hill where any visitor can either walk up to the top or get a chair lift to catch this wonderful view of the city. As per previous form, we took the chair lift. We had read that on top of the hill was a toboggan ride which would take us back down to sea level and we both fancied a go on this. When we arrived at the entrance to the ride, it turned out that it wasn't much of a toboggan but more like a plastic sledge with a pole in the middle that acted as a break.

This was a really cool way of getting back down to sea level as the run crossed over the main four-lane road that went through the park on the way down. I went, but a coach load of Russians had pipped us to the post and jumped on their toboggans first. Intent on catching their descent on video, they went very slowly so as not to drop it. Therefore whilst it was still fun, it wasn't quite the speed rush I had been expecting, but I wouldn't be surprised to find that I am now starring as the angry foreigner waving his fists and gesticulating in a short Russian home movie.

With a couple of hours to spare and nothing else taking our fancy for a visit, we decided that the smell of our body odour was too much for us to bear so we booked into a hotel for an hour and had a shower. This was just what the doctor ordered and Sarah was most pleased as she felt that her hair had developed an eco-system all of its own. Feeling refreshed and after grabbing some dinner, we made our way to the train station. As usual it was packed, but we knew when our train was coming in because the Tannoy played some rather annoying music to let us know that it was turning up.

The Sites, Sounds and Smell of Beijing #4

After our journey along the coast, we realized how little time we had left before we returned home. This was our cue to pull our fingers out, have a look in the Beijing Lonely Planet and visit those places that took our fancy.

The National Museum of China - The blurb said that in the past, this Museum had been prone to closures at unpredictable times, because the Government always has to revise its own history to make everything look fine and dandy[62]. Allegedly it was not open at all between 1966 and 1978 as everything was changing so fast due to the Cultural Revolution and the all of the fall out that came along with Mao's death they couldn't keep up!

On the entrance steps a massive countdown clock had been erected for the 2008 Olympics, so that everyone can see how many weeks, days etc there were until it started. The Olympics start on 8th August 2008. The number 8 may well be considered a lucky number in China but neither of us envied any of the competitors running in Beijing during the summer heat. Running at night or at a cooler time of year might be preferable. The outside was your typical Communist austere grey. It really would have benefited from some decoration or demolished and replaced with something else to make it more appealing to look at. We went into the special exhibition area which was all about the Incas. It was amazing to see the dazzling array of artefacts; proving that the Spanish Conquistadors hadn't destroyed everything to do with that civilization.

There was the obligatory souvenir shop located at the end of the exhibition, but it seemed to be selling more copies of the Terracotta Army soldiers than anything else. In fact, the same boxed set of five warriors, that I'd bought for 10RMB in Xi'an, were on sale in the shop for 60RMB. What a rip off, as they still looked as cheap and nasty as they had before. Most of the museum was closed, but the exhibitions on Imperial China were open and brilliant. As none of the captions were in English, it did make most of it impenetrable, but the artefacts spoke volumes by themselves.

Beijing's Natural History Museum - The only way to follow this up was with a visit to Beijing's Natural History Museum. The Lonely Planet had mentioned that it was full of the usual stuff; skeletons of prehistoric

[62] If that was the case, they wouldn't have had to keep changing it would they.

animals and early humans as well as more modern animals in containers of formaldehyde. The biggest selling point though was the exhibits of real human cadavers. We both found the place a bit boring but we continued looking on every floor and exhibition hall in the Museum without actually seeing the cadavers. Quite a few of the exhibition halls were closed for refurbishment when we were there, and we thought that this one had suffered a similar fate. We left disheartened.

On exiting the Museum, we saw a small sign for an exhibition and thought we would stick our noses in to see what it was all about. It turned out to be the exhibition of human cadavers and body parts. We both found this to be pretty disturbing. All of the exhibits were housed in tanks of preservation fluid and ranged from individual limbs to whole bodies! All of the full body exhibits had a plastic bag covering the face of the poor unfortunates who had been put on display. There were also foetuses, which was just as disturbing. We were shocked to see that families had taken their young children into an exhibition like this, but on reflection, why shouldn't they have? This was all a bit too much for our Western eyes though and we were glad that we had not gone into this place having just had something to eat, but we must confess it didn't stop us from going for lunch straight after!

It was whilst ordering our lunch (in a well known chain of Western Chicken restaurants) that I realised that I had been in China too long. As I was standing at the counter, the assistant asked me, in English, what I wanted. In my mind, I thought that she had spoken to me in Chinese and turned to Sarah to see if she had any idea what had just been said. Sarah could only look at me quizzically and say that the assistant had spoken to me in English. Feeling a little embarrassed, I could only apologise for my obvious lack of listening skills.

Dead Mao Part Deux - After our poor choice of day the last time, we wanted to go and see the body of arguably the greatest mass murderer in history; we thought that we should go on a day that it was actually open. Ray and I were keen to go, but Sarah was feeling a bit worn out (or just couldn't be bothered) so she decided to stay in bed. Mao had supposedly said that he didn't want to end up on public display like Lenin had been in the Soviet Union, but final wishes and what happens to you after you are dead, are two different things! We left early in the hope of avoiding the crowds, but by the time we got to the Mausoleum, it already had a massive queue snaking around it.

Even though the weather was its usual hot self, the queue was so long that it stretched from the front door almost around to the back of the building. The authorities do not allow bags or cameras in, but we could leave any items like this in a storage area for the princely sum of 30RMB! As Ray didn't want to pay this, because it is a bit over the top, he stayed out of the line and waited for me to come out the other side.

The whole thing smacked of a money making exercise. The mausoleum was free, but I had to pay for a paper guide before being allowed to enter. In the entrance lobby, there was massive statue of the man himself with flowers placed at his feet. These could be rented at the front door and bringing your own was strictly forbidden. The body itself looked like it was made of wax and a nasty golden hue was on the face. I couldn't really tell if this was from a spot light or that he actually looked like that; because no one was allowed to stand still! Once past the body, there was the obligatory Mao gift shop with everything a person could possibly want with the man's smiling face on it. There were a few other rooms in the building that could be visited detailing the exploits of other Communist leaders. No doubt the ones that didn't fall out of favour for some reason or another. I didn't bother with any of these as I just wanted to leave. There were rumours going about the place that Mao would finally be laid to rest in the ground before the 2008 Olympics because the Chinese authorities felt that they would lose face with the rest of the world when it was known that they had a dead body on public view. Another rumour is that the body disintegrated long ago and that it is a wax work on display.

On our way out of the square, I thought I would pay a visit to a site that's not listed on the tourist maps. It was one of the cleanest, if not THE cleanest toilet in

China. It was just off of Tiananmen Square, next to the Museum of Chinese History. Doug had told me about it and after visiting some of the standard (and rather disgusting) Chinese toilets. I thought that it would make a nice change to visit a classier one. I was not disappointed. It had marble floors, it had obviously been cleaned on a regular basis and the smell was not as potent as mustard gas. To cap it all, there was a Mao souvenir shop at the entrance. I did check to see if they had some toilet paper with Mao's face printed on it, but they didn't which was a shame. I could see why, as this might be seen as being a little disrespectful, but everything else seemed to have Mao's cheery face stamped on it so why not?

Going Bye-Bye #2

On a sad note, we said goodbye to Ray, Tana and the remainder of the restaurants outside of the West Gate. Tana was planning to stay in China for another six months to continue teaching at Beihang, but she wanted to spend the time off in the summer to visit Western China. A few of her students had said they would look after her, but Tana's planning was its usual self, as she seemed to be taking the biggest bag in her collection for the trip when a small backpack would have sufficed. We went with Tana for her goodbye meal outside the West Gate, and this was the last time we were able to eat out of it because over the next few days, the whole place was closed down and the demolition crews moved in with a vengeance. It was a shame seeing all of the nice little restaurants we had spent so much time and money in, being reduced to rubble. I am sure there wouldn't have been a dry eye from our students, as this was the location of one of the hotels that they had used to spend some quality time with the girlfriends they shouldn't have had!

Ray had decided not to continue teaching and concentrate on his business activities, but just as we were going to his farewell dinner, he received a phone call from an English-speaking radio station based in Beijing asking him to come in for an interview. He had only applied on a whim, and his interview was only a few hours before he had to be at the airport. Needless to say, he got the job and so his long awaited return to the US only lasted for a couple of weeks before he returned to China to broadcast his particular brand of radio over the airwaves.

The Saddest Thing I Saw in China #3

We always joked that any non-descript meat in our food was once somebody's pet, but the sale of animals was one of the things that disturbed me most during my stay. Xizhimen station was a great place to people watch but it was split in two and you had to walk a little distance to get from one part to the other. It was a busy station so it was the perfect place for street sellers to show off their wares. On our early visits, it was trinkets regarding the Olympics, but later on, we started to see people selling animals for pets. The animals were kept in what can only be described as terrible conditions. Turtles were in washing up bowls which were full to overflowing. The water they were kept in was full of excrement and if they did escape, the seller would just pick them up and put them back into the bowl or kick them back in with their feet. Kittens and puppies were also up for sale. The kittens were kept in cages that were not big enough for them to move around in. The puppies didn't even have it that good.

The seller would usual have one in his hand whilst trying to grab the attention of passers by. When we were going into town for Ray's leaving meal, I saw a commuter buy one of these puppies (and pay the princely sum of 100RMB for the pleasure). The commuter was just about to walk off with his purchase when the seller realized that they would be travelling by metro, the seller stopped the buyer and asked him to wait. The seller removed another plastic bag from his and proceeded to put the dog in it. We could not believe what we were seeing and we were sure the dog would die before it got too far through lack of oxygen. The only saving grace was that the bag was not tied at the top, which was common practice here whenever we would buy something. The seller then reached into the canvas bag that had been at his feet and pulled out another puppy to sell. It was then we realised that the bag was full of puppies and that the weight of those on top was surely crushing those underneath. I couldn't believe that the police would just walk past and it was obvious that the RSPCA doesn't have a branch out here.

Qingdao Or Bust

We had been talking about a trip to Qingdao for a while. On every occasion we tried to organise it, something always came up. It was either someone couldn't make the dates we wanted to go on or we couldn't get tickets. Originally, there were five of us going on this trip. Sarah, Tana, Rob, the irrepressible Doug and myself. We were also planning to meet up with Caroline, one of our fellow CIEE inductees as she was teaching about half an hour away from the city centre. Due to the delay, Caroline had actually gone back to the USA, Rob had gone home to Australia and Tana was off on her tour of Western China, leaving just the three of us. We had all been determined to go, mainly to visit the brewery and drink the semi-legendary beer in a bag on the beach. In fact, these were the only reasons to go! I think it might be a good idea at this point to stop and explain what the beer in the bag actually was.

Ever since we had met him, Doug had been telling us that some of his friends had gone to Qingdao and when they sat on the beach, the beer had been served to them in a bag. Intrigued by this curious concept; Doug was well up for examining this himself, and had raised my curiosity enough that I fancied one of them as well. Sarah was just happy to have a beer, no matter what container it came in!

On the last day that we saw him, Rob gave us the direct line phone number of a lady called Maggie who worked in a travel agency in the centre of Beijing. He told us that she would organise return train tickets to nearly anywhere in China (for a small fee of course). After contacting Maggie, she made a point of taking our mobile number so she could get in contact with us once she knew what she could do. What seemed to be the norm in China with anything like this, was that we ended up ringing her every morning to find out where our tickets

300

were and why she hadn't got them. In the end, she said that she had managed to get us three soft sleepers for the day and time we wanted to leave, but she wasn't able to get us any return tickets. This was fine, we thought. We would just book them ourselves when we got there. However, a spanner was most definitely thrown into the works and it looked as though we would never get there.

About a month before we organised this jolly to Qingdao, Doug had handed his passport over to his department and they had proceeded to do everything in their power not to get it back to him. This would have put the trip in jeopardy, especially for Doug, and we were not keen to go there without him. Passports were needed not only to book hotels, but flights as well. As Doug had also booked our hotel for us, we thought it would be to all our benefits for him to get his passport back.

The saga of Doug's passport is worth going into just in a little bit of detail to give another example of how the Chinese would do things that might be fine with them, but seemed designed just to annoy the hell out of us. He had handed his passport over to his departments' liaison four weeks earlier, as he needed to have his visa extended to continue teaching for another semester. As seems to be the way with Communist countries, the process for doing anything is long and complex, even though it doesn't have to be. They just do things that way but according to Doug's previous experience, the whole process should not take anything more than a couple of weeks. After two weeks had passed, Doug was curious to know why nothing had happened.

When he made some enquiries as to the location of his passport, he was fobbed off a couple of times with "it will be ready tomorrow" or "we don't have it". With time running out before we left, and with Doug having already forked out the money to go, he was justly becoming quite concerned about his passports location. With only a couple of days to spare, he was called by SAFEA to say that they now had his passport and it had been sitting in their safe for a week. It turned out that they had been trying to ring him for a week, but they had been ringing his old apartment which was currently being renovated. In fact, it was the same apartment that SAFEA had asked Doug to move out of precisely so they could renovate it.

Panic over, or so we thought anyway as all they had to so was open the safe and take out the passport. However, this is where it became even more frustrating. They only had one key for the safe and it was in the possession of one of the SAFEA's staff who was currently somewhere in the interior of the country visiting their family. SAFEA promised that they would organise for the key to be couriered over to Beihang so Doug would have his passport in time for the trip and luckily for all concerned, that is exactly what happened.

Anyway, back to our Qingdao trip. The train was leaving at 11:30pm so we decided to go to Steak & Eggs, a western restaurant, for a big feed. The food was great, but a little on the pricey side, so we only ever went there as a treat. My meal actually cost me over 100RMB and by was by far and away the most expensive meal I bought during my trip. The meal was huge and we were all completely stuffed which was handy because we didn't know when we would next eat. As we had soft sleeper tickets, we could sit in one of the exclusive soft sleeper seating areas. After spending so much time in the over crowded hard sleeper lounges, it was nice to spend some time in relative peace and comfort.

Day One - Qingdao had been ceded to Germany in the last years of the 19th Century and even though they were in control of the port for less than twenty years, their influence on architecture and business were still in evidence. These included the world famous brewery (even though it used the old spelling of the ports name – Tsingdao) and the railway station. According to the sign on the outside of the building, it is no longer in its original location. It was moved 50 meters when the station was expanded but it is still used as part of the modern railway building.

The first thing we did when we arrived in Qingdao was to go to the ticket office to book our return tickets. However, and as to be expected, they didn't have any for the times we wanted. It was especially important for Doug to be back at a certain time. He had set up a consultancy company and had to be back in Beijing as he

302

was expecting a call from a client. Being a bit peckish after queuing for a while, I continued my tour of Chinese KFC's, as this gave us an opportunity to decide what we were going to do next. We bought a map (with the landmarks written in English) and then caught a taxi to our hotel. We paid for our rooms and then headed to their business centre to see if they could get us some train tickets, but surprise, surprise, they couldn't.

That only left one thing and that was to catch a plane back to Beijing. The earliest plane was for the morning we actually wanted to be back in the capital. Booking the plane wiped out nearly all of our spending money (because they only accept cash at the business centre) therefore I had to pay a visit to a nearby ATM so we could do all of the things we had gone to Qingdao for. It also meant that we either had to book another night in the hotel or just not go to bed.

For some reason, we all decided to go with the latter so we spent a little while trying to figure out how we were going to do this. After looking in the Lonely Planet, it seemed that the only things that were open late were the bars. We agreed that we would find the bar that stayed open the longest and when that closed, we would make our way to the airport and crash out in the departure lounge. This wasn't the best arrangement we could have envisaged, but at least we wouldn't be late getting back to Beijing for Doug's business call.

We began by taking a stroll down one of the many beaches that Qingdao is famous for. The piles of broken glass we saw didn't make us want to actually walk on the sand, which didn't look that clean either, but instead we stayed on the paths. At no time did we see any of the fabled bags of beer that we were all desperate to try, even though we did see loads of stalls selling the stuff in bottles and even kegs all the way along the beachfront. The beach was crowded both days we were there and we were all quite surprised to see a Chinese woman wearing a bikini. For a country where it is better socially to have whiter skin, this was a real rarity indeed. During our stroll, we were stopped by a Chinese guy who tried to prevent us from walking along a small part of the beach.

As we stopped, he started to shout at us and pointed at a sign. Doug translated his ranting and told us that we were expected to pay 2RMB to continue walking along. As we saw some Chinese people walking past us and into this area for free, we felt that this was another case of discrimination against Westerners so we refused to pay and kept walking. I was a bit put out when he grabbed my arm but I was able to shrug him off and he didn't seem too keen to chase us. We spent the rest of the morning and early afternoon trying to find one of the numerous restaurants the Lonely Planet said was on the beach, but we couldn't find any so we headed in land to grab some lunch.

We caught a taxi to the brewery and found that it was surrounded by restaurants. After filling our boots, we headed over the road for our long awaited visit and it didn't disappoint. We decided to fork out for an English speaking guide and she really added to the experience. The first part of the tour involved visiting the older buildings that had been built by the Germans back in 1903 when the brewery was opened.

As usual, there was a little bit of propaganda that kept saying that the brewery had been poorly run before the Communists took over in 1949, but it didn't get in the way of a fascinating story. The tour was a bit quick for my liking because I was trying to read some of the captions that the tour guide hadn't mentioned, but this was only a minor grumble. We were then shown into the old fermenting rooms and we were given a free sample of unfiltered beer, which was very cloudy. Sarah actually preferred this to the normal Tsingdao because it was slightly sweeter.

The next part of the tour involved the newer brewery buildings to see the bottles being filled and packaged. It was in this section that they had installed something called the 'Drunken Room', where the floor was at such an angle to make it quite difficult to stand up straight. The tour guide didn't initially come in with us as she said she didn't like going in there, but we were having so much fun that she came in to find out where we were. Cue the guide crashing face first in to the wall.

We couldn't help but laugh, but she had a smile on her face so we didn't feel too guilty about it.

The tour guide said a couple of interesting things that we didn't expect. The first was that she said Tsingdao was exported to Taiwan, but it did occur to me that as China claims the island is part of the PRC, they shouldn't need to export it? That would be like us saying we were exporting London Pride to the Isle of Wight. The second was after watching a programme about Tsingdao's product placement in American films, the guide said that there were different grades of the beer. The best is exported to the USA and the worst is kept in China, because the Chinese don't care as much about the quality.

The last part of the tour was definitely the best. We were given a free pitcher of filtered beer and a presentation glass. This was a really nice touch and when the family next to us offered us their pitcher because they couldn't finish it and didn't want to see it go to waste, we knew we were in for a good afternoon. After trying a few more of the different varieties of Tsingdao, we decided to get some dinner. Doug, who had not slept very well at all on the train, decided he wanted an early night, so we went back to the hotel. As he went to bed, Sarah and I went for a walk down by the waterfront. There we saw loads of children riding around on roller blades as well as people trying to ride triplet bikes (bikes made for three, like the one the Goodies had) and failing. Very amusing! We called it a night after this, but the hotel did have BBC World so it was nice to watch some proper TV in English instead of putting up with CCTV9.

The Longest Day - For some reason, we had to check out of the hotel at 10am, even though it was written on the reception desk that is should have been noon. Chinese double standards at work here again! That extra hour or two in bed could have made all of the difference as we needed to stay up quite late that evening. We left our bags in the hotels' left luggage store as we didn't want to have to carry them around on our backs all day, and then headed off for breakfast. Our first point of call after breakfast was Zhongshan Park. The entrance to the park was full of displays of the Olympic mascots. We also decided to check out what were supposedly the remains of an ancient village, but they were conspicuous by their absence.

It was just a fenced off area with some trees in it. In the middle of the park was the local TV tower. This was at the top of a hill so we decided to get the cable car up to it. The view was very impressive, but we decided not to actually go to the top of the tower because of the low cloud cover and pollution. We could see the Tsingdao brewery from the base of the TV Tower and we liked the fact that the stacks on the roof had been painted to resemble beer cans. A nice touch!

Once we went back down to ground level and wandered through the park, we came across a mini fun fare. Like the one in Hohhot, it looked a bit dangerous but what they did have were go-karts. Doug and I instantly wanted a go and prepared for some serious racing. However, the lawn mower engines on the back were not designed for speed so after a gentle plod around the course, that was it. I was quite sure that I was over taken by an express snail whilst in the kart but it was worth the 10RMB we paid for the experience.

We next planned to go over to Qingdaoshan Park where there were the remains of a hill fort built by the Germans when it was their treaty port. However, the taxi driver took us to a different park. Even though it had been designated in the top ten attractions in Qingdao, it wasn't quite what we were after even if, as according to the Lonely Planet, all that remains of the hill fort is a hole in the ground. What this park did have though was a selection of models of some of the historically important buildings in Qingdao. None of them were in particularly good condition and could have done with some restoration. Well, they had been very keen to restore everything else so why not these.

Whilst we were wandering around, I received a text from Maggie the travel agent telling me to check my email. She had some news about ticket availability for another trip Sarah and fancied doing, so we went in search of a Net Bar. The one we found could possibly be the best Net Bar in the world. Everything in it was new with nice big sofas, big screens (ideal for computer games), web cams and all for 1RMB an hour. Doug checked out the opening times and it stayed open 24 hours a day, even though the price went up to 2RMB an hour after midnight. We then decided that this would be our last port of call before catching the plane, even if staying awake was still going to be a problem. With the day coming to an end, we gave up trying to locate the mythical beer in a bag. The closest we came was beer served in a plastic beaker to be drunk out of a paper cup. It still tasted okay though!

Doug had found a highly recommended German restaurant listed on the tourist map that he heard about from his friends that had visited in the past, and we decided to go there for dinner. It was a lovely meal. The portions were generous and the price not too expensive. After this, we went to the Lennon Bar (or Lenin bar as Sarah insisted on calling it). This was a Beatles themed bar and things looked good as we pulled up to it as there was a massive painting of John Lennon looking at us. Unfortunately the place was dead and only one Beatles song was played all night. They only seemed to have one tape, because we heard the same song about five times before we couldn't stand it anymore and went to the Net Bar.

Our journey there was not as straightforward as it could have been. Doug got a bit confused and thought that the taxi driver was taking us for a ride, and going the wrong way. After a few strong words, we exited the cab and decided to walk to where we thought the station was. All that happened was that we walked around in a big circle and realised that the driver was taking us the right way all the time. One thing this little stop off did though was to waste over an hour.

When we eventually arrived at the Net Bar, it was around 2am and the first thing we saw was a punter asleep on his computer. The staff didn't care so we knew that if we did konk out, we would be okay. Sarah was the only one of us who actually went to sleep, sprawled out on one of the sofas. Doug spent the night emailing and updating his blog. I spent my time emailing, looking at the football news and then watching YouTube for anything that took my fancy.

It was a bit weird walking into the Net Bar at night and walking out in the daytime. By the time we got to the airport, I was beginning to flag and I fell asleep as soon as I sat in my plane seat. As with all the other internal flights we had taken in China, there was a delay in taking off. I slept through most of the journey and I only woke up for the last part, which was a bit scary. The plane was being buffeted all over the place and I hoped that I would be able to walk away from this experience. If the plane journey wasn't bad enough, we all thought that this was the worst landing any of us had ever had! The pilot seemed to be coming in too fast and it felt that the plane was bouncing on the runway before we finally hit the ground. This didn't stop a lot of the Chinese passengers from undoing their seatbelts as quickly as they could even though plane was still taxiing down the runway.

This was another feature of every internal flight we had taken. As soon as any of these planes landed, all of the Chinese people on board would have already unclipped their seatbelts and would stand in the aisle even though they might be standing there for a about 15 minutes as the plane made it's way to the terminal. Even repeated requests for them to sit back in their seats where unheeded, but some did make a concession to sit down just sat in the aisle ready to spring for the door as soon as it opened.

The trip had been a fantastic experience but we were glad to be back, especially as we were all so knackered from having stayed up for the best part of twenty four hours.

A Grand Day Out

Even though we had travelled around a bit, we still had some money left to burn so we decided to take a day trip to Dandong. It is on the border of North Korea and is separated from it by the Yalu river. It is famous for the point where the Chinese 'Volunteer' army crossed to help the government of Kim Il Sung during the Korean war. Having spoken to Paul the Goalie about his time looking over the border from South Korea[63], it would be interesting to compare what he had said about the place with what we were about to see. Our now well worn copy of The Lonely Planet only listed three things to see whilst we were there, and we planned to see them in this order;

1) The Tiger Mountain Great Wall
2) The Border between China and North Korea
3) The Museum to Commemorate US Aggression (or the Korean War to us).

With only limited tourist options, we knew that these would only take us a day to visit, so we went to the same travel agent that had booked us the train tickets to Qingdao, hoping that on this occasion Maggie would be able to secure us the return journey. Without that in place before we left, we wouldn't go.

We were still in Qingdao when we received confirmation that the train tickets for both legs of the trip had been secured. With a journey that would last 14 hours on the over-night train there, and the same amount of time on the way back, we hoped that it would be worth the effort. Sarah was not overly keen on the idea, especially as the weather had not been great and nearly everything to do in Dandong involved being outside. Maggie said that we would have to pay for the return tickets when we arrived at Dandong. She gave us the contact name and details of the person we needed to see. So far so good!

We left from the main Beijing Railway station and as soon as the train pulled away, I was accosted by someone wishing to have their photograph taken with me. Nothing unusual there, but it was the first time it had happened on a train. This was also the first time I had seen the staff on the train selling souvenirs and they

---

[63] Paul had told me that on the North Korean side of the border was a village that was only ever populated when the NK authorities knew that there was going to be a procession of tourists in the area. On a trip to the border, Paul could see loads of people in this village milling around doing mundane things but all looking inanely cheerful. When he came back later when the majority of the tour groups had left, the village was deserted.

were all related to North Korea. Very strange! We arrived at Dandong at 7:30am and I was surprised not to see a KFC outside of the station but before we could have breakfast, we wanted to pick up our tickets and proceed with our sightseeing, especially as time was against us. We went in search of the tourist office Maggie had told us to go to which we could see on our map was not that far from the station. First of all, we went the wrong way. I had had a mishap with the symbols on the map and it turned out that we were actually headed towards the local Net Bar. This did not make that much of a difference because the tourist office did not open until 8am.

After wandering around for a few minutes (and actually finding the nearest KFC to the station), we asked for directions in a hotel where, luckily for us, the receptionist spoke enough English that we could communicate with each other. They were very helpful and pointed us in the right direction. The tourist office was located in a hotel and was not that clearly sign-posted, so it was lucky we had asked where it was because I could see us walking past without ever seeing it. It was however, almost opposite the station, so we had walked around in a big circle! Our contact wasn't there, and the woman who was spoke very little English. I was desperate for the toilet, so I disappeared for a moment.

When I got back, Sarah was very upset. Between Sarah's basic tourist Mandarin and the lady's non existent English, Sarah had concluded that the return tickets they had secured were for the train leaving at 10:30am that day. Sarah was not happy about this believing we had come too far to spend only three hours in the place. Sarah would not let it be, feeling we had been conned yet again as gullible westerners, and continued in her best Chinglish to try and get some sense out of the lady. We'd been in China long enough by now to really know better than to try and get any sense out of anyone. However, the woman managed to say that our contact would be arriving at 8:30am, so we waited around, as we were very concerned that this would be another one of those China moments.

Once our contact arrived, she explained that the tickets were not there yet and we could pick them up at

10:30am, which was what the first lady was trying the say but we did not speak enough of each others languages to get to this point. This left Sarah feeling very guilty for arguing with the lady who we now realise must have thought we were very strange to be so upset about them getting the booking right. The tickets were for the train leaving for Beijing at 6:30pm as had been guaranteed by Maggie. With that sorted out, we were told to go down to Yalujiang Park, which is on the Yalu River. There were at least a couple of hours worth of things to see and do before our train tickets would be ready.

The first thing we saw when we arrived at the banks of the river was the Sino-Korea Friendship Bridge which connects Dandong to the town of Sinuiji on the Korean side of the border. It is one of the few ways of actually getting in and out of North Korea carrying road (which all seemed to be trucks) and rail traffic (where the trains only had three carriages instead of the twenty or so on most of the other trains we had seen in China). What was strange is that all of the transport seemed to be going into Korea with nothing coming back the other way. This was also our first chance to have a look at North Korea. Apart from some boats, trees and a house, there were numerous smoke stacks (with nothing coming out of them) and a massive Ferris wheel (which stayed stationary for the whole of our trip).

Behind this (and not visible at this stage) was the Old Bridge which was 'accidentally' bombed by the United Nations forces during the Korean War to try and stop the Chinese from supplying the North Koreans with arms and men. The Japanese built this bridge in 1903 when they ruled most of this area of China. To aid with the flow of larger boats and ships going up and down the river, they did not build it to be raised, but it would in fact turn 90º to let ships continue up the river. All that remained on the Korean side of the bridge were the support columns as they pulled the rest of it down instead of trying to repair it. The Chinese side was open to the almighty tourist pound and well worth a visit. There were telescopes at the far end of the bridge which I used to have a look into North Korea, even though the tree line on their side has been planted in such a way that I couldn't see very much at all.

Another site worth seeing were the panels detailing the history of the bridge. The most memorable one for me was of a woman holding a child showing how distraught she was at its destruction. On closer examination, it was very hard to see any of the background as it was blurred and therefore could have been taken anywhere and of anything. For all I knew, it could have been taken during one of Mao's many bright ideas that led to starvation and the death of millions. Was this another great example of Communist propaganda at work? You betcha!

The entrance to the bridge has what can only be described as the obligatory collection of military hardware, but on this occasion none of them were jet fighters but instead were howitzers. There was also a concrete tower, but I could only guess at its actually purpose. Even though it had what looked like gun holes in it, there weren't any information panels about so we can only assume that it was built to protect the border during the Korean War. We did go in and climb to the top, but these days it seems to be used as a public toilet as the smell of stale urine was almost overpowering, even though there are no signs to this effect either.

The main reason I wanted to come down to the river was to hop on to a speedboat and go on a trip down the border. We walked along the bank for a while whilst continually being accosted by people trying to get us on their boats. Most of the ones we saw were designed to take large groups but we would have to wait for it to fill up before it would set sail. We both felt it was unwise to stop at the pier which had a fight going on between a coach load of Chinese tourists (it is very unusual to see the Chinese loose their composure like so they might have been Korean or Japanese.

We found it very difficult to be able to spot the difference) so we figured the trip must have gone seriously wrong. We eventually settled on one of the last boat stops as there wasn't a queue and the women who did all of the talking could speak English. The speedboat didn't look to be in best of shape, but as long as it didn't sink, we didn't mind too much as we would not be out there that long. The guy driving the boat took us within spitting distance of the other shore and we were sure that we were actually in North Korean territory. There were loads of boats following the same route as us and we did get the odd wave off of some Koreans who were there fishing.

There were a number of boats moored up but the majority of them were North Korean police launches which were all seemingly fully manned. I was so tempted to take a photo of the NK border guard sitting in his gun turret eating a sandwich, but I didn't think he would be too happy about that and might open fire. He did give me a nasty Paddington bear type stare and the double barrelled machine gun he was sitting behind looked equally menacing. This might be seen to be a bit over the top, but I wasn't keen to push my luck. The amount of police boats down the Korean bank should be enough to put anyone off trying to land there, but to be honest, why would you want to go there. This is as near as either of us wanted to get.

The speedboat trip was an excellent, if short experience but there is one extra item of note. There was a building quite near to the bombed bridge, about three stories high. The building was clearly visible from the Chinese side of the river and all that could be seen were loads of people swimming in the river, seemly having fun. It looked a bit like a Butlins holiday camp. Reminded of what Paul the Goalie had said, I was suspicious of the whole thing. Were they told to be there or were they genuinely having a good time considering that there were so many policemen around. When we walked past this area later in the day when there were hardly any tourists on the river, there didn't seem to be anyone there. Strange that.

Once we were back on dry land, we were accosted by the first beggar of the day. Even with our experiences of seeing beggars in China, there seemed to be more than anywhere else on the banks of the river. A small boy ran up to me with his hand out and did everything in his power to stop me getting past. As this was never going to happen, the kid did the only thing he

313

could do to get my attention. He jumped onto my leg and refused to let go until Sarah (who was laughing her head off) pulled out some coins (simply for being the best act of begging she had ever seen) and he was off. If only she had been as quick with the camera, this would have been a sight to see. After grabbing a quick drink because the temperature was beginning to heat up, we made our way back to the tourist office where our tickets were ready and waiting for us.

Next up was a trip out to what is the most easterly part of the Great Wall. We caught a cab but the road to the wall was still under construction but that didn't stop the traffic from going along at its usual high speeds. The wall itself was very impressive as it had been built up some quite steep slopes. Like the other bits of the wall we had been to, it had been completely restored. Once we started to climb it, I remembered why I had wanted to come here in the morning. It was almost midday by the time we started to climb, and this was a real slog of a wall. Neither of the other two sections we had visited before were as steep as this, and the sun was unforgiving. It was so hot that it was possible to follow the trail of sweat I was leaving behind me as we walked. I say a trail, but it was actually forming a river of its own!

When we reached the tower at the highest point of the wall, there was a little concession stall with a freezer where we could buy a cold drink. The water was more expensive than we normally would consider paying, but at that point we would have paid just about anything to have some. We relaxed in the tower until I had stopped sweating before we decided to continue. We both felt relieved that our journey was downhill from now on.

According to the Lonely Planet, at the bottom of the wall was a small museum and from there, visitors could catch a launch to take them back along the river to the entrance. This was our initial plan, but what we didn't realised was that the path split into two. On examination of this junction, we could see one did go to a large building (which we assumed was the museum), but we couldn't tell where the other went. It was signposted in Chinese characters but we could only read about half a dozen of these between us (which were male, female, chicken, lamb, beef, Beijing, gate) so we decided to be adventurous and went that way. What we didn't expect was an Indiana Jones style walkway around the mountain. It had everything; overhanging rocks, caves, a suspension bridge and most mad of all, a metal beam going all the way around which gave us something to hang onto. Whoever put that up deserves a medal or a one-way ticket to the loony bin. In some ways, this was even tougher than coming up the wall, but it was absolutely fantastic and not listed in the Lonely Planet. Shame on them!

Two sights on the wall really impressed us. Firstly when we were half way up there were two elderly Chinese men climbing the wall that kept taking time out to stop and sing to everybody that passed them. They found us very amusing and kept shouting "ok" whenever we saw them. We had a sneaky feeling that if we collapsed from the heat and the pure physical exertion they'd have slung us over their backs and carried us up! They were very fast at climbing up the wall and also took the Indiana Jones path back. Speaking of which we think they would be much better to play Indiana Jones in the next movie. There's no way an aging Harrison Ford could compete with these guys!

The second sight was that of a lady who, at first, we weren't sure whether she was impressive or just stupid. She had come to the wall looking like she was in her Sunday best wearing strappy shoes with thin fashionable lady like heels. How she managed to walk along this path in those shoes was beyond us. Once we arrived at the steepest climb of the day, we actually felt a rope would have been a good accessory; we were convinced that this woman would take the path down to the boat and take the easy option out. But no, she climbed up and over the rock face and whilst that was impressive in itself at the end of it all she didn't have a single hair out of place, showed no sign of sweating and looked like she had the energy to do it all again!

This part of the wall was a complete contrast to Badaling. We only saw a handful of people all day so we felt that we owned the place. It is the more scenic area to go to, and the best part of the wall we had seen. Even though it did give one a sense of achievement to have walked all around it, there were occasions when a cable car would have been most appreciated.

Our next task was to try return back to the town itself, not an easy task as it turned out. We went back to the sites entrance but the only available taxi was one that a Chinese couple from Dalian had booked for the day. We managed to convince them to let us share it back to town. In exchange for helping us out, all we did was pay the fare and have our picture taken with them. A small price to pay as it turned out. The driver took us to our third and final destination, the Museum to Commemorate US Aggression.

In its defence, this was the best Museum I had seen in the whole of China. It looked new, it was full of interesting information panels that (unlike the section of the Military Museum in Beijing dedicated to this conflict) were written in English as well as Mandarin. The artifices were not stuck on the wall with glue or pins and it was kept at a regular temperature. It is a shame therefore that there was so much wrong with it.

As expected, it was a mass of propaganda to the point that it was almost funny. This included the following:

1) The whole museum kept inferring that America was the instigator of the war because it sought to increase it's Imperial gains after World War 2 (conveniently forgetting that is was the US and it's allies that helped defend China during that conflict).

2) We were informed that the UN forces committed War Crimes all over the place and that they used all sorts of dirty tricks to prevent the war from finishing when all the Chinese/North Korean forces wanted was peace and didn't employ any of the above themselves.

3) There were charts showing the amount of UN dead but it would seem that the Chinese did not lose a single person throughout the whole conflict because their casualty lists were conspicuous by their absence.

4) There were quite a few bits of military hardware outside; most of it looking like it had come from the USSR which had allegedly been neutral during the whole thing.
5) The Chinese forces were constantly referred to as volunteers where as in reality they were all Chinese army regulars who were sent in to Korea to give China a buffer zone much like the Soviet Union had with Eastern Europe.
6) We were told that American ships sailed into the Taiwan straight to prevent the People's Army from claiming what is theirs by right. America didn't care about Taiwan until China entered the Korean War.
7) The one thing that was shockingly missing from this whole place was at no point did it actually say why the war started in the first place. I was a bit disappointed that there was not a visitor's book so I could have asked why this was.

We walked back into town and went to a lovely restaurant that was reminiscent of London tea shops in the 1920's. All of the waitresses wore black dresses with white 'pinnies' and there was even a grand piano on the second floor. It was an absolutely lovely place and the food was gorgeous. Sarah got particularly excited because hers was presented in a glossy case with individual compartments. This led us nicely to the time to catch the train but before we left, I did have to take a picture of the large statue of Mao. There have not been that many statues of this pie eating champion around the place so it was nice to get one of him in all his glory.

We were both tired and looking forward to as good a night sleep as you can get on a moving train. The people in our berth were very friendly and one of guys was keen to practise his English, telling us that he either last studied it when he was 14 years old or started studying when he was 40 – we couldn't really understand what he was saying! They also found the size of my footwear very amusing as I was wearing my Timberland style boots. I got a laugh out of them by spraying my feet and shoes with deodorant but I was just taking precautions just in case I killed anyone with the smell. In fact, I am surprised that I didn't get complaints about my general smell because I must have reeked, even by the standards of the Chinese, as I had spent most of the day sweating.

Every so often their conversation would go back to my shoes and there would be pointing and mumbling between themselves. In the morning, they even felt brave enough to actually pick them up to see how heavy they were. I say brave because the smell was still lingering! It was nice to get back to Beihang. The shower felt so good and I was glad that that was going to be our last journey before going back home.

Drifters Epilogue #2

I might have stopped, but the Drifters played on. Club Football continued to organise competitions over the summer for any team willing to play in them. I had glanced at the fixtures and noted that none of these competitions would finish before I went back home, so I thought I would continue my retirement especially as it had all finished on such a high. Well, that and the fact that my knee had started to hurt from all of the travelling about we were doing. That was until two days before we were set to leave Beijing. Rupert had sent out one of his customary emails and after looking at the player list, I noticed that they didn't have a goalkeeper.

Volunteering my services, I made my way one last time to the pitches near the Lido Hotel to meet my relieved team mates (none of whom had fancied playing in goal themselves). For the first time, I was actually scared to be playing football. After the warm up, my knee was really painful but I said I would play and I didn't want to let the team down. It gave me a chance to meet up with Christophe once more and pick up my copy of the official DVD of that eventful night when we had won promotion.

We were scheduled to play two games and the first was against some of the better players from the British School Accies and Athletico. In the first game we were beaten by a 3-0 score line. I blamed myself for two of the goals because I was a little out of practise and

318

lacking in the confidence to be throwing my body around the place. Before the second game, I was keen to point out that a double defeat would mean a Christophe match report written in French, something I was keen not to see. The team rallied and we managed to bag ourselves quite a convincing win. It was nice to go out on a victory and I was indebted to Marcus who said he would go in goal for me so I could have a run out in my last game. I turned him down as I didn't want to risk my knee anymore than I had already.

I was very sorry to be seeing the back of The Drifters. Being in that team may have raised my blood pressure but it was a great laugh. I miss them all and I don't think anything will ever replace the feeling of actually winning something with a team that had never won anything before. It was a shame that looking at their results from afar for the next 5-a-side season that they went straight back down and the team disbanded less than a year after my departure.

And In The End

Apart from my one last appearance for the Drifters, we spent the last few days in China for the most part sitting around waiting for the time to pass. We were fed up with all the tourist trappings and there was nothing really left in Beijing that we felt would be of a great loss to us if we didn't see them. We made an effort to do some last little bits of shopping, watch some DVD's, packed our bags and mucked around on the Internet. I met up with some of the Drifters for an end of season bash, as well giving the team a chance to say goodbye to Stuart and I.

Rupert brought along the first piece of silver ware that the Drifters had ever won. However, he decided to bring it along on the back of his moped and it turned out not to be as solid as it looked. In fact, it didn't look that solid even after a couple of attempts to repair it. It turned out to be a few bits of plastic held together with screws, and to cap it all; it wasn't even silver but gold in colour. It didn't matter how naff it looked though; because we all felt proud that we had actually won something. Cue too many beers and some really nice food as we went to the Russian for the usual steak wrapped with bacon.

Our last act was to go to the big tourist market for one last taste of the Chinese selling experience and it didn't let us down. They were still trying to sell us anything and everything, but I did succumb and bought a tourist style red guard bag. I could not lower myself to buy another one with Mao's smiling face on it and went for one with a big red star on it.

We had planned to go to Ashtray for our last meal but it was still closed, which was very annoying as the flat fired bread with sultanas was a personal favourite of mine, and I had not seen for sale anywhere else. We therefore went to the Dongbei restaurant out of the east gate, as we wanted to eat ribs with a plastic glove! Annoyingly they didn't have any of this left, so we had to make do with the dishes that we would have had out of the West Gate, if they had not all been demolished the week before!

In an attempt to beat jet lag and make the plane journey shorter by sleeping through it, I thought we should stay up all night. To help with this, we watched a film with Doug and Karen. They managed to stick with us until 2am but after they had gone, it became a lot harder to stay awake. It was especially sad to say goodbye to Doug as he had been an absolutely brilliant person to have had around as well as making the whole experience a lot more fun. We knew we were both going to miss him a great deal. Sarah gave up the ghost around 4am but with the aid of some sugary, caffeine filled soft drinks, I managed to make it through to the morning. Someone had to make sure we got to the airport on time.

It was strange getting into the taxi to drive away from the University for the last time. It was a lovely sunny morning and the taxi driver got us to the airport in plenty of time. We had been really worried by the weight of our suitcases, but it was a relief when they turned out to be under the limit. We were surprised when the bloke on the check in desk didn't ask either of us if we had packed our bags. It was the departure lounge that I finally conked out and fell asleep. Annoying, our flight home was late()getting in, but once on board the pilot said he would put his foot down to get us back on time! We had so much hand luggage that it took up the whole of an over head locker. Sarah now felt like a total hypocrite and her favourite airport game is no longer 'tutting' at people with too much hand luggage.

We were joined in our section by a group of Chinese students that were flying to Britain for a cultural holiday. The girl sitting next us started talking to Sarah about her trip and even gave her a present of a hair grooming set. Sarah rapidly switched back to HR mode and spent the rest of the flight wondering if:

1) It was appropriate for her to accept the gift.
2) What would happen if she was stopped at customs and asked if anyone had given her anything to carry on and,
3) What if it was really a ploy to get her to unwittingly smuggle drugs.

However, in between periods of sleeping, I also joined in the conversation. She was the first Chinese person I had heard mention Falun Gong and she also wanted to talk about how the West viewed China. Unfortunately for her, I no longer felt that I had to bite my tongue over all the bullshit the Chinese Government comes up with to cling on to power, and ranted a little bit. I felt a little sorry for her afterwards, but conversely, much better for getting everything off of my chest!

It was great to walk into the terminal at Heathrow and to see some signs that were only in English. Sarah was worried when we were walking through customs, due to the amount of bootleg DVD's we had in our bags, but they seemed to be pre-occupied with someone who had brought banned food into the country in her hand luggage! We were met by my parents who had come along with a bottle of Irn Bru for me to drink. It was wonderful to finally be back home, even if my application for the PGCE was once again, unsuccessful.

Afterward

In the Sunday Times Magazine dated 22nd October 2006, there was an article about Ernai which are the Chinese equivalent of mistresses. The one piece of information that caught the eye was that in an attempt to cut down on this practice, Chinese law prohibits 'cohabitation outside of marriage' so we effectively broke the law the whole time we were out there; and that would explain why they gave us separate rooms even though they knew we were a couple.

Further Reading

Chang, Gordon G.
The Coming Collapse of China (2003) Arrow Books

Chang, Iris
The Rape of Naking: The Forgotten Holocaust of World
          War II (1998) Penguin

Fenby, Jonathan
Generalissimo: Chiang Kai-shek and the China he Lost
          (2005) Free Press

Gascoigne, Bamber
A Brief History of the Dynasties of China (2003)
          Constable and Robinson

Hastings, Max
          The Korean War (2001) Pan Books

MacFarquhar, Roderick & Schoenhals, Michael
Mao's Last Revolution (2006) The Belknap Press

Manthorpe, Jonathan
Forbidden Nation: A History of Taiwan (2005) Palgrave
          MacMillan

Menzies, Gavin
1421: The Year China Discovered the World (2004)
          Bantam

Min, Anchee
Becoming Madame Mao (2001) Allison & Busby

Nathan, Andrew J. (Ed) & Giley, Bruce (Ed)
China's New Rulers: The Secret Files (2004) The New
          York Review of Book, Inc

Li, Zhisui
The Private Life of Chairman Mao (1996 Edition) Arrow

Roberts, J. A. G.
The Complete Illustrated History of China (2003) Sutton
Sun, Tzu (Yuan Shibing, trans.)
The Art of War (1993) Wordsworth Reference

Wu, Cheng'En (W. J. F. Jenner, trans.)
Journey to the West (2004 Edition) Foreign Language
        Press

Yanchi, Quan
Mao Zedong Man, not God (1992 Edition) Foreign
        Language Press

Zhang, Liang (Ed.)
        The Tiananmen Papers (2002) Abacus

19295293R00180

Printed in Great Britain
by Amazon